# THE CLASSIC TECHNIQUES

LIFE WORLD LIBRARY
LIFE NATURE LIBRARY
TIME READING PROGRAM
THE LIFE HISTORY OF THE UNITED STATES
LIFE SCIENCE LIBRARY
GREAT AGES OF MAN
TIME-LIFE LIBRARY OF ART
TIME-LIFE LIBRARY OF AMERICA
FOODS OF THE WORLD
THIS FABULOUS CENTURY
LIFE LIBRARY OF PHOTOGRAPHY
THE TIME-LIFE ENCYCLOPEDIA OF GARDENING
THE AMERICAN WILDERNESS
THE EMERGENCE OF MAN
THE OLD WEST
THE ART OF SEWING
FAMILY LIBRARY:
    THE TIME-LIFE BOOK OF FAMILY FINANCE
    THE TIME-LIFE FAMILY LEGAL GUIDE

TIME
LIFE
BOOKS
®

THE ART OF SEWING

# THE CLASSIC TECHNIQUES

BY THE EDITORS OF TIME-LIFE BOOKS

TIME-LIFE BOOKS, NEW YORK

TIME-LIFE BOOKS

FOUNDER: Henry R. Luce 1898-1967

*Editor-in-Chief:* Hedley Donovan
*Chairman of the Board:* Andrew Heiskell
*President:* James R. Shepley
*Chairman, Executive Committee:*
James A. Linen
*Group Vice President:* Rhett Austell

*Vice Chairman:* Roy E. Larsen

MANAGING EDITOR: Jerry Korn
*Assistant Managing Editors:* David Maness,
Martin Mann, A. B. C. Whipple
*Planning Director:* Oliver E. Allen
*Art Director:* Sheldon Cotler
*Chief of Research:* Beatrice T. Dobie
*Director of Photography:* Melvin L. Scott
*Senior Text Editors:* Diana Hirsh, Ogden Tanner
*Assistant Art Director:* Arnold C. Holeywell

PUBLISHER: Joan D. Manley
*General Manager:* John D. McSweeney
*Business Manager:* John Steven Maxwell
*Sales Director:* Carl G. Jaeger
*Promotion Director:* Paul R. Stewart
*Public Relations Director:* Nicholas Benton

THE ART OF SEWING
SERIES EDITOR: Carlotta Kerwin
EDITORIAL STAFF FOR
*THE CLASSIC TECHNIQUES:*
*Assistant to the Editor:* David L. Harrison
*Designer:* Virginia Gianakos
*Text Editors:* Helen Barer, Jay Brennan
*Staff Writers:* Marian G. Goldman, David Lawton
*Picture Staff:* Clara Nicolai, Kathleen Shortall,
Gabrielle Smith
*Research Staff:* Sondra Albert,
Malabar Brodeur, Catherine Ireys,
Peggy Jackson, Nancy Jacobsen, Nancy Miller,
Vivian Stephens, Sandra Streepey
*Art Staff:* Patricia Byrne, Robert McKee
*Editorial Assistant:* Kathleen Beakley

EDITORIAL PRODUCTION
*Production Editor:* Douglas B. Graham
*Assistant:* Gennaro C. Esposito
*Quality Director:* Robert L. Young
*Assistant:* James J. Cox
*Copy Staff:* Rosalind Stubenberg (chief),
Susan B. Galloway, Joan Minors, Mary Orlando,
Florence Keith
*Picture Department:* Dolores A. Littles,
Jessy S. Faubert

Portions of this book were written by Mary
Batten, Margaret Elliott, Audrey Foote,
Eileen L. Hughes and Mary Williams.
Valuable assistance was provided by these
departments and individuals of Time Inc.:
Editorial Production, Norman Airey,
Nicholas Costino Jr.; Library, Benjamin Lightman;
Picture Collection, Doris O'Neil; Photographic
Laboratory, George Karas, TIME-LIFE News
Service, Murray J. Gart; Correspondents
Margot Hapgood (London), Maria Vincenza Aloisi
(Paris), Ann Natanson (Rome).

THE CONSULTANTS:
Gretel Courtney is a member of the staff of the
French Fashion Academy in New York. She has
studied pattern making and design at the Fashion Institute of Technology and haute couture at
the French Fashion Academy in New York.

Annette Feldman is a knitting and crocheting designer, both for clothing and interior decoration.
She is the author of *Knit, Purl and Design.*

Vivian Landsman studied sewing and clothes design at the Fashion Institute of Technology, and
pattern drafting and design at City College in
New York. A professional clothes designer for
custom houses in New York and Chicago, she
was formerly the costumer for the Dallas (Texas)
Repertory Theater.

Julian Tomchin is a textile designer who has been
awarded the Vogue Fabric Award and a special
American Fashion Critics' Award (Coty). A graduate of Syracuse University's Fine Arts College,
he has been chairman of the Textile Design Department at the Shenkar College of Fashion and
Textile Technology in Tel Aviv and now teaches
at the Parsons School of Design in New York.

Erica Wilson, a graduate of the Royal School of
Needlework in England, is a designer, teacher
and writer on all aspects of needlecraft. She is the
author of *Crewel Embroidery, Fun with Crewel*
and *Erica Wilson's Embroidery Book,* and has
had her own instructional television series.

# CONTENTS

INTRODUCTION TO THE CLASSIC TECHNIQUES

ashion is spinach, one knowledgeable commentator wrote. Hemlines go up this year and down the next. Sweaters shrink to reveal the figure, then expand to baggy concealment. Embroidered pillows seem to be everywhere, only to disappear as fine crewelwork comes to adorn walls. The world watches, shaking its perplexed and often annoyed head. But actually the whole business is not quite as wayward as it may seem. Fashion indeed

# ENDURING STYLES: UNDERSTATED AND ADAPTABLE

is in a constant state of change, but the nature of that change is always a response to a society that is in search of yet another ideal of beauty. Baudelaire, the French Symbolist poet, once pointed out that "there are two elements in beauty, the one permanent, the other fugitive." It would seem that, much of the time, fashion is chasing the latter. But in the hunt after the ephemeral it often paints an indelible, ineffable portrait of a moment or a decade.

Fashion indubitably reflects; like Baudelaire's poetry, it is symbolistic. The wide, heavily padded shoulders and the nipped-in waists seen on the late-show movies tell the viewer instantly that she is looking at a movie made in the early 1940s; ankle-length skirts inform watchers that they are observing the "new look" of the postwar era; mini-skirts make clear that it was just the day before yesterday—or tomorrow morning. Not that fashions necessarily express some deep significance, reflecting the character of the period. Styles may be rakish and the times staid, morals virtually nonexistent and modes demure.

It is not the fugitive, however, but rather the permanent that concerns this book. For there are certain shapes and general looks that have appealed to people of many countries over many decades and even centuries. While these shapes and looks change subtly from year to year, they never go in and out of style as the most chic fashions do. They are always popular because they look well in every circumstance.

Distinctions that will mark a style as classic in both clothing and home decoration apply to all needlecrafts —embroidery and knitting, as well as sewing and dressmaking. They are, however, best seen in clothing. Classic clothes are never extreme; basic simplicity is what makes them so adaptable to most occasions and almost any figure. Indeed a tolerance for the variations of the human body is one of the hallmarks of the classic design in clothing, just as a range of sympathetic characterizations is one of the strengths of a classic in literature.

Take the classic easy-fitting suits of the Spanish designer Balenciaga for example. They follow the human form without imposing demands of slimness or firmness that many women could never quite meet. One of the designer's fitters is actually reported to have said, "Balenciaga *likes* a little stomach." In any case he was tolerant of figure imperfections, and so many grateful women adopted his clothes that they indisputably rank as classics.

What makes classic clothes look beautiful is the excellence of their cut and proportion. Although constantly adapting in certain small ways as a nod to the current fashion, they nevertheless maintain their essential shapes—shapes that include the tailored shirt, the A-line skirt, the straight, easy dress, the pullover sweater. Like the circle and the square in architecture, they remain the major building blocks of fashion.

The colors of classics tend to be conservative, often neutrals like black and white, gray and beige, and, of course, navy blue. Once again the reason is adaptability. All are colors appropriate for many occasions; many of them lend themselves well to a variety of accent marks like scarves, belts, gloves and jewelry—and the addition or subtraction of such accessories can create widely different and pleasing looks with the same basic costume.

The fabrics for classic styles must also meet the requirements of simplicity and adaptability. They do not draw attention to themselves but to the design of the garment. Generally they are soft and inconspicuously structured: flannel, gabardine, plain weaves, thick weaves, jersey. The designs on these fabrics, if they have any, are as understated as the fabrics themselves. They are the subdued pin stripe, the herringbone, the small check, the polka dot. All of these elements—cut and proportion, color and fabric—combine to produce a look of quiet, functional beauty.

Many of the classic styles that are most popular today follow specific designs created in the 1920s by one woman, Gabrielle (Coco) Chanel, the great French couturière. Her genius lay in her realization that women were ready to break with the traditional trappings of the haute couture: the heavy fabrics, the linings, the stiffeners and what she called "ludicrous trimmings and fussy bits and pieces."

Chanel took women's fashion in the opposite direction, aiming for natural-looking ease and comfort. "A dress that is not comfortable is a failure," she said. "To be elegant is to wear clothes that permit you to move easily, gracefully, comfortably." Understatement in design, Chanel believed, was also essential to true elegance. "Always take off, never add," she urged.

She made simple, natural clothing stylish not alone through her House of Chanel in Paris, but through the impact of her own style—and her extraordinary beauty. On a cool day in Cannes, she picked up a man's pullover sweater and tied it at the waist with a scarf; soon the sweater was a Chanel fashion. Returning from a Mediterranean cruise aboard the yacht of the Duke of Westminster, she appeared in a sailor outfit that set off a face deeply tanned by the sun. Previ-

ously, women had avoided the sun; now the fair look was abandoned for a tan à la Chanel. Even her famous perfume—Chanel No. 5, so named because Coco thought five her lucky number—leaned toward the natural. Although a blend of flower fragrances, it was so concocted, at her direction, by a Riviera chemist that it had a fresh and airy note, lacking the heavy floral scent of then-popular perfumes. "Women are not flowers," she said. "Why should they want to smell like flowers?"

This philosophy led to styles, widely copied at home and in ready-to-wear factories, that have been worn ever since the 1920s by women of all ages and shapes: the short skirt, the simple jersey dress, the loose cardigan jacket, the tailored pants. Chanel did not, however, invent these enduring favorites. Their roots lie deep in antiquity.

The skirt—essentially any garment that hangs from the waist without wrapping the legs—is depicted in 12,000-year-old cave paintings that show women wearing long skirts of animal hide. Similarly, the shirt, a favorite of men and women, dates back to prehistoric times (right). The sheath—a garment that hangs freely from the shoulders and touches the body only at the bust and hips—is probably just as venerable; it was a favorite of the Greeks and Romans.

Such classic garments are certainly not the result of a linear evolution but rather are variations on age-old themes. When the sheath, for example, gained renewed popularity in the late 18th Century, it was clearly a dress, not a Greek chiton. Then the Napoleonic Empire replaced the First Republic, and the sheath changed again, subtly, as it was gathered in under the bust. Decades later, when Victorian corsets and stays were eventually put aside, it emerged once more, now adorned with beading or fringe but almost straight from shoulder to a hem that might zig and dip.

By 1919 the sheath had been varied still again by the French couturière Madeleine Vionnet, who used black crepe de Chine for an unlined dress that slipped over the head. This was the first example of the "little black dress," soon to be *de rigueur* as Chanel and other designers made it part of the emerging classic wardrobe. Then, in the 1960s, the American designer Mainbocher simplified the sheath still further into the memo-

rable "little nothing dress"—a sleeveless dress that had a round neckline and touched the body at the bust and hips. Quintessentially elegant, this was almost a reincarnation of the ancient chiton, enjoying one of its finest hours.

In all ages, the classic look has been simple—and therein lies the difficulty in achieving it. With simple, straightforward lines, most of them clearly visible, the design demands quality. Only the highest of standards—in selection of pattern and fabric, in preparation of fabric and in final assembly—can make such simple clothing classic rather than commonplace.

Choosing a pattern for a classic garment

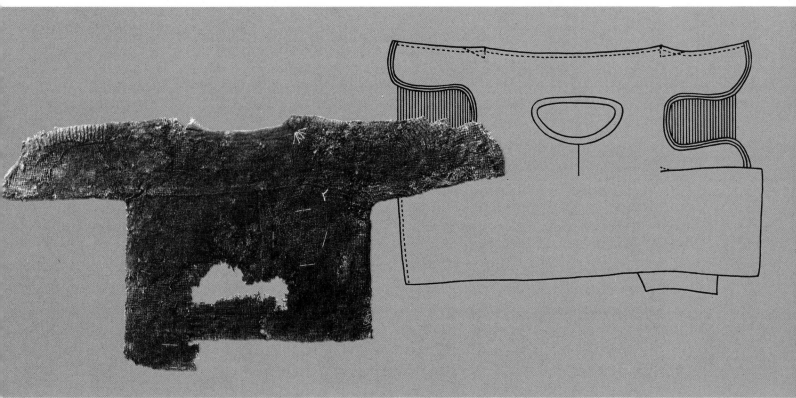

Evidence of the antiquity of the shirt, this short-sleeved garment was worn by a Danish woman more than 3,000 years ago. The shirt was made from one piece, as sketched at right. Two side flaps folded over to meet in the vertical seam; the top half folded down to meet the upper edges of the flaps, thus joining the body of the shirt at the horizontal seam, leaving the neck opening properly positioned and closing the ribbed sleeves.

seems easy at first glance. Superficially, one shirt-dress looks like another—if there were no such strong family resemblance, the style would not be classic. The differences from one version to another must, by definition, be so subtle that they escape any but the most knowing eye. Paradoxically, this very subtlety makes stylistic variations crucially important. A longer seam here, extra fullness there or a picayune change in collar size can make dramatic alterations in the look of the garment, for a small change often serves to emphasize—or conceal—body structure.

A shirt with a high-standing collar, for instance, will engulf a woman with a short neck, but a softer, looser collar will fall gracefully away from the neckline and actually give the impression of a longer neck. Wide, floppy pants look elegant and graceful on a tall, slender woman but will swamp the shorter, fuller figure. A matter of an inch or two in the length or the width of a skirt can mean the difference between good proportions and dumpiness. Most patterns available today make it easy to adjust the lengths and widths of simple garments. But the basic cut cannot be altered by such minor changes in measurement; the style you choose necessarily has to be one that is coordinated to, and generally flatters, your basic shape.

It is equally important to use forethought when selecting material for a particular style. Medium-weight flannel, for instance, is splendid for a skirt or straight pants, but something softer, such as a silky knit, is better for a blouse, while a medium-weight jersey makes an elegant A-line dress. Patterns may be woven into or printed on the fabric but their color should be flattering to you and coordinated with other parts of your wardrobe. Generally, solid-colored fabrics are more elegant and versatile because they readily combine with prints and stripes and other designs. Patterned fabrics are often used for blouses and also frequently serve as linings, panels or borders for a variety of garments. But if you decide on using a print, make sure the scale of the design and texture are right for your figure. A bold stripe or print in a stiff or bulky fabric may overwhelm a small figure or accentuate a big one, yet can produce a very attractive silhouette if it is used on a lightweight fabric such as jersey or voile.

When choosing pattern and fabric, you have to select from other people's work. The standard of sewing is one you set for yourself. The way pieces are cut, joined and finally stitched together plays the final, definitive role in determining quality. A good eye and mechanical skills are required, but they are readily developed if you understand the basic principles.

Perhaps the first thing to appreciate about sewing is that it is totally logical. Virtually every seam or line of stitching in clothes is there for an important reason. They shape the cloth either to fit around the contours of the body or to allow the body ease of movement and action.

In simple garments such as those that are included in this volume, the functional quality of the design is relatively easy to see. The special seam called a dart, for example, enables the fabric to curve gracefully over the bust. The shaped side seam of a skirt neatly follows the outward curve of the body from waist to hip. Thus it fits the waist but allows for the movements of the hip.

In more complicated styles, where the seaming is more intricate, this functional aspect of the stitching lines may be less apparent. But regardless of the fashion details, all clothes are meant to be worn on the body —to be moved in, sat in, breathed in, walked in—and this relationship of design to fit and movement remains the basic factor in their overall construction. The pattern of cutting and stitching always follows these functional dictates, and as you put any garment together, you are actually sewing these aspects—fit and movement—into their appropriate places.

Take the fitting of a sleeve into a shoulder section, for example. It makes a good illustration of this relation of fit and movement to the actual process of sewing. Think of it as the joining of two curves, one longer than the other. The curve made by the sleeve opening is in every case longer than the curve made by the shoulder opening because you have to move your arm much more extensively than you have to move your shoulder. The longer curve must fit into the shorter curve in such a way that the arm can move freely and the sleeve will hang straight and gracefully from the shoulder when the arm is down. To achieve this combination of fit and movement the extra material in the top of the sleeve is made to match the smaller armhole with the help of a row of gathering stitches. Directions showing how to perform this critical procedure—beginning with the first pinning steps and continuing through the basting, the machine stitching and the final pressing —can be found on pages 118-125.

Once you grasp the importance of this relationship of fit and movement to the actual sewing techniques, as in the sleeve, much of the apparent mystery of sewing will disappear. The logic of what you are doing, why you need to put two pieces of shaped fabric together in a particular fashion, becomes considerably clearer. This understanding can help you in a number of ways. First of all, it makes fitting a much more straightforward business; instead of guessing how you should correct a seam that is pulling or a dart that is awry, you will see what the seam or dart is supposed to be accomplishing and adjust it so it can do its job more smoothly.

Sewing techniques also begin to make more sense. A curved seam, for example, needs to be stitched in one continuous line and then carefully trimmed. This is the only way it will produce a smooth, uninterrupted arc. The more you understand about how clothes are cut and shaped and how you can contribute to their fit and quality by using the proper sewing techniques, the more satisfying a pastime sewing will become. How to begin and end a seam, how to insert a zipper, how to put on a waistband —these operations are the veritable staples of sewing. Master them and they will enter your repertory forever.

Such an approach to sewing enables you to produce clothes that have a truly professional quality to them—and it also serves to make the related arts of embroidery, knitting and crocheting the useful pleasures they are meant to be.

# Variations on the classic themes

They may seem worlds apart—but the handsome garments at left have a great deal in common. The coat, the dresses and the jacket, all are variations on the basic classic style. Like the skirts, shirts and pants pictured on the following pages, they owe their timelessness to simple lines and good proportions. So long as these two classic requisites remain dominant, a wide assortment of design details can be introduced to create clothes for many different moods. The final effect will depend on the length in which the garment is made, the fabric chosen—its texture, weight or pattern—and the addition or subtraction of such design elements as sleeves, pockets, collars or buttons. The result can be as sophisticated as the long magenta evening dress at left, as sedate as the tailored navy dress and jacket at far left, or as jaunty as the pink tunic at upper left—but still classic.

# Versatility in simple skirts

Typical of the many ways in which a basic skirt can be varied while still retaining the simplicity of classic design are the three versions shown here. One straightforward variation is provided by the choice between a side zipper, back zipper or, as at left, no zipper at all but buttons down the front. Embellishments—like the patch pockets on this skirt as well as on the short, pert skirt at near right, and the unpressed inverted pleat on the long, graceful skirt at far right—create further variety within the classic format.

# Soft blouse, tailored shirt

The timeless brown wool shirtwaist dress *(below)* is little more than an overgrown shirt. Even with the addition of a tie belt, the use of lustrous fabric and the substitution of a collar attached directly to the garment body for the crisper collar set on a collarband, the gold evening dress at right is nonetheless based on the same design as the men's and women's tailored shirts in the foreground.

# Pants for both sexes

At the opposite extreme from the snug, fly-front yellow pants at far left, cut like boys' jeans, are the feminine, flowing, blue palazzo pants beside them. At right is the compromise that goes anywhere pants can be worn: trim red slacks, form-fitting yet comfortably relaxed in their cut. Framing all three are their prototype, men's slacks in a blue knit.

# 2
## THE SEWING MACHINE
## THE IRON
## NEEDLE, THIMBLE, THREAD

Whether you are sewing a simple apron, a pleated skirt or a well-tailored dress, the basic tools required are not numerous; needles and thread, a thimble, a sewing machine and a steam iron will accomplish the job.

Today many women come to these marvelous instruments quite untutored. But a couple of generations ago, young women learned the fundamentals of sewing and its

# EQUIPMENT FOR A WELL-STOCKED WORKROOM

accompanying equipment along with their reading and sums. Sometimes, the instructions were even set to music. "How should a little girl be prepared for sewing?" asked one such lyrical primer. "By having clean hands, clean nails, a clean face, tidy hair and a clean apron." Another verse went on to ask whether the little girl should "stoop over her work," and the singsong reply went: "No, because it cramps the lungs. She should bring her work to her eyes, rather than her eyes to her work." The little girl learned, too, that "a good sewer's workbasket" should at the minimum contain: "a thimble, pin cushion, needle box with sewing needles, darning needles, a tape . . . and a box to hold spools of cotton."

Sound advice then, and a good starting point for the well-equipped workbasket today. Of the countless other devices now crowding notion counters, the majority are needed only for special tasks. But there are some valuable items of hand-sewing equipment not to be found in a 19th Century kit and that will simplify a number of tasks. A 60-inch tape measure with numbers on both sides is best for body measurements as well as for gauging curved stitching lines. The glass-fiber rather than the cloth or plastic type is preferred; it will not fray or stretch. A transparent plastic draftsman's drawing aid, called a French curve, that enables you to trace smooth curves instead of drawing them freehand is also handy. A 2- by 18-inch transparent plastic ruler should be available for short measurements, as well as a yardstick for longer ones. You will also want pressing cloths of both the see-through and thick cotton varieties, as well as a sleeveboard for ironing sleeves. One useful gadget is an emery bag—a small pincushion that contains abrasives similar to those used for sharpening knives. Pins and needles are quickly sharpened when thrust in and out of it. In addition to the larger scissors, shears and other tools used for cutting and marking (pages 78-79), you will need a pair of pointed, 4-inch scissors for cutting buttonholes, snipping thread and other small jobs.

With all this equipment on hand, the old-fashioned sewing basket no longer suffices for storage. Some women are blessed with a special sewing room, perhaps with a large table on which to spread out materials and tools. But such luxuries are rare, and generally equipment must be squirreled into a closet or a cabinet.

Even minimal room need not interfere with efficient—and attractive—storage of sewing gear. Much of it can be displayed with pride, the way a good cook shows off pans and spice jars in her kitchen. A plastic silverware tray, for example, can simultaneously store and display the riot of colors available in your supply of spools of thread. If the spools are laid on their sides, colors are instantly identifiable. Large clear plastic boxes can hold patterns separated by identifying index cards. Wicker baskets serve as handsome containers for materials—a laundry hamper, for example, can store bolts of fabric standing up. (Remember, however, to line the hamper to prevent snagging.) And an old trunk makes still another capacious receptacle for fabrics, while cigar or old-fashioned tin candy boxes hold notions.

Neither the old sewing basket nor any substitute, of course, can provide proper storage for two crucial tools: steam iron and sewing machine. Each should be kept near your other sewing equipment where it will be handy for frequent use yet safe from accidental damage—on a sturdy stand, in a case or upon a protected shelf.

For the machine and iron are the keys to modern sewing. The steam iron (pages 36-

*37)*, properly used, eliminates problems of puckered seams and prominent darts that formerly made good fit so difficult to achieve at home. And today's versatile sewing machines *(below and following pages)* can automatically perform wonders of intricate stitching that once were the awe-inspiring accomplishments of professionals and a few talented amateurs.

# The invention that automated needlework

Some of today's sewing machines are marvels of ingenuity. They sew forward, backward and zigzag. They hem, gather, quilt, ruffle and overcast. Once the technique of using one has been mastered, about all you have to do is turn a dial or two and, presto, you have an elegantly smocked bodice.

The goal of the first sewing machines was simply to make a straight seam, and even that was difficult to achieve. All the inventors tried to copy hand sewing, using a single thread and a single needle to create a chain of stitches. The chain, however, was a string of weak links; if one broke, the entire chain could be easily pulled out.

The key to success was to create a system employing two threads—one carried through the fabric by a needle on one side and the other held on the reverse by a shuttle, or bobbin, around which the first thread could lock. Essential to such a lock-stitch system was the placement of the eye in the needle. Ever since prehistoric times, the eye had been in the top and the entire needle passed through the fabric. But in machine sewing, a needle clamped in the machine could not pass its entire length through the fabric. The eye therefore had to be placed in the tip of the needle to enable the upper thread to lock onto the lower in a swift, dip-in dip-out motion.

Dozens of men participated in the evolution of the basic lock-stitch machine. Three, however, made the all-important breakthroughs. In the early 1830s, Walter Hunt, an inventor in the classic mode of the Yankee tinkerer, put together a workable model employing a needle with the eye at its tip. But Hunt failed to see the potential in his machine and sold his rights to it. Elias Howe, a farmer and machinist, is generally credited with inventing the sewing machine, and in fact did patent one in 1846, but his machine aroused little interest.

It was Isaac Singer, a one-time actor, who created the real prototype of the modern sewing machine in the 1850s. He borrowed liberally from earlier efforts but managed to put them all together into a smoothly functioning package. His machine used the needle with an eye in its tip that both Hunt and Howe had employed. But he incorporated into it the now-standard presser foot to hold the material, a toothed wheel to move the fabric forward after each stitch, and a foot treadle that enabled the operator to use both hands while working.

Singer's machine was an almost instant success, and the lock stitch that he employed is the basis of most machine stitching today. The zigzag stitch, which is now a standard part of almost all new machines, is simply a lock stitch made as the needle swings alternately from left to right. There are many other variations as well, to make possible the performance of a number of intricate sewing tasks.

In selecting a machine it is important to consider how many of these innovations make sense for you. There are some accessories that are practically essential: for example, a foot that facilitates the insertion of zippers, and another that will finish a buttonhole in a trice. There are other things —embroidering and monogramming, for example—that contemporary models can do, but that most sewers may need only occasionally. When deciding on a machine, make sure it can perform all the essential operations—and a few more.

In general, heavier machines will perform better than light ones, which tend to skitter and slip. In any event, remember that your sewing interests are likely to expand. It makes good sense to have a machine that will accommodate your widening horizons. But whatever level you are now working at, or aspire to, the essential first step is to learn how to use the modern machine at your disposal—a subject that is discussed on the following pages.

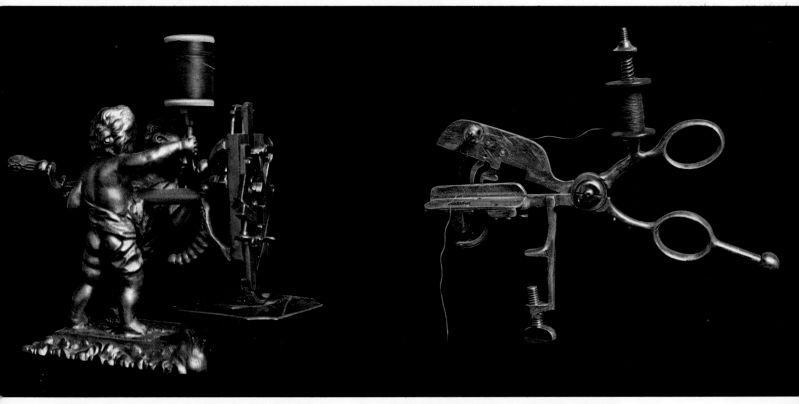

These two table-model sewing machines were among dozens that appeared in the 1850s after the success of Isaac Singer's expensive machine. The Cherub model, at left, was crank operated; the Shears machine worked with a scissors-like handle. Each retailed for under $25. Neither, however, was capable of sewing a sturdy, lock-stitched seam, as Singer's could; they managed only a chain stitch for minor chores like repairing tears.

# Techniques of sewing by machine

Certain fundamentals concerning needles, threads and stitching apply to all sewing machines. The standard Size 14 needle is suitable for all medium-weight fabrics except knits; the latter are best sewn with a Size 14 ballpoint needle. The standard thread is No. 50 mercerized cotton or a synthetic. If your fabric is all synthetic, the thread must be synthetic too. Set the machine to sew at 12 stitches per inch; to machine baste change the setting to six stitches per inch. Unless your machine makes stitches designed for knits, they need special procedures (page 33).

The most frustrating mishap in machine stitching occurs when the thread slips out of the needle at stopping points. To prevent that, start and stop with needle and take-up lever at the highest positions.

...e hand wheel until
... needle and the
...ake-up lever are at
...hest positions. Pull
...ches of thread from
...dle and the bobbin.

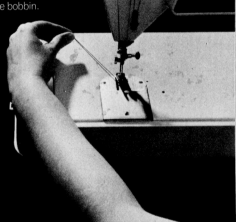

## AFTER SEWING

Raise the take-up lever to its
highest position, raise the
presser foot and pull out the
fabric. Use the thread cutter
on the back of the machine,
or scissors, to cut off the
needle and bobbin threads.

If, when the threads are cut
*(above, right)*, both are on
the same side of the fabric
(as on darts), tie a knot close
to the stitching and trim the
excess with scissors.

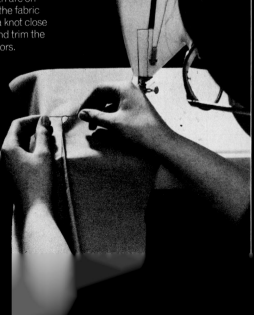

If, when the threads are cut
*(above)*, one shows on the
top, tug the lower thread to
pull down a loop from the
upper thread. Catch it with
a pin and pull it through.
Knot and trim.

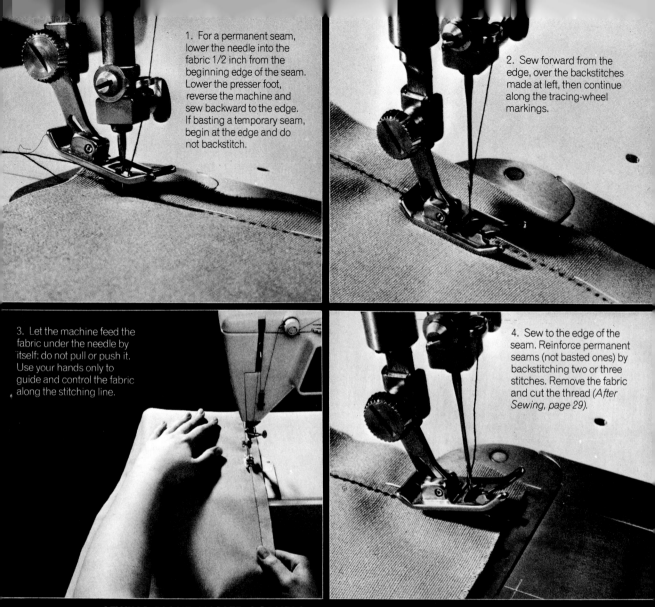

1. For a permanent seam, lower the needle into the fabric 1/2 inch from the beginning edge of the seam. Lower the presser foot, reverse the machine and sew backward to the edge. If basting a temporary seam, begin at the edge and do not backstitch.

2. Sew forward from the edge, over the backstitches made at left, then continue along the tracing-wheel markings.

3. Let the machine feed the fabric under the needle by itself: do not pull or push it. Use your hands only to guide and control the fabric along the stitching line.

4. Sew to the edge of the seam. Reinforce permanent seams (not basted ones) by backstitching two or three stitches. Remove the fabric and cut the thread (*After Sewing, page 29*).

## SEWING RIGHT-ANGLED CORNERS

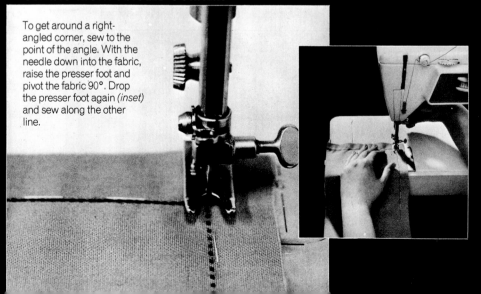

To get around a right-angled corner, sew to the point of the angle. With the needle down into the fabric, raise the presser foot and pivot the fabric 90°. Drop the presser foot again (*inset*) and sew along the other line.

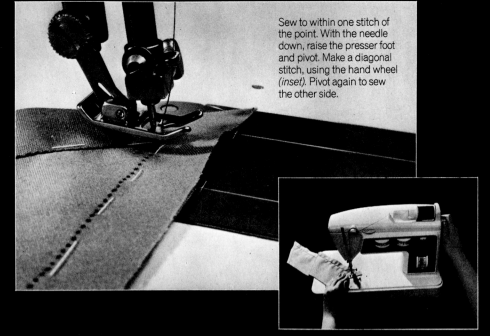

Sew to within one stitch of the point. With the needle down, raise the presser foot and pivot. Make a diagonal stitch, using the hand wheel *(inset)*. Pivot again to sew the other side.

## SEWING AROUND CURVES

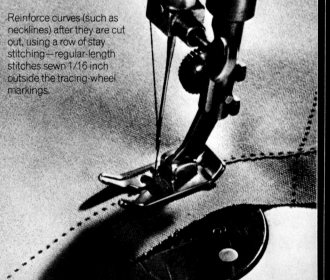

Reinforce curves (such as necklines) after they are cut out, using a row of stay stitching—regular-length stitches sewn 1/16 inch outside the tracing-wheel markings.

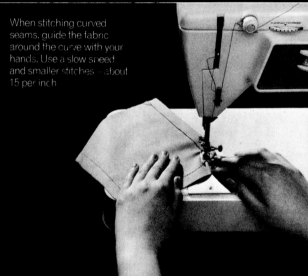

When stitching curved seams, guide the fabric around the curve with your hands. Use a slow speed and smaller stitches—about 15 per inch.

## SEWING EASED SEAMS

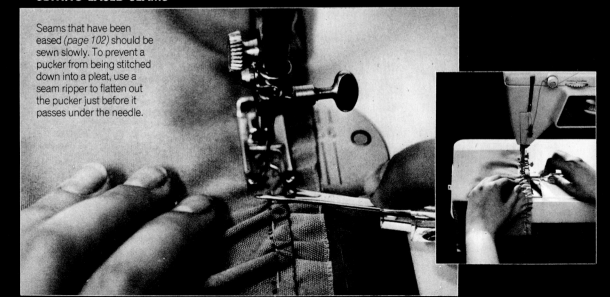

Seams that have been eased *(page 102)* should be sewn slowly. To prevent a pucker from being stitched down into a pleat, use a seam ripper to flatten out the pucker just before it passes under the needle.

## EDGE STITCHING

1. Use the presser foot to guide you in edge stitching—sewing a straight line of decorative stitching close to the edge of the fabric. Using a straight-stitch foot, follow the inside edge of its short toe; using an all-purpose foot, follow its right toe.

2. To turn the corner, pause at the point with the needle in the fabric, raise the presser foot and pivot. Push the point under the presser foot with the tip of a seam ripper.

## TOPSTITCHING

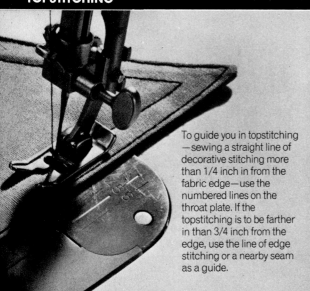

To guide you in topstitching—sewing a straight line of decorative stitching more than 1/4 inch in from the fabric edge—use the numbered lines on the throat plate. If the topstitching is to be farther in than 3/4 inch from the edge, use the line of edge stitching or a nearby seam as a guide.

## SEWING ZIPPERS

When sewing on a zipper by machine, use the special one-toed zipper foot. Move the foot to the left of the needle if the zipper is to the right, and vice versa, so as to prevent the zipper tab and teeth from interfering with the stitching.

## RIPPING OUT A LINE OF STITCHING

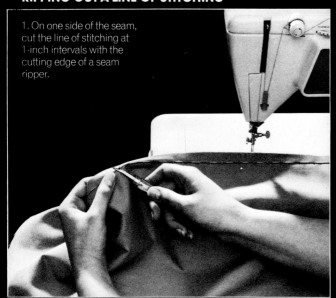

1. On one side of the seam, cut the line of stitching at 1-inch intervals with the cutting edge of a seam ripper.

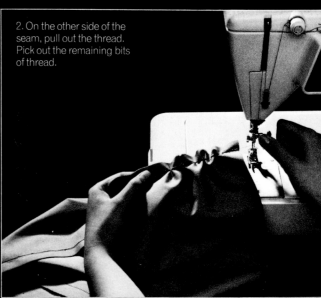

2. On the other side of the seam, pull out the thread. Pick out the remaining bits of thread.

# SPECIAL TIPS FOR SEWING KNIT FABRICS

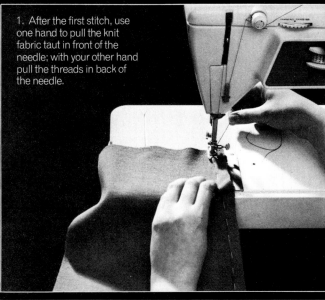

1. After the first stitch, use one hand to pull the knit fabric taut in front of the needle; with your other hand pull the threads in back of the needle.

2. When enough fabric has passed by the needle to grasp from behind, stretch it taut from behind the needle as well as in front. Keep the fabric taut throughout your sewing.

3. Reinforce curved seams by slowly sewing a row of small stitches—15 per inch—on the stitching line, then sewing a second row 1/16 inch outside the first.

4. To rip out a seam, spread it open and snip the thread with a seam ripper. Continue spreading and snipping.

5. Finish raw seam edges with a zigzag stitch 1/2 inch in from the seam. Trim (*page 101*).

# From sad iron to steam iron

Today, the iron, a gleaming model of functional efficiency, is as much at home in the sewing room as in the laundry room. Indeed, it is as essential to understand the use and importance of ironing and pressing techniques as it is to be able to sew a straight seam. For it is the iron that can change a seam from a simple row of stitches into an integral and often indistinguishable part of a finished garment.

In the last few years new irons especially designed for sewing have become available. They have smaller soles and narrower, more tapered tips than conventional irons, facilitating work in tight spots like sleeve interiors. They are light in weight, which not only makes them easier to work with but also helps the user to avoid the conventional mistake of using too much pressure when ironing a freshly constructed seam, for example. The use of heavy pressure makes an impression of the seam visible on the other side of the material.

But there are cautions to be observed with these irons as well as the older, heavier models, particularly when working with synthetic fabrics and blended fabrics. Such materials are extremely sensitive to heat. Most women tend to set their temperature controls too high, causing an expensive fabric to melt or stick to the iron.

Unfortunately, there is as yet no way that precise guidelines can be prescribed.

You must either use a pressing cloth or experiment with the iron and a snippet of fabric. Start with temperatures slightly lower than those recommended by the fabric manufacturer. This is especially wise when working with fabrics that contain newly developed fibers or chemical finishes; not until they have been in general use for some years will anyone be certain what the precise temperature setting should be.

Before the coming of the electric iron, no one worried much about precise temperature controls. People worried instead about getting the iron hot, a task that took up a great deal of time. There were a number of methods, none of them quick, easy or very reliable. Probably the most common way of heating the old cast-iron, wooden-handled flatiron was simply to put it on the kitchen stove and wait. When it was hot, it was often too hot and promptly scorched the cloth. When the iron cooled off too much, back it went to the stove to heat again. This continual stop-and-go routine made ironing an irksome affair. One manufacturer tried to capitalize on the problem by offering a small pot-bellied stove with a ledge around its middle so that as many as eight irons might heat at one time. These and other flatirons (*opposite*) were also known as "sad" irons — but not, as might be supposed, because of the depressing nature of the whole wretched business. "Sad" had the archaic meaning of "heavy" or "dense."

While the ledge-heated irons represented an efficient step forward, the real solution lay in placing the source of heat within the iron itself, as many people realized. One manufacturer produced an iron with an internal cavity into which a hot iron slug could be inserted. The slug iron usually came with several extra slugs so one was always hot, ready for use. Another attempt was the charcoal iron—a "self-heater." The self-heater was particularly recommended for use in hot weather, presumably so that the ironing could be done in some cool room away from the cook stove. But self-heaters were relatively heavy. Some weighed as much as 14 pounds.

The modern iron, with its heat source now placed firmly inside where it belongs, is a far cry from great-grandmother's—or grandmother's, for that matter. The popular spray-steam iron makes it easy to accom-plish the skillful blending of stitch and fab-ric. The built-in steam feature eliminates the old need to dampen entire areas from a sprinkling bottle, and the spray permits the operator to spot-press darts and puckers. Some modern steam irons are designed so that they do not need mineral-free water and can be filled with tap water without risk that minerals will cause clogging. Some have adjustable cord attachments to adapt them to either left- or right-handed use.

The variety is great. Once, however, you have found the iron that suits your needs, you will discover it is a major instrument of sewing success. It is worth knowing, and knowing well, how to make it work best.

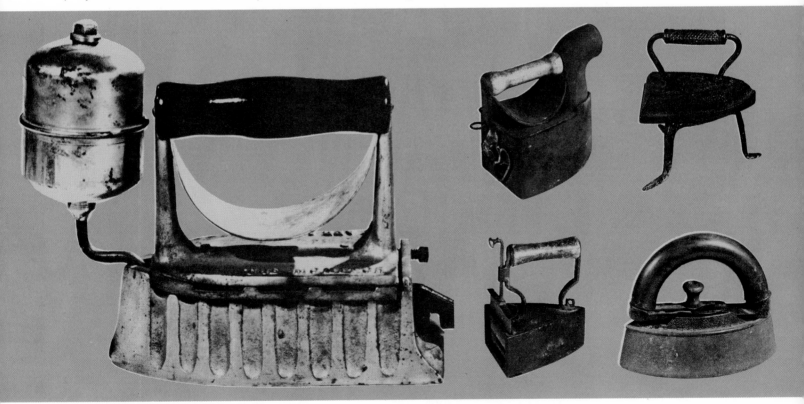

Before electricity, irons were ungainly—though often ingenious—contrivances. The iron at left was heated by natural gas. The irons at right are *(top)* a "self-heater" into which hot charcoal was placed, and a conventional flatiron, heated on a stove. At bottom are a brass iron with a removable metal core that was heated in a stove, and an early-20th Century iron. Its wooden handle was detached when the iron was heating.

# The dissimilar skills of ironing and pressing

Use the iron as soon as you begin a project, to smooth the material and pattern. The secret of perfect ironing is to glide, not push, the iron forward.

Pressing is a very different technique, used to flatten details such as pleats or seams, as soon as they are permanently sewn. The trick here is to set the iron down vertically, directly on the spot to be pressed.

It is easier to press a seam during the sewing process than it is to wait until later, when the iron must be wiggled into the corners of the completed garment. A combination steam-dry iron is best.

Final ironing and pressing are done on the right side of the fabric (the side that is visible in the completed garment). Use a cloth over the material to protect it from scorching or from developing a shine—a silicone cloth for heavy fabrics and cheesecloth for lightweight materials. To get the right ironing temperature, it is a good idea to experiment with a swatch of extra material.

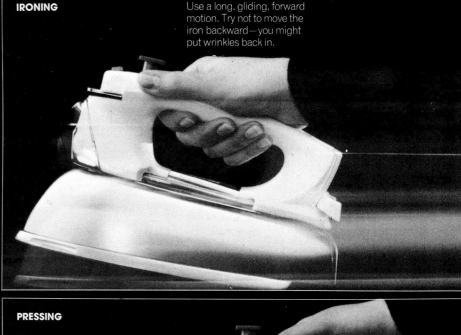

**IRONING**

Use a long, gliding, forward motion. Try not to move the iron backward—you might put wrinkles back in.

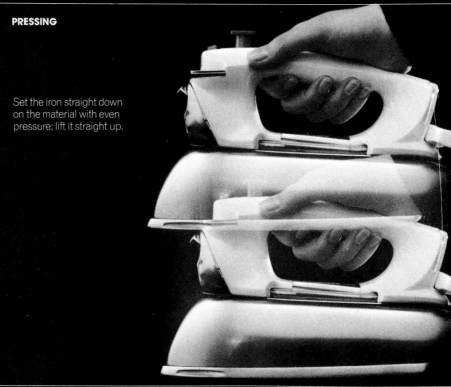

**PRESSING**

Set the iron straight down on the material with even pressure; lift it straight up.

**DETAIL PRESSING**

With your free hand, open up angles and folds in the fabric. Use only the point of the iron to press confined spaces.

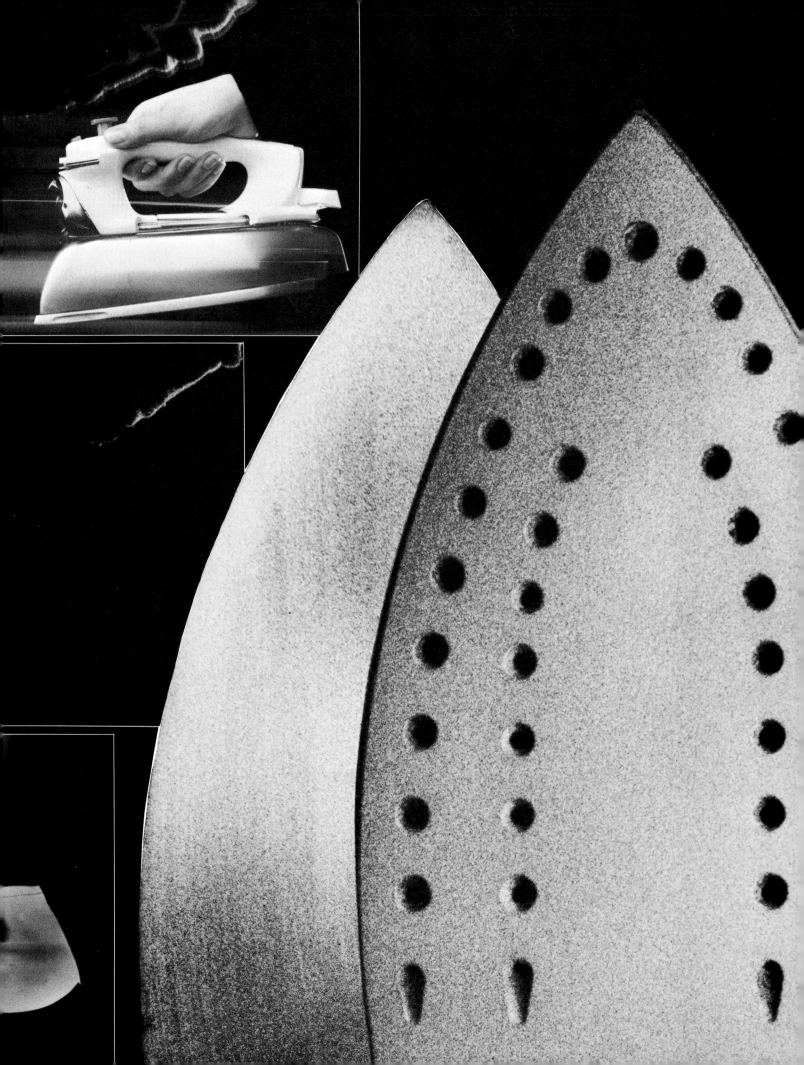

# Ancient tools to sew a fine seam

They are small things, the basic tools of sewing—the slender, shiny needle, the fine length of spun thread, the pebbled hump of the thimble—and, rather sadly, they are considered fairly unremarkable today. They are simply taken for granted. But this has not always been so.

Before the craft of needlemaking became well known and, of course, long before modern manufacturing procedures made them so plentiful, good needles were highly prized possessions. In England as late as the 16th Century, particularly in the smaller villages and rural areas, most goods and tools were provided by traveling fairs or peddlers, and both appeared only intermittently. So a lost needle might not be replaced for months, and often a household might have only one. So prevalent was this problem that it became the theme of *Gammer Gerton's Needle,* a popular play of the time that sent a number of characters trotting across the boards in search of the missing implement. Needlemakers of the time tried to help with the actual problem of the easily lost needle; they placed a little kink halfway down the shaft so that the needle would not slip out of the material when the sewing was put aside. Apparently, the kink did not make the in-and-out movement of the needle

much more difficult. But then the work done in these small rural cottages was not the fine hand sewing we think of today.

According to Chinese legend, a lowly worm changed that. Around 2500 B.C., Empress Hsi-ling dropped a silkworm cocoon into a bowl of warm water and, to her astonishment, saw it soften and turn into a gauzy mass. The tradition does not tell us why the Empress bothered to pull on the loosened cocoon, but tugging gently, she discovered that she had one long continuous filament in her hand. This was raw silk, so fine that several strands must be twisted together to form thread for sewing. Legend further says that the Chinese went on to invent the steel needle, the better to use this fine silk thread. Here the story falls apart; there was no steel in China until centuries after Hsi-ling's time.

If the claim of the Chinese to a first in needlemaking seems shaky, bolts of fine silk nonetheless did begin to travel along the caravan routes from the Orient to Europe, and by the Middle Ages skilled metalworkers in Damascus and Antioch were supplying the Continent with its first steel needles. Slowly the expertise involved spread to Western Europe, and by the reign of Elizabeth I steel needles were gradually replacing the clumsy bronze ones of medieval England.

The very names of needles tell us what great changes steel brought to hand stitching over the years. Needles employed in common household use came to be known as sharps, as they are even to this day, for steel had made it possible to grind a far finer point than could be achieved with soft bronze. Steel also made it possible to produce long, slender milliner's needles, sometimes known as straws—perhaps because they were used to make straw hats. Young girls, whose unskilled fingers might have been pierced by sharps, were given "blunts" for their endless stitching exercises (the samplers they made with blunts actually were training runs never intended for framing). Tailors also used blunts, as did glovers and shoemakers, for the heavier fabrics and for leather work.

Variety and abundance marked the heyday of sewing accomplishment in the West. Ladies competed in the fineness and intricacy of their work. Clothes were exquisitely finished and decorated. Perhaps the ultimate in fine stitchery came into being with reproductions on white silk of small engravings and etchings. The sewing was minute, performed with needles less than one hundredth of an inch in diameter and the finest of gray or black thread.

Such dedication may seem astonishing today. Certainly it is not the style of most modern sewers. We tend to concentrate on the more prosaic accomplishments of hand sewing: a handkerchief's rolled edge, the hem of a dress, a careful buttonhole. But the needle and thread, however we may use and mechanize them, remain the essential tools of all sewing.

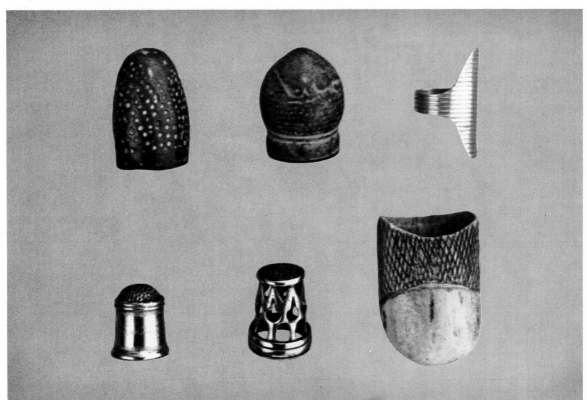

A gallery of thimbles, from diverse areas and eras, indicates the manifold forms and materials used for this basic sewing tool. Top from left: Spain, bronze, 14th or 15th Century; Syria, domed bronze, 300 B.C.; British West Indies, ring-shaped silver, 19th Century; bottom: Mexico, gold cylinder with a steel tip, 19th Century; Peru, open gold and silver latticework with a bone tip, 18th Century; and Alaska, bone, 19th Century.

# How to work with needles and thread

The easiest sewing tool to select is the thimble; it should be lightweight and fit snugly on your middle finger.

Next to be considered is the thread, which should be about two shades darker than the fabric color. Mercerized cotton is the commonest thread; use it to sew cotton, linen, rayon and cotton-synthetic blends. Silk thread of the type called A is superior for silk, wool, wool-silk blends and synthetics; it is elastic and leaves no lint. Use polyester thread for knits, and silk buttonhole twist for buttons and buttonholes.

Needles are available in 24 sizes —the higher the number, the larger the needle. The eye must be large enough for thread to pass through freely and the shank must be heavy enough not to bend—but the point must be fine enough to pierce fabric without marring. Use Sizes 7 or 8 for polyester and mercerized thread, Sizes 8 or 9 for silk thread, and 4 or 5 for buttonhole twist.

Simplistic as they may seem to some, poking the thread through the needle eye and knotting the end securely are often troublesome. The pictures at right present straightforward methods of accomplishing both fundamental steps.

## THREADING THE NEEDLE

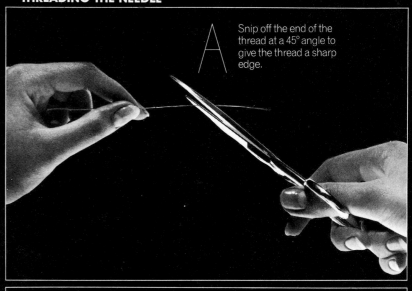

A  Snip off the end of the thread at a 45° angle to give the thread a sharp edge.

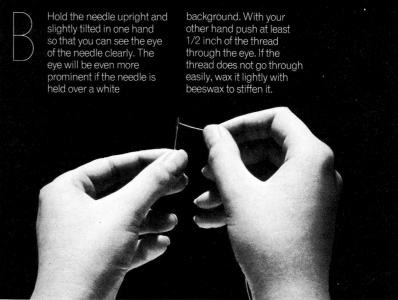

B  Hold the needle upright and slightly tilted in one hand so that you can see the eye of the needle clearly. The eye will be even more prominent if the needle is held over a white background. With your other hand push at least 1/2 inch of the thread through the eye. If the thread does not go through easily, wax it lightly with beeswax to stiffen it.

C  From the other side of the needle, pull the thread through the eye.

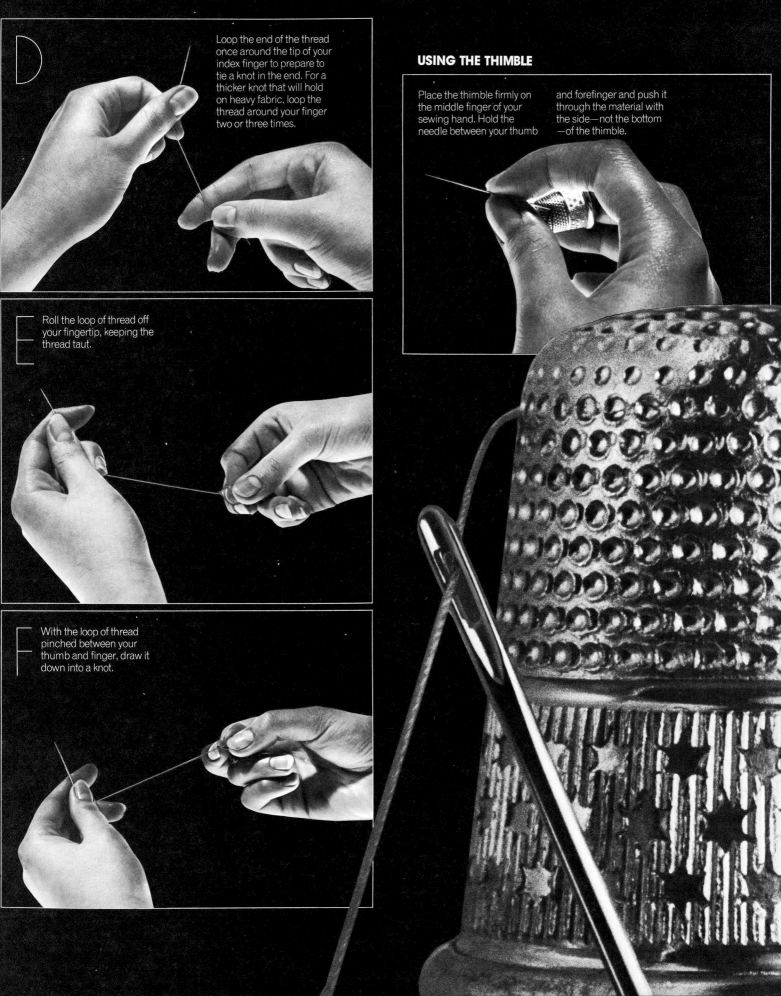

**D** Loop the end of the thread once around the tip of your index finger to prepare to tie a knot in the end. For a thicker knot that will hold on heavy fabric, loop the thread around your finger two or three times.

**E** Roll the loop of thread off your fingertip, keeping the thread taut.

**F** With the loop of thread pinched between your thumb and finger, draw it down into a knot.

## USING THE THIMBLE

Place the thimble firmly on the middle finger of your sewing hand. Hold the needle between your thumb and forefinger and push it through the material with the side—not the bottom —of the thimble.

# Stitches for sewing by hand

No matter how sophisticated your sewing machine, there will always be a time and place for hand stitches —not only temporary basting and marking stitching but the permanent finishing stitches that can make the difference between an amateur and a professional look.

Basting stitches are sewn with a single strand of thread no more than 30 inches long. When used to indicate a stitching line, they are sewn directly on the seam line markings; when used to hold garment pieces together for fitting purposes, they are sewn a fraction inside or outside the seam line, wherever they will leave no visible trace. On knit fabrics, they begin and end with a loose fastening stitch. Bastings on knits are sewn very loosely and the stitch length is shorter than specified in the instructions that follow.

Permanent hand stitches are usually made with a single strand of thread no more than 18 inches long. Each stitch shown on these pages performs a definite function; the choice of stitch depends on the purpose for which it is intended, and the fabric to be sewn.

**THE FASTENING STITCH:** To anchor thread

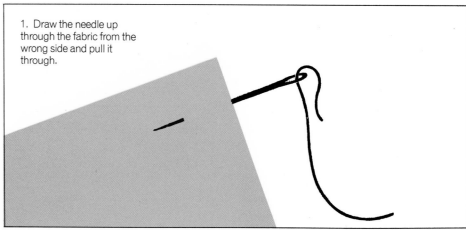

1. Draw the needle up through the fabric from the wrong side and pull it through.

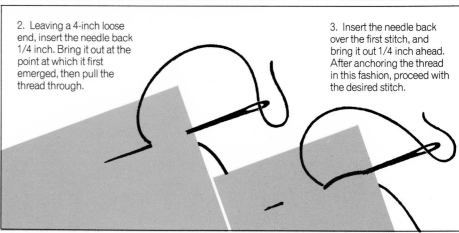

2. Leaving a 4-inch loose end, insert the needle back 1/4 inch. Bring it out at the point at which it first emerged, then pull the thread through.

3. Insert the needle back over the first stitch, and bring it out 1/4 inch ahead. After anchoring the thread in this fashion, proceed with the desired stitch.

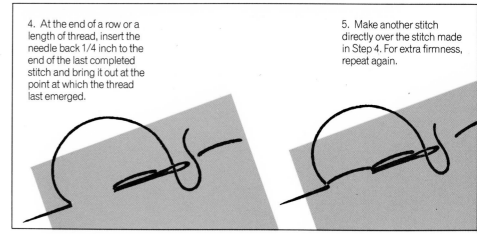

4. At the end of a row or a length of thread, insert the needle back 1/4 inch to the end of the last completed stitch and bring it out at the point at which the thread last emerged.

5. Make another stitch directly over the stitch made in Step 4. For extra firmness, repeat again.

6. To remove stitches secured with fastening stitches, first snip the double fastening stitches, then other stitches at 5-inch intervals; pull out the threads.

**IF YOU ARE LEFT-HANDED...**
Follow the directions in Steps 1-5, proceeding from left to right and inserting the needle as shown below. Remove the stitches as shown in Step 6.

## THE BASTING STITCH: For markings and temporary sewing

1. Using a knotted thread (or in the case of knits, a loose fastening stitch, and in the case of markings, a 4-inch loose end), take a 1/2-inch stitch in the fabric; pull the thread through.

2. Take another 1/2-inch stitch 1/2 inch beyond the first; pull the thread through firmly, but loosely enough not to pucker the fabric. Continue the process.

3. When you are finished, a row of 1/2-inch stitches will appear on both sides of the piece or pieces of fabric. Secure the end of the line of stitches with a fastening stitch (opposite) or leave a 4-inch loose thread, in the case of markings.

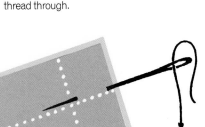

4. To remove the basting stitches, first snip the stitch next to the knot, next snip the fastening stitches and then continue to snip at 5-inch intervals; remove the threads. Never pull knots through fabric.

**IF YOU ARE LEFT-HANDED...**
Insert the needle as shown; follow the directions in Steps 1-3, proceeding from left to right. Remove the stitches as in Step 4.

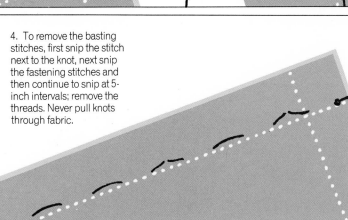

## THE RUNNING STITCH: To mark or baste small areas and to topstitch

1. Insert the needle through the fabric to be basted or marked and pull the thread through, leaving a loose end 4 inches long; for topstitching, use a knotted thread.

2. Weave the needle in and out of the fabric several times in 1/8-inch, evenly spaced stitches; pull the thread through. Finish with a loose end when marking, and a fastening stitch (opposite) on the fabric's wrong side when topstitching.

**IF YOU ARE LEFT-HANDED...**
Follow the directions in Steps 1 and 2, proceeding from left to right as shown below.

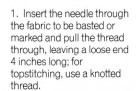
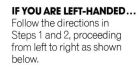
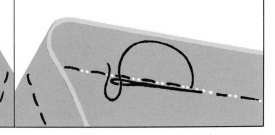

## THE OVERCAST STITCH: For seam edges

1. Anchor the first stitch with a knot on the wrong side of the fabric and draw the needle through to the other side, 1/8 to 1/4 inch down from the top edge.

2. Hold the needle toward you and at a right angle to the fabric. With the thread to the right, insert the needle under the fabric from the wrong side, 1/8 to 1/4 inch to the left of the first stitch.

3. Continue to make evenly spaced stitches over the fabric edge. End with a fastening stitch (opposite).

**IF YOU ARE LEFT-HANDED...**
Follow the directions in Steps 1-3, proceeding from left to right as shown below.

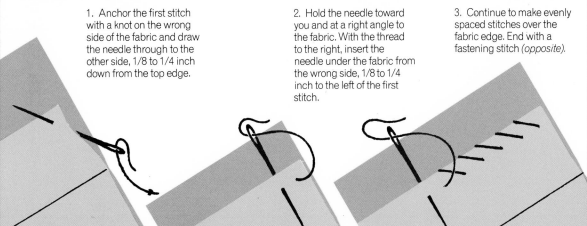

## THE HEMMING STITCH: For bound or raw edges

1. Anchor the first stitch with a knot inside the hem; then, pointing the needle up and to the left, pick up one or two threads of the garment fabric close to the hem. Push the needle up through the hem 1/8 inch above the edge; pull the thread through.

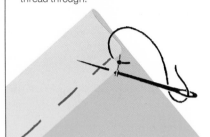

2. Continue the same process—picking up one or two threads, and making 1/8-inch stitches in the hem—at intervals of 1/4 inch, creating a tiny slanted stitch on the inside and an almost invisible stitch on the outside. Do not sew too tightly or the fabric will pucker. End with a fastening stitch (page 42).

**IF YOU ARE LEFT-HANDED...**
Follow the directions in Steps 1 and 2, inserting the needle as shown below and proceeding from left to right.

## THE ROLLED-HEM STITCH: For lightweight fabrics

1. Turn the edge of the fabric over 1/8 inch and, using a knotted thread and pointing the needle to the left, make a horizontal stitch 1/4 inch long at the top corner of the fold.

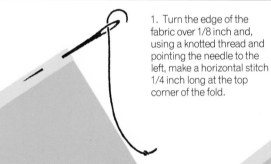

2. Pick up one or two threads on the main fabric, below and on a line with the stitch made in Step 1.

3. Take another horizontal stitch in the fold, 1/16 inch to the left of the stitch made in Step 1.

4. After repeating Steps 2 and 3 for approximately one inch, hold the sewn section of fabric securely, and gently but firmly pull the thread taut with your other hand. The material will roll over on itself and the stitches will disappear. Continue the rolled-hem stitches, pulling the thread taut every inch and ending with a fastening stitch (page 42) hidden in the fold.

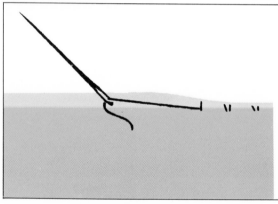

**IF YOU ARE LEFT-HANDED...**
Follow the directions in Steps 1-4, inserting the needle as shown at right and proceeding from left to right.

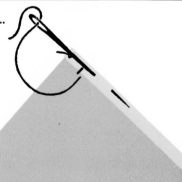

## THE CATCH STITCH: To hem knits, heavy fabrics

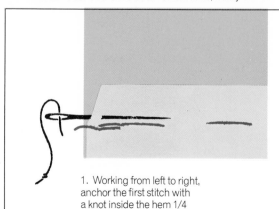

1. Working from left to right, anchor the first stitch with a knot inside the hem 1/4 inch down from the edge.

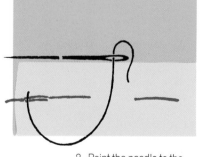

2. Point the needle to the left and pick up one or two threads on the garment close to the top edge of the hem; pull the thread through.

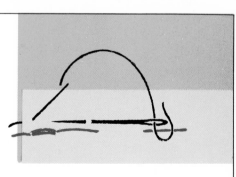

3. Take a small stitch in the top layer only of the hem, 1/4 inch down from the edge and 1/4 inch to the right of the stitch in Step 2.

4. Continue to pick up a few threads on the garment and to take a small stitch in the hem, creating a triangular pattern on the inside and a line of almost invisible stitches on the side that shows. End with a fastening stitch *(page 42)* on the turned-up hem.

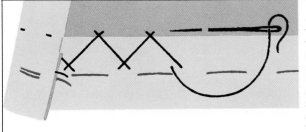

**IF YOU ARE LEFT-HANDED...**
Follow the directions in Steps 1-4, proceeding from right to left and pointing the needle to the right, as shown.

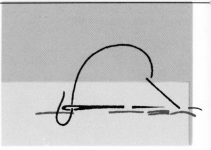

## THE SLIP STITCH: To hem folded edges

1. Fold under the edge of the hem and anchor the first stitch with a knot inside the fold of the hem.

2. Point the needle to the left and pick up one or two threads of the garment fabric close to the edge of the hem and directly below the stitch made in Step 1.

3. Slide the needle horizontally through the folded edge of the hem 1/8 inch to the left of the previous stitch; the stitches will be almost invisible. Keep the stitches firm but not tight; end with a fastening stitch *(page 42)* inside the fold.

**IF YOU ARE LEFT-HANDED...**
Follow the directions in Steps 1-3, picking up a few threads, then sliding the needle through the folded edge of the hem as shown below and proceeding from left to right.

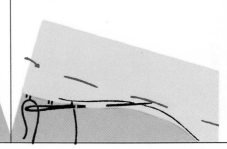

## THE BUTTONHOLE STITCH

1. Using a knotted thread, insert the needle from the wrong side of the fabric 1/8 inch down from the top edge.

2. Form a loop with the thread by swinging it around in a circle counterclockwise.

3. Insert the needle from the wrong side of the fabric through the same point at which the needle emerged in Step 1, keeping the looped thread under the needle.

4. Draw the thread through, firmly pulling it straight up toward the top edge of the fabric.

5. Repeat Steps 2-4 directly to the left of the first stitch, and continue to make close stitches of even length, forming a firm ridge along the top. End with a fastening stitch *(page 42)* on the wrong side of the fabric.

**IF YOU ARE LEFT-HANDED...**
Follow the directions in Steps 1-5, proceeding from left to right and looping the thread around the needle as shown below.

# 3
## PATTERNS
## FABRICS
## CUTTING,
## MARKING

Happily, the rather rigid rules that once prevailed in the fashion world have been considerably relaxed in recent years. But if the rules are gone, certain principles remain. There are guidelines that can help you make the kind of clothes that will be most flattering to your figure and personality.

The key to making clothes that will suit you lies in choosing pattern lines and fabric colors, weights and textures properly pro-

# MATCHING THE LOOK TO THE FIGURE

portioned to one another and to the scale of your figure. Both pattern and fabric can be artfully utilized to correct whatever is disproportionate or imbalanced in your figure and create an illusion of natural perfection.

Measurements alone should not be relied upon to analyze your figure. A more important procedure is to stand in front of a full-length three-way mirror, preferably in a revealing bathing suit or leotard, and examine your figure from all angles. Virtually every figure has a flaw or two, but they should be thought of as problems to be resolved rather than bemoaned.

Choose a pattern that emphasizes good features while drawing attention away from unattractive ones. For example, an empire waistline nicely accentuates a small-busted, trim-shouldered figure, and conceals a prominent bottom. Pleated and gathered skirts can pad out hips that are slim, but they make heavy hips even more noticeable. Form-fitting silhouettes look best on well-proportioned figures with minor problems. The A-line that falls free from the shoulders is a flattering silhouette for most figures —and an ideal cover-up for many flaws.

Visualizing how a silhouette will look on you can be difficult. An excellent way to find out—and a good deal of fun—is to go to the "better dresses" department in a store and try on several of the smartest outfits until you find the styles that are most becoming. Then select a pattern that has the same silhouette and lines.

After the pattern is selected, look for a fabric suitable to that style. A tailored suit with severe lines loses its distinctive qualities if made from soft fabric such as single knits or crepes. Yet many patterns adapt to a variety of fabrics, taking their character from the material used. A basic A-line style is easy and free-flowing if made of a light, soft fabric; it becomes crisper and more tailored with firmer fabric. To be certain that the weight and texture of the fabric will not distort the silhouette of your pattern, consult the list of recommended fabrics on the back of the pattern envelope.

The fabric must also suit you. Before buying material, hold it up to you in a mirror in both natural and artificial light. If the color does not complement your skin, hair and eye coloring, do not buy it, no matter how appealing its texture or weight.

Be sure the color is as flattering to figure as to face. Light, bright and warm colors, such as red, yellow and orange, enlarge the shape because they reflect light more vividly than somber hues. White satin, for example, can make a large woman appear enormous. Subdued colors in blues, greens and violets make the figure appear smaller. That does not mean that large figures must be clothed solely in dark colors and thin figures in vivid colors. Colors you like can be used as accents, perhaps in collars, cuffs or a scarf.

Stripes can be disconcertingly deceiving. Vertical stripes, traditionally thought to impart a slimming effect, can, if they are widely spaced, lead the eye across the body; they then appear to decrease height and increase girth. On the other hand, horizontal stripes, often thought to make a short woman look dumpy, can actually move the eye upward if they are both narrow and narrowly spaced. With them, a figure often seems taller and thinner.

Before buying any fabric, check the care-and-treatment label and the fiber-content label. Fabrics made from natural fibers (wool, silk, cotton and linen) breathe and move more freely, but they are generally more expensive and need more care than synthetics. Synthetics, on the other hand, are sometimes harder to sew. Blended fabrics, containing combinations of natural and synthetic fibers, are a good compromise.

When looking for fabrics, it is a sound idea to buy the best you can afford and forgo the apparent bargain. A well-chosen, quality fabric can make the critical difference in the look of a finished garment.

# In search of the perfect pattern

Modern patterns, with their careful guide lines for marking, cutting and assembling, are sophisticated aids to sewing—and a long evolutionary step from those of the past. It was not, in fact, until the sewing machine came into widespread use in the late 19th Century and created a demand for patterns for home use that anything like those known today became available. Until that time, women had to construct their dresses from simple patterns that came in only one size, adjusting them by eye and feel, or attempt to make their own patterns from complicated diagrams that fashion magazines printed alongside their colored fashion plates (opposite).

To meet the need, an ingenious Yankee tailor, Ebenezer Butterick, began manufacturing patterns that were guaranteed to "make a perfectly formed garment." Butterick not only hit upon the idea of using tissue paper for his patterns, an innovation that greatly simplified the chore of tracing the outline on the fabric, but also provided them in a variety of different sizes. Butterick's patterns were so superior that in one year alone six million were sold.

Over the years, patterns have become increasingly useful. In 1921 McCall's introduced patterns printed with cutting, marking and sewing guide lines. And when the major pattern companies adopted a uniform standard for sizes in 1968, selecting the correct size became simpler than ever before, although it is of course still necessary to adjust patterns to the individual figure. Today, even personal adjustments can be eliminated by using the computer-fitted patterns that are becoming available. For such a pattern, as many as 17 measurements of an individual figure are made. These are fed to a computer, which activates a "plotter" whose stylus traces a custom pattern needing no adjustments whatsoever. The only drawback is that the pattern is good only as long as the pattern owner's weight remains stable; if she gains or loses, the computer cannot help until she sends in new measurements.

Patterns were late arrivals in the sewing world because there was for many centuries no need for them. From earliest times, clothes had simply hung loosely on the body. In ancient Greece and Rome they came to be based on geometric shapes—rectangles, squares, triangles, circles—that draped over the body, like the multifold Roman toga or the short, graceful Greek tunic, the chiton. Even after the fall of Rome, the loose tunic continued to be the standard costume—short for men, long for women.

Patterns became essential only when

clothes began to be constructed to conform to the shape of the body, a gradual development in fashion that reached a climax in the 12th Century. The Crusaders' contacts with the opulent East had aroused a demand for more stylish clothing. Europe was simultaneously undergoing an economic revival; there was an unprecedented expansion of woolen cloth manufacture, and tailors' guilds sprang up in the burgeoning cities. The new fitted style required much more complicated construction in garments. Stitching together a few rectangles or circles no longer sufficed; a large number of sections had to be assembled in special ways, and the only way to reproduce

these sections accurately was to use patterns. They served not only as handy outlines of the garment pieces, but more important, they enabled tailors to avoid wasting cloth, which remained expensive despite its increasing availability.

At first made of paper, and later of cloth, these early patterns were outlines and nothing more. They came in one size; the tailor adjusted his cutting by eye to allow for bigger or smaller customers, but even so a lot of taking-in and letting-out was necessary during the sewing to get the garments to fit.

Only tailors were allowed to use patterns and sew clothes until Louis XIV granted seamstresses the right to make women's

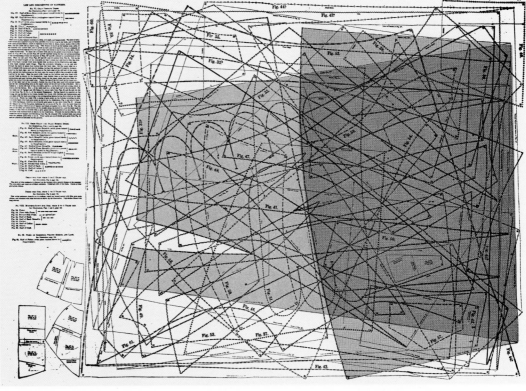

Patterns in 19th Century fashion magazines, from which dresses like those at left above could be made, were not easy to follow. Several patterns were superimposed, with keyed numbers that enabled the seamstress to pick out the one selected. Since cutting out one pattern would destroy the others, it was necessary to trace it. To compound the difficulty, a pattern piece often overlapped on itself, like the skirt section outlined here in gray.

and children's apparel in the 17th Century. Louis made still another contribution to the art of reproducing clothing styles. In keeping with his belief that he was meant to lead not only France but Europe in all things, including fashion, he established an unusual way of disseminating the Paris mode. He began sending life-sized dolls, cunningly dressed in the latest styles, to the courts of Europe so that noble ladies throughout the Continent could imitate the dolls' costumes and follow French leadership.

The use of costumed dolls as models for dressmakers continued long after Louis's time. They shrank to a more convenient size *(right)* and took on simpler forms *(overleaf)*, but the miniature dresses helped women dress in fashion until Butterick's tissue papers made them collectors' prizes.

# Keeping up with fashion by copying dolls

Probably the most charming patterns ever made derived from dolls like these. They circulated in Europe and America in the 19th Century. The most elaborate models were of china or alabaster. The dolls' clothes were beautiful and painstakingly correct in every construction detail. So true were they that dressmakers could remove the clothes and use them as patterns in miniature, to be copied in the measurements of their customers.

Dolls of the 19th Century—like the six French examples shown above—were dressed in costumes that dressmakers copied.

This two-dimensional doll is one of a type called *poupées modelles* (model dolls), manufactured in Paris in the 19th Century to convey fashions to dressmakers in the provinces and abroad. The *poupée* pictured is a homemade copy, probably based upon a European original. It is made out of stiff paper and hand painted in the late 1820s in New York. The dress, a theatrical or dance costume, slips over the doll's head.

Boston's *Sunday Herald* of 1895 offered readers a cardboard doll—two of which are shown, in petticoats and yachting dress, left of the box—and supplied additional clip-on costumes weekly *(counterclockwise):* evening wrap, formal dress, cycling outfit, two dinner gowns, afternoon dress, tea gown, walking dress, opera gown, walking dress, traveling outfit, tennis dress, walking dress, formal afternoon dress and bathing dress.

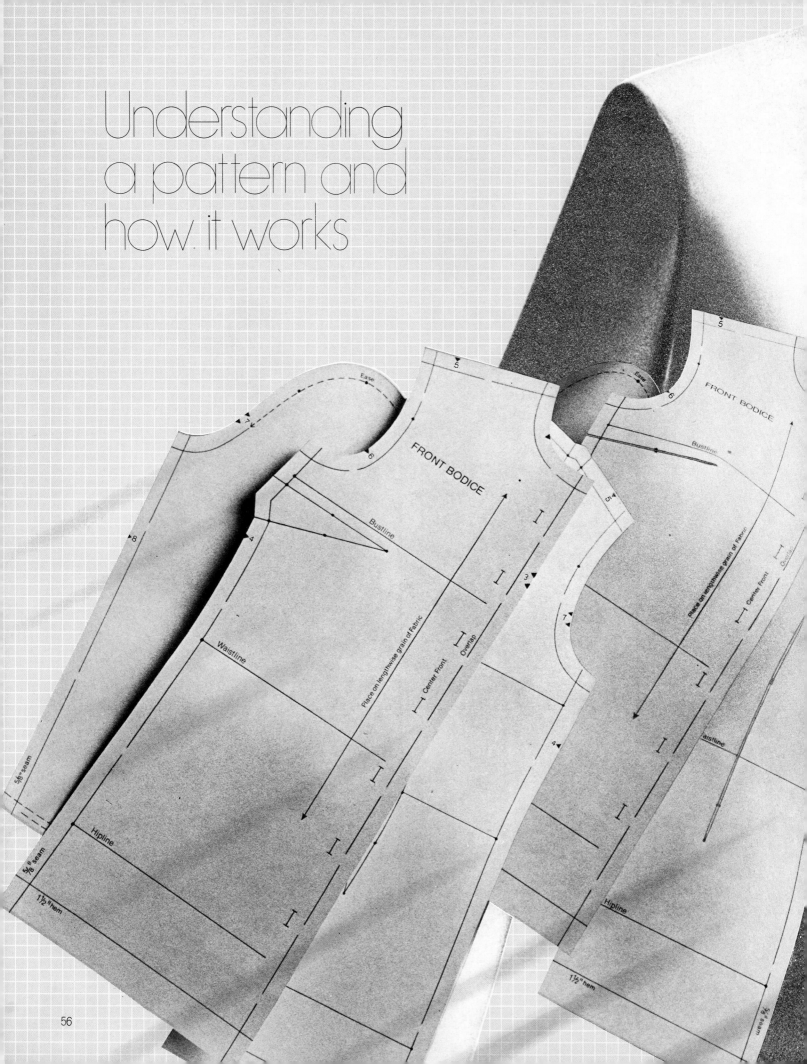

# Understanding a pattern and how it works

Since fabric is flat and the human body is not, the paper patterns that are used as a guide for cutting and sewing garments include numerous instructions—some of them in the form of symbols—to help you convert a one-dimensional fabric into three-dimensional clothing.

For example, the grain line and fold line (glossary below) tell how to align the pattern piece with the weave so that the fabric curves properly. Other symbols guide such steps as the joining of two pieces to conform to general body contours (numbered notches) and the seam-ing of individual pieces to fit around pronounced curves such as the bust or buttocks (broken lines).

The photograph at left illustrates how a flat paper pattern can produce a shaped, three-dimensional garment. The three sections at far left include, in order, a sleeve, front bodice and back bodice (partly concealed). These pieces are shown in the center group shaped as if they were material: the rounded top of the sleeve has been curved and the bodice shaped. At near left, the bodice and the sleeve have been stitched together to fit the body like a mold.

# PATTERN MARKINGS AND SYMBOLS

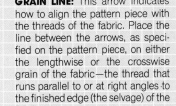

**GRAIN LINE:** This arrow indicates how to align the pattern piece with the threads of the fabric. Place the line between the arrows, as specified on the pattern piece, on either the lengthwise or the crosswise grain of the fabric—the thread that runs parallel to or at right angles to the finished edge (the selvage) of the fabric.

**FOLD LINE:** Either of these two symbols indicates how the edge of the pattern piece aligns with the fabric fold: the bold line of the arrow should line up with the fold.

**SEAM ALLOWANCE:** Either of these two symbols indicates the distance between the cutting line, where the pattern piece is cut, and the stitching line (sometimes called the seam line), where it must be sewn. This distance, usually 5/8 inch, is marked in numerals in at least one place on the pattern piece.

**CUTTING LINE:** A heavy solid line, frequently accompanied by a drawing of scissors, marks the exact line along which the pattern piece must be cut.

**STITCHING LINE:** A thin broken line, frequently accompanied by a drawing of a sewing machine presser foot, marks the exact line along which seams, darts and other construction areas must be stitched. An arrow along the stitching line, or seam line, shows the direction in which the seam must be sewn.

**ADJUSTMENT LINE:** A heavy double line indicates the points on the pattern piece at which it may be shortened or lengthened. To lengthen the piece, cut the pattern between the printed lines and add paper. To shorten, pin the pattern up between the double lines.

**NOTCHES:** These symbols, which are used alone, in pairs or in threes, are always numbered. They mark the exact points along the outer seam lines where sections are joined together; the single notches are joined to single notches, No. 8 notches to No. 8 notches, etc.

**CONSTRUCTION SYMBOLS:** Large dots, squares and triangles guide construction of a garment—indicating the center front of a sleeve, for example, or marking the point where pieces such as collars and neckline facings must be attached to the garment body. Small dots guide alignment of seams.

**FABRIC LAYOUT SYMBOLS:** A black star indicates that the fabric must be laid out in one thickness, wrong side down, and a single piece of fabric cut. The shaded bar indicates that the pattern piece shaded in the pattern cutting layout is to be placed on the fabric with its printed side down. The other three construction symbols—the large asterisk, dagger and double dagger—are keys to special cutting directions in the pattern instruction sheet.

**BUTTON MARKING:** The horizontal line on this symbol shows exactly where the buttonhole is to be placed and its length is the buttonhole length. The button drawing is the size of the button to be used (the pattern envelope also specifies button sizes).

**ZIPPER MARKING:** This symbol on the pattern marks the position of the zipper on the garment, and the symbol length is the exact opening length. The top of the slider tab indicates the top of the zipper opening, and the bottom stop, the bottom of the opening.

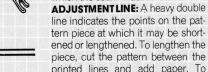

# Figure types and sizes

Women's patterns are much more rigidly standardized than ready-to-wear clothes, so your ordinary dress size is not a reliable guide to the correct pattern size. Pattern sizes are divided into seven figure types, based on measurements. The Misses type *(opposite)* is considered average; six others are shown overleaf. Men's patterns are all based on the average male figure, as defined at right.

To determine your figure type, first note your measurements, shown by red bands on the figures at right. Find your height in the charts opposite and overleaf, then look for any special characteristics in the descriptions, such as narrow shoulders or a high bust. Select the categories that best describe your overall figure, then compare the measurements for bust and hip. Use these dimensions to make the final selection; ignore pattern labels, such as Women or Junior, which are intended to describe figure type, not age.

Within your figure type, choose the size nearest your horizontal measurements. (Vertical measurements are easier to adjust.) For dresses and shirts, be guided by bust size; for skirts and pants, hip size. (If the circumference of your body at the thighs, abdomen or buttocks exceeds that at your hips, use the larger dimension to determine size.)

If all measurements fall between sizes, take the smaller size if you are small-boned, the larger if big-boned.

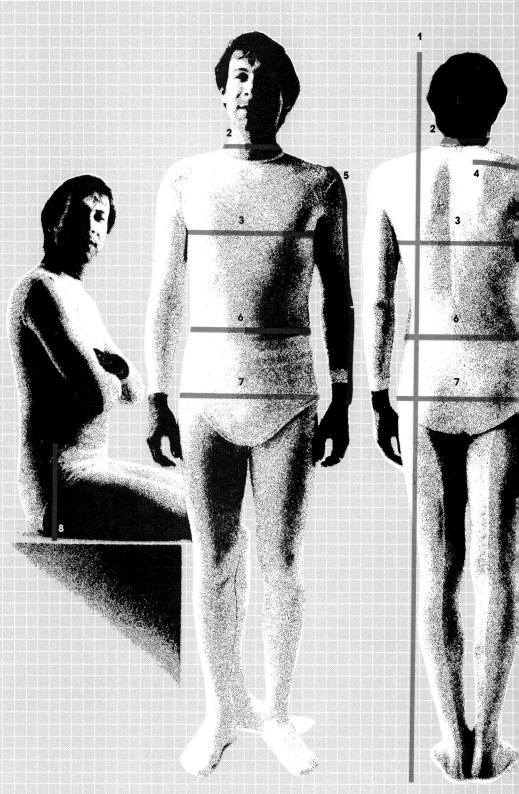

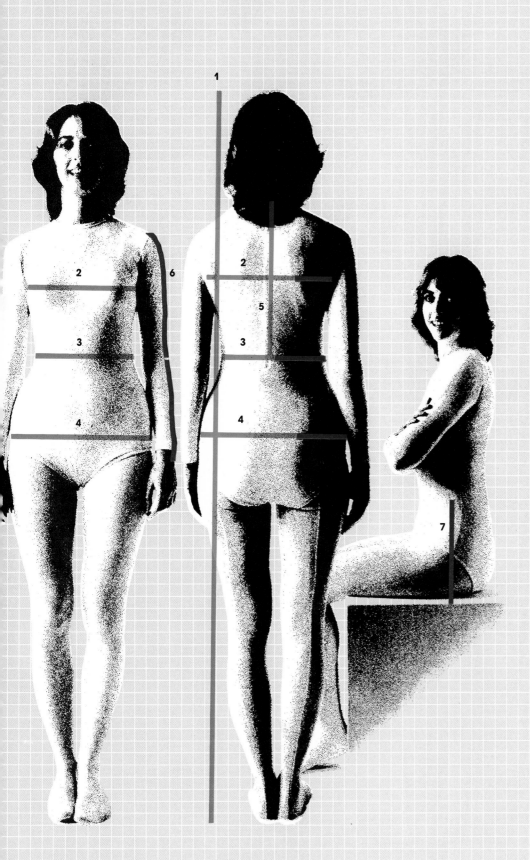

# TAKING MEASUREMENTS

Measure yourself with a tape held snugly against the body. The red lines on the figures at left indicate measurements on pattern envelopes; the blue lines are additional measurements for further fitting. Wear the underwear and shoes that you will with the finished garment.

### WOMEN'S MEASUREMENTS

**1. HEIGHT:** Stand erect, without shoes, against a wall. Place a ruler flat on your head and mark the point where the ruler touches the wall. Measure from the mark to the floor.

**2. BUST:** Measure around the fullest part with the tape slightly raised in back.

**3. WAIST:** Tie a cord around the narrowest part; measure around from behind. Leave the cord for other measurements.

**4. FULL HIP:** Measure from behind around the fullest part, usually 7 to 9 inches down from the waist.

**5. BACK-WAIST LENGTH:** Measure from the top of the spine to the waistline cord.

**6. ARM LENGTH:** Measure from the shoulderbone point to the elbow. With the elbow bent, measure under the elbow to the wristbone.

**7. CROTCH LENGTH:** Sitting on a hard surface, measure from the waistline cord to the surface.

### MEN'S MEASUREMENTS

**1. HEIGHT:** Measure as for women.

**2. NECK:** From about an inch above the top of the spine, measure around the neck.

**3. CHEST:** With the chest slightly expanded, measure from the shoulder blades across the fullest part, with the tape under the armpits.

**4. SLEEVE LENGTH:** Measure from the top of the spine across to the shoulder-bone point, then down to the elbow. Bend the arm to a right angle and measure from under the elbow to the wrist.

**5. ARM LENGTH:** Measure as for women.

**6. WAIST:** Start at the navel and measure around the body.

**7. HIP OR SEAT:** Measure at the widest part of the hips or buttocks and at the midpoint of the pelvic bone.

**8. CROTCH:** Measure from the waistline cord as for women.

# MISSES

Designed for the female American figure of average proportions, 5'5" to 5'6" tall without shoes.

| SIZE | 6 | 8 | 10 | 12 | 14 | 16 | 18 | 20 |
|---|---|---|---|---|---|---|---|---|
| bust | 30½" | 31½" | 32½" | 34" | 36" | 38" | 40" | 42" |
| waist | 23" | 24" | 25" | 26½" | 28" | 30" | 32" | 34" |
| hip | 32½" | 33½" | 34½" | 36" | 38" | 40" | 42" | 44" |
| back-waist length | 15½" | 15¾" | 16" | 16¼" | 16½" | 16¾" | 17" | 17¼" |

# MEN

Designed for the male American figure of average proportions, 5'10" tall without shoes.

| SIZE | 34 | 36 | 38 | 40 | 42 | 44 | 46 | 48 |
|---|---|---|---|---|---|---|---|---|
| chest | 34" | 36" | 38" | 40" | 42" | 44" | 46" | 48" |
| waist | 28" | 30" | 32" | 34" | 36" | 39" | 42" | 44" |
| hip (seat) | 35" | 37" | 39" | 41" | 43" | 45" | 47" | 49" |
| neckband shirt | 14" | 14½" | 15" | 15½" | 16" | 16½" | 17" | 17½" |
| sleeve | 32" | 32" | 33" | 33" | 34" | 34" | 35" | 35" |

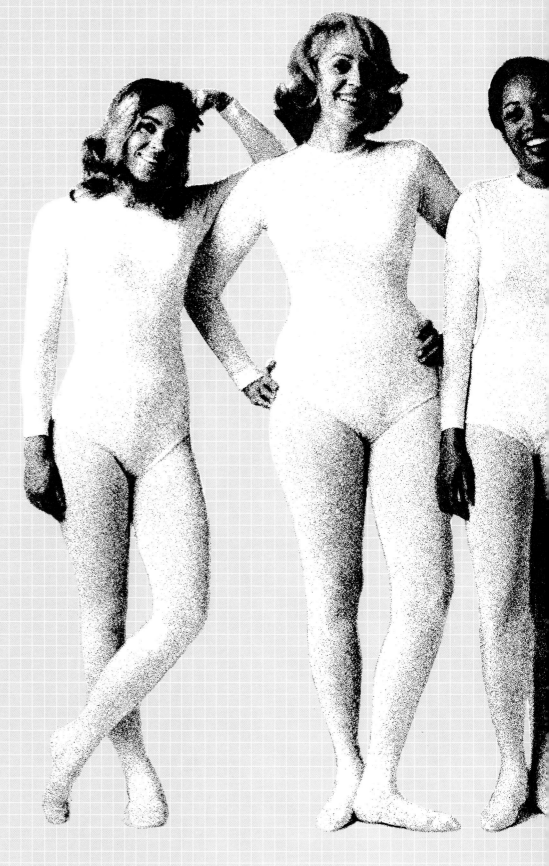

# JUNIOR/TEEN

Designed for girls, 5'1" to 5'3" tall without shoes; the waist is large in proportion to the bust.

| SIZE | 5/6 | 7/8 | 9/10 | 11/12 | 13/14 | 15/16 |
|------|-----|-----|------|-------|-------|-------|
| bust | 28" | 29" | 30½" | 32" | 33½" | 35" |
| waist | 22" | 23" | 24" | 25" | 26" | 27" |
| hip | 31" | 32" | 33½" | 35" | 36½" | 38" |
| back-waist length | 13½" | 14" | 14½" | 15" | 15⅜" | 15¾" |

# WOMEN

Designed for figures 5'5" to 5'6" tall without shoes, with larger bust and hips than the Misses figure.

| SIZE | 38 | 40 | 42 | 44 | 46 | 48 | 50 |
|------|-----|-----|-----|-------|-----|--------|-----|
| bust | 42" | 44" | 46" | 48" | 50" | 52" | 54" |
| waist | 35" | 37" | 39" | 41½" | 44" | 46½" | 49" |
| hip | 44" | 46" | 48" | 50" | 52" | 54" | 56" |
| back-waist length | 17¼" | 17⅜" | 17½" | 17⅝" | 17¾" | 17⅞" | 18" |

# HALF SIZE

Designed for figures 5'2" to 5'3" tall without shoes with short back-waist and large waist and hips.

| SIZE | 10½ | 12½ | 14½ | 16½ | 18½ | 20½ | 22½ | 24½ |
|------|------|------|------|------|------|-------|------|-------|
| bust | 33" | 35" | 37" | 39" | 41" | 43" | 45" | 47" |
| waist | 27" | 29" | 31" | 33" | 35" | 37½" | 40" | 42½" |
| hip | 35" | 37" | 39" | 41" | 43" | 45½" | 48" | 50½" |
| back-waist length | 15" | 15¼" | 15½" | 15¾" | 15⅞" | 16" | 16⅛" | 16¼" |

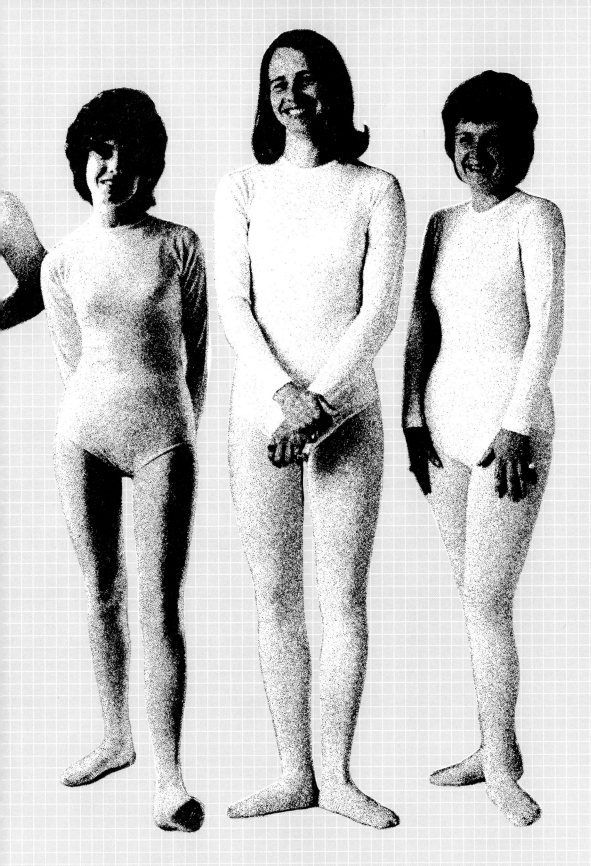

## MISS PETITE

Designed for figures 5'2" to 5'4" tall without shoes, with back-waist lengths shorter than Misses.

| SIZE | 6MP | 8MP | 10MP | 12MP | 14MP | 16MP |
|---|---|---|---|---|---|---|
| bust | 30½" | 31½" | 32½" | 34" | 36" | 38" |
| waist | 23½" | 24½" | 25½" | 27" | 28½" | 30½" |
| hip | 32½" | 33½" | 34½" | 36" | 38" | 40" |
| back-waist length | 14½" | 14¾" | 15" | 15¼" | 15½" | 15¾" |

## JUNIOR

Designed for figures 5'4" to 5'5" tall without shoes, with high busts and short back-waist lengths.

| SIZE | 5 | 7 | 9 | 11 | 13 | 15 |
|---|---|---|---|---|---|---|
| bust | 30" | 31" | 32" | 33½" | 35" | 37" |
| waist | 22½" | 23½" | 24½" | 25½" | 27" | 29" |
| hip | 32" | 33" | 34" | 35½" | 37" | 39" |
| back-waist length | 15" | 15¼" | 15½" | 15¾" | 16" | 16¼" |

## JUNIOR PETITE

Designed for figures 5' to 5'1" tall without shoes, with high busts and very short back-waist lengths.

| SIZE | 3JP | 5JP | 7JP | 9JP | 11JP | 13JP |
|---|---|---|---|---|---|---|
| bust | 30½" | 31" | 32" | 33" | 34" | 35" |
| waist | 22½" | 23" | 24" | 25" | 26" | 27" |
| hip | 31½" | 32" | 33" | 34" | 35" | 36" |
| back-waist length | 14" | 14¼" | 14½" | 14¾" | 15" | 15¼" |

# Adjustments for your measurements

Few figures are so perfectly proportioned that they match all the body measurements on which a pattern is based. The time to check your measurements against those on the pattern envelope is before you cut, while you can still adjust the pattern.

How you adjust the pattern is important. It is tempting just to cut the fabric a little wider at the hips or to add an inch or so at the hem. But unless adjustments are made at the right spot the lines of the garment will be ruined.

See how your measurements differ from those for which the pattern was designed—they are printed on the pattern envelope—and make any necessary adjustments on the basis of these differences. Do not compare your measurements with the dimensions of the pattern pieces themselves; *most* pieces allow extra room for comfort and style. Sleeve, crotch and hem lengths, however, are exceptions; here you can compare your measurements directly with the pattern pieces.

Before you adjust, trim your pattern close to the cutting line and iron each piece with a warm, dry iron. Work first on vertical adjustments, then on the horizontal ones; mark all measurement changes on the pattern piece and then draw new cutting and stitching lines as shown on the following pages.

## LENGTHENING A PATTERN SECTION

**BASIC STEPS FOR LENGTHENING**

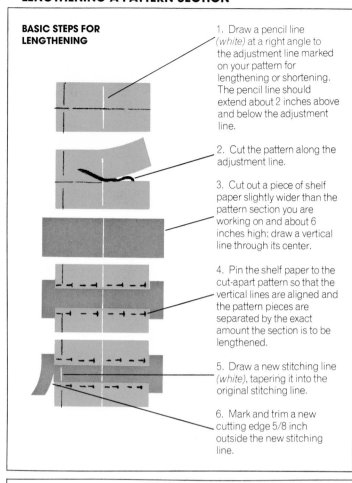

1. Draw a pencil line (*white*) at a right angle to the adjustment line marked on your pattern for lengthening or shortening. The pencil line should extend about 2 inches above and below the adjustment line.

2. Cut the pattern along the adjustment line.

3. Cut out a piece of shelf paper slightly wider than the pattern section you are working on and about 6 inches high; draw a vertical line through its center.

4. Pin the shelf paper to the cut-apart pattern so that the vertical lines are aligned and the pattern pieces are separated by the exact amount the section is to be lengthened.

5. Draw a new stitching line (*white*), tapering it into the original stitching line.

6. Mark and trim a new cutting edge 5/8 inch outside the new stitching line.

## LENGTHENING AT THE WAISTLINE

1. For a one-piece dress, compare your back-waist length measurement (*page 59*) with the measurement printed on the pattern envelope. If your measurement is longer than specified, lengthen the pattern at the waist before you set the hem length.

2. Add the pattern insert as shown in the basic steps for lengthening, working on the front section of your pattern.

3. Extend the stitching line (*white*) of the side seam across the pattern insert; taper it into the original stitching line, a few inches above and below the insert, making a smooth line from the seam intersection at the dart or armhole down to the intersection of the original stitching line and the bottom of the pattern piece.

4. Mark and trim a new cutting edge 5/8 inch outside the new stitching line.

5. Repeat on the back section of your pattern.

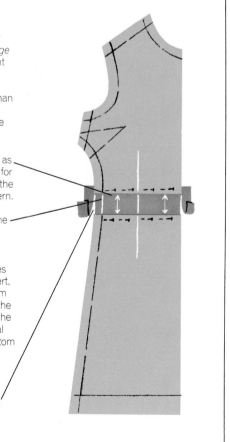

## LENGTHENING THE LOWER PORTION OF A GARMENT

1A. For a dress or a skirt, measure from your center front waistline the desired length of the garment. Mark the length on the center front of the pattern. This step should be done after any necessary lengthening or shortening at the waist.

1B. For pants, mark your pants length measurement on the side seam of the pattern piece. This step should be done after any necessary lengthening or shortening at the crotch.

2. If the mark is below the hemline indicated on the skirt or pants pattern, you will have to lengthen the pattern by an amount equal to the difference between your mark and the original hemline.

3. Add the pattern insert as shown in the basic steps for lengthening, working on the front section of your pattern.

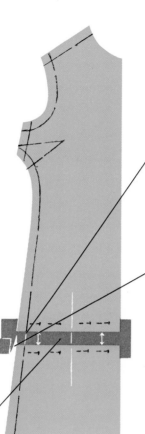

4. Extend the stitching line (*white*) of the side seam across the pattern insert. Taper this line into the original stitching line, a few inches above and below the insert, making a smooth line from the side seam at the waistline down to the intersection of the original stitching line and the bottom of the pattern piece.

5. Mark and trim a new cutting edge 5/8 inch outside the new stitching line.

6. Repeat on the back section of your pattern.

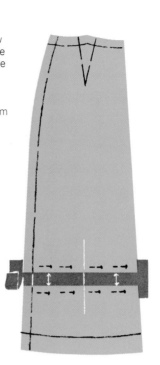

## LENGTHENING AT THE CROTCH

1. For pants, compare your crotch length measurement (*page 59*) with the pattern's, measuring along the side of the pattern from the waist seam allowance to a point opposite the bottom of the crotch seam allowance. If your measurement is longer than the pattern's, you will have to lengthen the pattern at the crotch before you set the hem length.

2. Add the pattern insert as shown in the basic steps for lengthening, working on the front section of your pattern.

3. Extend the stitching line (*white*) across the pattern insert. Taper this line into the original stitching line, a few inches above and below the insert, making a smooth line from the waistline down to the intersection of the crotch seam and the inner leg seam.

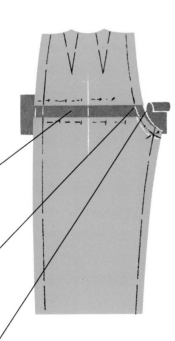

4. Mark and trim a new cutting edge 5/8 inch outside the new stitching line.

5. Repeat on the back section of your pattern.

## LENGTHENING A SLEEVE

1. Compare your arm length measurement (*page 59*) with the pattern piece measurement, measuring from the center of the seam allowance at the top of the sleeve to the hemline. If your measurement is longer than the pattern's, you will have to lengthen the pattern.

2. Add the pattern insert as shown in the basic steps for lengthening.

3. Extend the stitching lines (*white*) of the underarm seam across the pattern insert, working on both sides of the pattern piece. Taper these lines into the original stitching lines, a few inches above and below the insert, making smooth lines from the intersection of the underarm seams and the armhole seam down to the intersection of the original stitching lines and the bottom of the pattern piece.

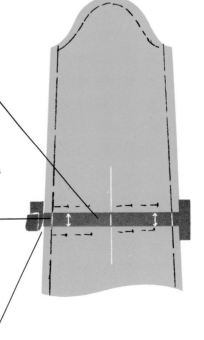

4. Mark and trim a new cutting edge 5/8 inch outside the new stitching line.

# SHORTENING A PATTERN SECTION

## BASIC STEPS FOR SHORTENING

1. Draw a line *(white)* above the adjustment line marked on your pattern for lengthening or shortening. The distance should be exactly equal to the amount the pattern section is to be shortened.

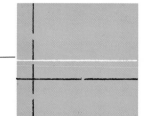

2. Fold the pattern so that the adjustment line meets the new line.

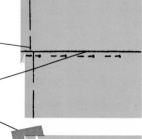

3. Press the fold flat with a warm iron; then pin as shown.

4. Pin a paper extension to your pattern.

5. Draw a new stitching line *(white)*, tapering it into the original stitching line.

6. Mark and trim a new cutting edge 5/8 inch outside the new stitching line.

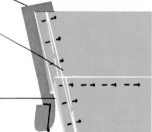

## SHORTENING AT THE WAISTLINE

1. For a one-piece dress, compare your back-waist length measurement *(page 59)* with the measurement printed on the pattern envelope. If your measurement is shorter than specified, shorten the pattern at the waist before you set the hem length.

2. Fold and extend the pattern as shown in the basic steps for shortening, working on the front section of your pattern.

3. Draw a new stitching line *(white)* across the folded pattern piece and extension. Taper this line into the original stitching line of the side seam, a few inches above and below the fold, making a smooth line from the seam intersection at the dart or armhole to the intersection of the original stitching line and the bottom of the pattern.

4. Mark and trim a new cutting edge 5/8 inch outside the new stitching line.

5. Repeat on the back section of your pattern.

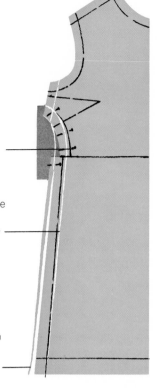

## SHORTENING THE LOWER PORTION OF A GARMENT

1A. For a dress or a skirt, measure from your waistline the desired length of the garment. Mark the length on the pattern. This step should be done after any necessary lengthening or shortening at the waist.

1B. For pants, mark your pants length measurement on the side seam of the pattern piece. This step should be done after any necessary lengthening or shortening at the crotch.

2. If your mark is above the hemline indicated on the pattern, shorten the pattern by an amount equal to the difference between your mark and the original hemline.

3. Fold and extend the pattern as shown in the basic steps for shortening, working on the front section of your pattern.

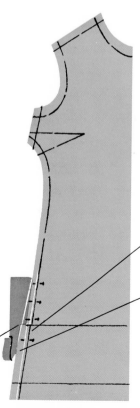

4. Draw a new stitching line *(white)* across the folded pattern piece and the extension. Taper this line into the original stitching line, a few inches above and below the fold, making a smooth line from the side seam at the waistline down to the intersection of the original stitching line and the bottom of the pattern.

5. Mark and trim a new cutting edge 5/8 inch outside the new stitching line.

6. Repeat on the back section of your pattern.

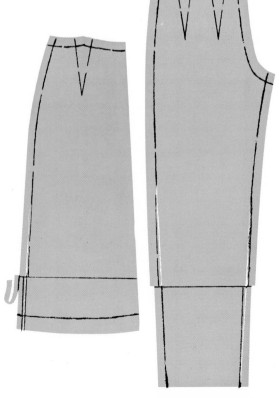

## SHORTENING AT THE CROTCH

1. For pants, compare your crotch length measurement (*page 59*) with the pattern's, measuring from the waist seam allowance to a point opposite the bottom of the crotch seam allowance. If your measurement is shorter than the pattern's, shorten the pattern at the crotch before you set the hem length.

2. Fold and extend the pattern as shown in the basic steps for shortening, working on the front section of your pattern.

3. Draw a new stitching line (*white*) across the folded pattern piece and the extension. Taper this line into the original stitching line for the crotch seam, a few inches above and below the fold, making a smooth line from the waistline to the intersection of the crotch seam and the inner leg seam.

4. Mark and trim a new cutting edge 5/8 inch outside the new stitching line.

5. Repeat on the back section of your pattern.

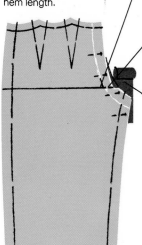

## SHORTENING A SLEEVE

1. Compare your arm length measurement (*page 59*) with the pattern piece measurement, measuring from the center of the seam allowance at the top of the sleeve to the hemline. If your measurement is shorter than the pattern's, you will have to shorten the pattern.

2. Fold and extend the pattern as shown in the basic steps for shortening.

3. Extend the stitching lines (*white*) for the underarm seam across the folded pattern piece and the extension, working on both sides of the pattern piece. Taper these new lines into the original stitching lines, a few inches above and below the fold, making smooth lines from the intersection of the underarm seams and the armhole seams down to the intersection of the original stitching lines and the bottom of the pattern piece.

4. Mark and trim a new cutting edge 5/8 inch outside the new stitching line.

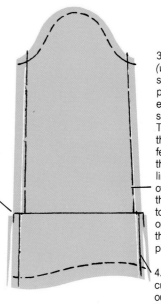

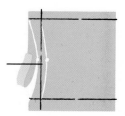

# REDUCING A PATTERN SECTION

## BASIC STEPS FOR REDUCING

1. At the point where you need to reduce your pattern piece, measure in from the stitching line and mark (*white*) 1/4 of the total amount to be reduced on each side seam.

2. Draw a new stitching line (*white*) making a graduated curve from the point of reduction to the original stitching line.

3. Mark and trim a new cutting edge 5/8 inch outside the new stitching line.

## REDUCING AT THE WAISTLINE

1. For a one-piece dress, a skirt or pants, compare your waist measurement (*page 59*) with that printed on the pattern envelope. If your measurement is less than specified you will have to reduce the pattern at the waist.

2. Working on the front section of your pattern, measure in and mark as shown 1/4 of the amount to be reduced on each side seam.

3. Mark as shown (*white*) the location of the fullest part of your hips.

4. Draw a new tapered stitching line, starting at the new waistline mark made in Step 2 and continuing until the new line merges into the original stitching line. Come as close as possible to the hipline mark made in Step 3 while maintaining the original contour of the pattern's stitching line. For a dress, extend the new stitching line above the waistline, tapering it into the dart or armhole seam.

5. Mark and trim a new cutting edge 5/8 inch outside the new stitching line.

6. Repeat on the back section of your pattern.

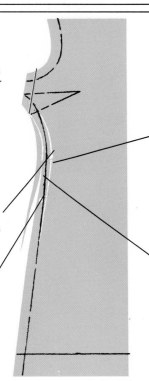

## REDUCING AT THE HIPLINE

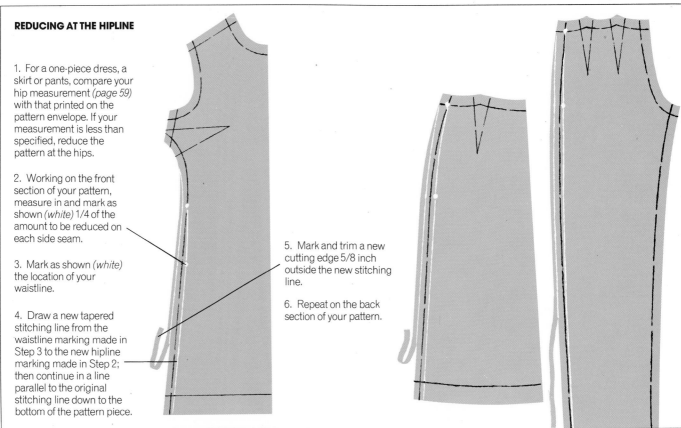

1. For a one-piece dress, a skirt or pants, compare your hip measurement *(page 59)* with that printed on the pattern envelope. If your measurement is less than specified, reduce the pattern at the hips.

2. Working on the front section of your pattern, measure in and mark as shown *(white)* 1/4 of the amount to be reduced on each side seam.

3. Mark as shown *(white)* the location of your waistline.

4. Draw a new tapered stitching line from the waistline marking made in Step 3 to the new hipline marking made in Step 2; then continue in a line parallel to the original stitching line down to the bottom of the pattern piece.

5. Mark and trim a new cutting edge 5/8 inch outside the new stitching line.

6. Repeat on the back section of your pattern.

## ENLARGING A PATTERN SECTION

### BASIC STEPS FOR ENLARGING

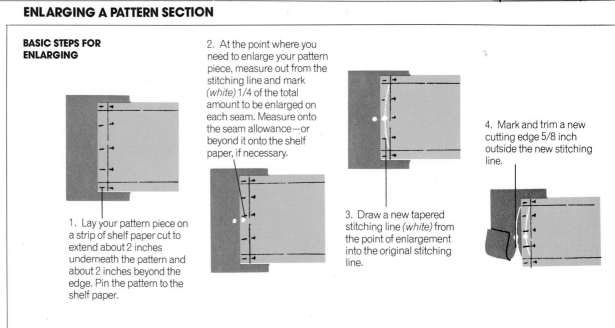

1. Lay your pattern piece on a strip of shelf paper cut to extend about 2 inches underneath the pattern and about 2 inches beyond the edge. Pin the pattern to the shelf paper.

2. At the point where you need to enlarge your pattern piece, measure out from the stitching line and mark *(white)* 1/4 of the total amount to be enlarged on each seam. Measure onto the seam allowance—or beyond it onto the shelf paper, if necessary.

3. Draw a new tapered stitching line *(white)* from the point of enlargement into the original stitching line.

4. Mark and trim a new cutting edge 5/8 inch outside the new stitching line.

## ENLARGING AT THE WAISTLINE

1. For a one-piece dress, a skirt or pants, compare your waist measurement *(page 59)* with that printed on the pattern envelope. If your measurement is larger than specified, you will have to enlarge the pattern at the waist.

2. Working on the front section of your pattern, extend the pattern as shown in the basic steps for enlarging.

3. Measure out and mark as shown *(white)* 1/4 of the amount to be enlarged on each side seam.

4. Mark as shown *(white)* the location of the fullest part of your hips.

5. Draw a new stitching line, starting at the waistline mark made in Step 3 and tapering it into the original stitching line. Come as close as possible to the hipline mark made in Step 4 while maintaining the original contour of the pattern's stitching line. For a dress, extend the new stitching line above the waistline, tapering it into the dart or armhole seam.

6. Mark and trim a new cutting edge 5/8 inch outside the new stitching line.

7. Repeat on the back section of your pattern.

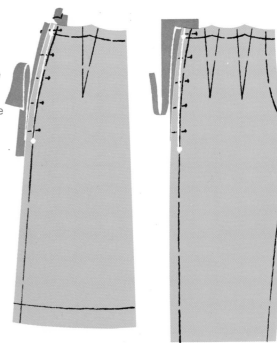

## ENLARGING AT THE HIPLINE

1. For a one-piece dress, a skirt or pants, compare your hip measurement *(page 59)* with that printed on the pattern envelope. If your measurement is larger than specified, enlarge the pattern at the hips.

2. Working on the front section of your pattern, extend the pattern as shown in the basic steps for enlarging.

3. Measure out and mark as shown *(white)* 1/4 of the amount to be enlarged on each side seam.

4. Mark as shown *(white)* the location of your waistline.

5. Draw a new tapered stitching line from the waistline marking made in Step 4 to the new hipline marking made in Step 3; then continue in a line parallel to the original stitching line down to the bottom of the pattern piece.

6. Mark and trim a new cutting edge 5/8 inch outside the new stitching line.

7. Repeat on the back section of your pattern.

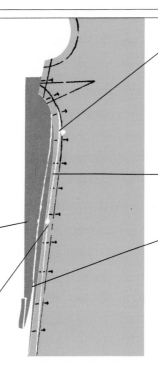

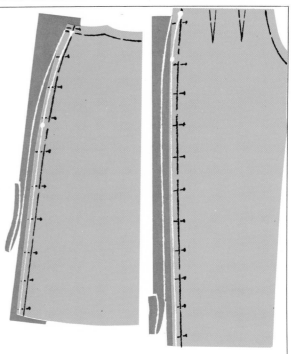

# Heritage of the weaver's art

Fabrics are cheap and plentiful today, largely because of the flood of man-made textiles from power looms. But long before their coming, cloth held enormous significance in human affairs. Empires were founded and nations prospered on cloth, and the processes of producing it were fiercely safeguarded. In ancient China, death by torture was the penalty for spreading the secrets of silk-making beyond the borders of the land. When England became the center of European wool-producing in the Middle Ages, the penalty for smuggling wool out of the country was exile.

Wherever cloth-making flourished, rulers set stringent regulations covering every phase of its manufacture including standards of quality, conditions of sale and the manner of its use for apparel. In Flanders sellers were constrained from talking to potential buyers, standing near them during transactions, or even coughing. In France during the Middle Ages, even members of the nobility were permitted to own only four garments each; unmarried women were restricted to a single gown.

Perhaps the earliest fabric was felt, made in prehistoric times by pressing animal fibers together. At some unknown time in the past, weaving evolved. Crude textiles were created by twisting fibers together to create strands of yarn that then could be woven by working horizontal lengths—called the woof—one at a time over and under vertical lengths called the warp. The process, clearly, was laborious and to create fabric for even a small, loosely woven garment required inordinate amounts of time.

Very gradually, solutions to the problem evolved. One innovation consisted of two short sticks called the distaff and the spindle. The distaff held a small mass of raw fibers. The operator pulled some of the longer fibers out of this mass, twisted their ends together slightly and then attached them to the spindle. Twirled, the spindle spun the fibers into yarn.

Another technological breakthrough was the loom, which probably originated in the Middle East more than 8,000 years ago. It held the warp threads so that the woof could be drawn through more easily. The loom took several forms: it could be a raised horizontal bar from which weighted threads hung to form the warp, or poles lying on the ground with the warp threaded between them or a rectangular wooden frame.

Early weavers developed three major weaves—plain, in which the woof yarns are simply woven under and over the warp; twill, in which the woof passes over two or more warp yarns before being run over and under; and satin, in which the warp floats over a number of woof strands before being passed through. All are still basic to the creation of woven fabrics, including those made from the four major natural fibers —flax, wool, cotton, silk—and synthetics.

The first of the man-made fibers was rayon, which was introduced to the American market in 1911. It was produced by weaving long filaments made from cellulose molecules. Such filaments lack the roughness and the crimp, or twist, of natural fibers. The fabrics produced from them therefore presented a smooth, lustrous appearance that made them eminently suitable for evening gowns and coat linings, but less suitable for other clothing. In time the textile industry met that challenge by a number of methods. Some filaments are chopped into short lengths typical of natural fibers and given artificial crimp by subjecting them to heat and pressure. Other filaments are distorted by heat and pressure, in a process called mechanical texturing, to reduce luster and impart the softness, bulk and hairiness of natural fibers. In these and other ways manmade fabrics are produced in forms used for all manner of garments.

While synthetic fabrics have achieved success in the market by imitating the characteristics of natural fabrics, their ultimate advantage lies in the fact that they require less care and give longer wear. They rapidly spring back into shape, dry quickly after washing and generally require less ironing. But they are sometimes harder to sew, and many people prefer the "blended" fabrics, combinations of man-made and natural fibers that encompass the qualities of both.

Clad in brightly colored woven tunics, a procession of nomads from Canaan enters Egypt in this detail from a wall painting discovered in a 4,000-year-old tomb. Even at this early stage of the weaver's art, certain enduring motifs had emerged: the geometric designs on the costumes—including not only those of the women on the right but also the donkey's protective blanket—are precursors of patterns that have emerged as classics.

1. square (windowpane check)

2. square (with striped elements)

3. circle (stylized)

7. square (gingham check)

4. stripe (herringbone)

5. square (small plaid)

6. stripe (hard, regular)

10. square (hard, regular)

8. circle (large floral — Paisley)

9. circle (regular — polka dots)

12. stripe (with floral motif)

# The designs: circles, squares and stripes

A key to the classic style is the design of the fabric. The uncluttered, understated look that signifies "classic" is based on geometric shapes —circles, squares and stripes, generally fairly small and arranged in regular patterns of repetition. Of these, the stripe is most often seen; it can, of course, be zigzagged as in a herringbone or be created out of other shapes—circles, squares or even small flowers.

Each fabric design creates a special look. Squares and stripes give garments a tailored appearance. Circles, by contrast, will create a softer, more fluid look. Large, rigid stripes (such as No. 6 at left) will produce a much harder look than small, circular flowers (11). A combination of circular elements and stripes (14) will soften the hard look normally imparted by the stripe and still provide a tailored appearance.

In the choice of a fabric, the sewing problems presented by the design must also be considered. The pieces of a regular design (4) must be carefully matched; the larger the pattern, the greater the difficulty in matching. Having chosen a fabric, one must consider other sewing problems relating to the texture and fiber content of the material, a subject dealt with overleaf.

14. stripe (with circular motif)

square (with circular elements)

15. circle (polka dot variation)

16. square (houndstooth check)

Different fabrics, whatever their design, present varying sewing characteristics, depending on their fiber content and construction. The chart below outlines the important traits of 16 popular, easy-to-handle fabrics. They are shown magnified in the photographs to reveal the dramatically different textures various fibers and constructions produce.

Natural fibers are usually easier to work with than synthetics or blends of natural and synthetic fibers. They tend to stretch or slip less when being machine stitched, and they are less apt to fray.

Plain weaves, composed of fibers interlaced at right angles, present the fewest sewing problems. Twills, crepes and piqués—which are angled, twisted or patterned weaves—usually are somewhat more difficult. Knits are linked, not woven, and are the most difficult.

| FABRIC | TEXTURE | STRETCH | FRAY | RECOMMENDED GARMENT |
|--------|---------|---------|------|---------------------|
| 1. | smooth and thin | some stretch | minimal fray | shirt, dress |
| 2. | rough and bulky | minimal stretch | slight fray | skirt, pants, dress |
| 3. | slightly bumpy | minimal stretch | some fray | pants, shirt |
| 4. | smooth and slightly bulky | minimal stretch | minimal fray | skirt, pants |
| 5. | smooth and thin | minimal stretch | slight fray | shirt |
| 6. | rough and slightly bulky | slight stretch | minimal fray | pants |
| 7. | slightly rough and slightly bulky | slight stretch | minimal fray | pants |
| 8. | smooth and slightly nubby | minimal stretch | some fray | dress, pants |
| 9. | smooth and slightly shiny | minimal stretch | slight fray | pants, dress, shirt |
| 10. | rough and thin | slight stretch | slight fray | dress, shirt |
| 11. | smooth and bulky | minimal stretch | minimal fray | skirt, dress |
| 12. | very rough and very bumpy | minimal stretch | slight fray | dress |
| 13. | rough and ridged | minimal stretch | minimal fray | pants, jacket |
| 14. | very smooth and slightly shiny | minimal stretch | slight fray | shirt |
| 15. | rough and bulky | minimal stretch | slight fray | skirt, pants, dress |
| 16. | very smooth | minimal stretch | some fray | shirt, dress |

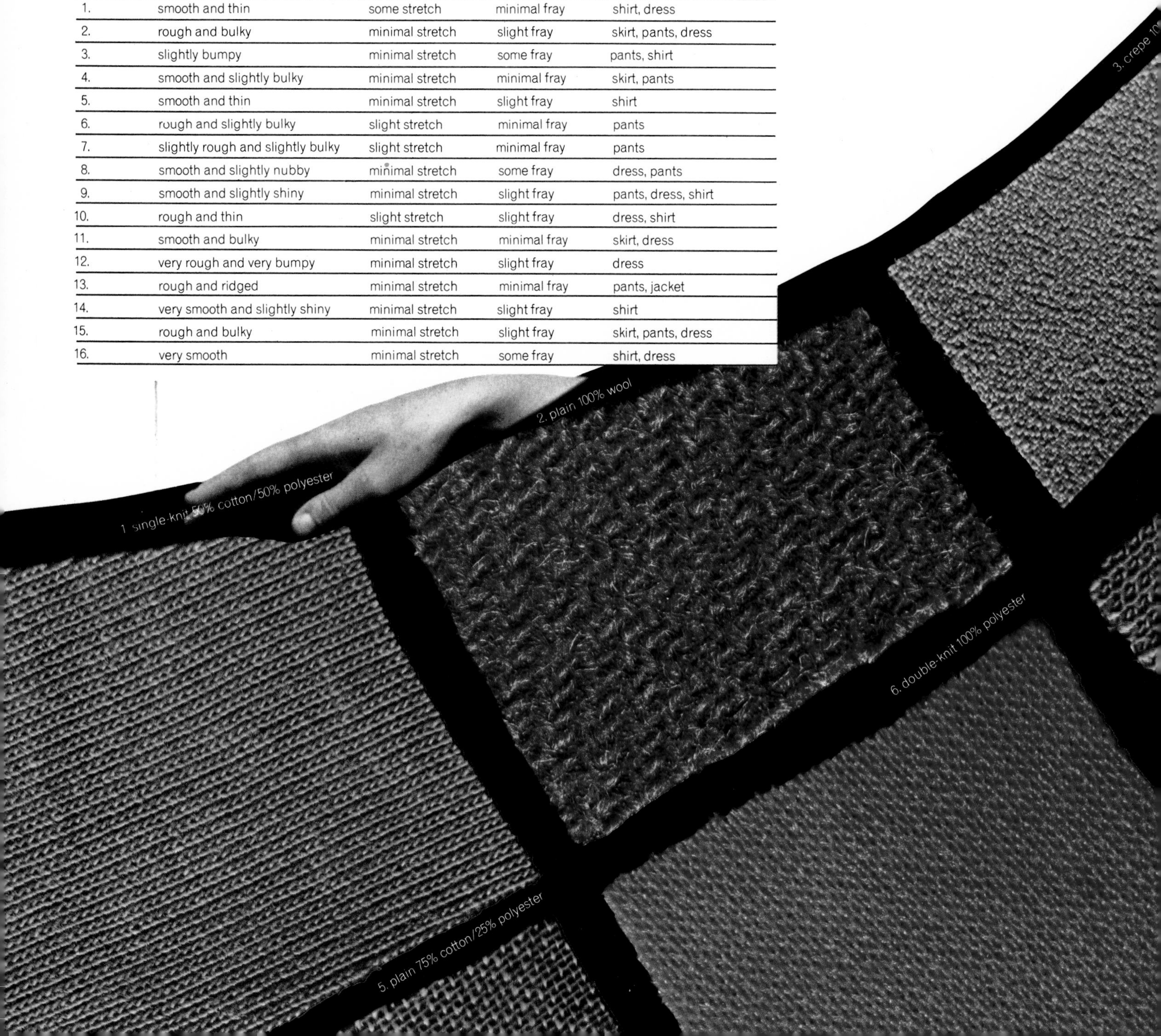

3. crepe 10

2. plain 100% wool

1. single-knit 50% cotton/50% polyester

6. double-knit 100% polyester

5. plain 75% cotton/25% polyester

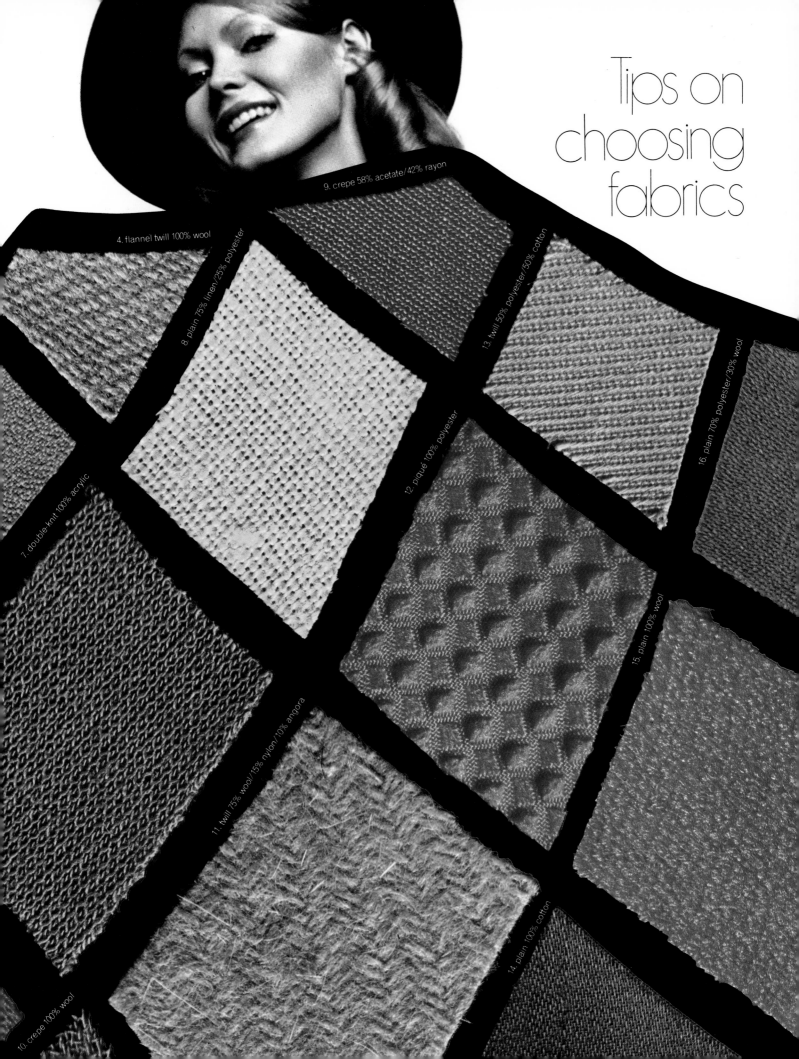

Tips on choosing fabrics

9. crepe 58% acetate/42% rayon

4. flannel twill 100% wool

8. plain 75% linen/25% polyester

13. twill 50% polyester/50% cotton

16. plain 70% polyester/30% wool

12. pique 100% polyester

7. double-knit 100% acrylic

15. plain 100% wool

11. twill 75% wool/15% nylon/10% angora

14. plain 100% cotton

10. crepe 100% wool

# Aligning and straightening the material

Unless your fabric has been pre-shrunk—and has a label saying so —it is essential that you shrink it yourself before cutting. If the material is nonwashable, take it to a dry cleaner to be preshrunk. If it is washable, follow the instructions in Step 14, opposite.

An equally important preparatory step, and one that is more frequently neglected, is straightening the fabric. If it was stretched out of shape prior to being placed on the bolt, or if it was not cut on the true grain—that is, with the lengthwise and crosswise threads at right angles to each other—the finished garment will not fit properly or hang evenly; a sleeve will not fall naturally from the armhole or a hem will sag.

In general, natural fibers are more easily cut on the true grain than synthetics and, even if slightly off, are easier to adjust. Synthetic fabrics and those that are a mixture of natural and synthetic fibers may need more straightening. Both can be adjusted by following the instructions at right for aligning the crosswise and lengthwise, or selvage, edges.

## A FINDING THE CROSSWISE GRAIN LINE

1. Iron the fabric on the wrong side to remove wrinkles and any lines made by folding.

2. If your fabric is knit, skip to Step 8. If your fabric is woven, spread it wrong side up on a flat surface. Snip into the selvage (lengthwise) edge near one end, at a point where a single thread runs the entire width of the material.

3. Using a pin, snag a crosswise thread from the snipped edge.

4. Pull gently on the thread, easing it along as though you were gathering the fabric; the pulled thread will show up as a puckered line.

5. If the pulled thread breaks as you pull it, cut along the pulled line to the point of the break and pick up the same or nearest crosswise thread. Continue to pull the thread.

6. Cut along the pulled line from one selvage through to the other; this is the true crosswise grain.

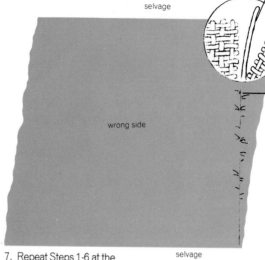

7. Repeat Steps 1-6 at the opposite end of the fabric.

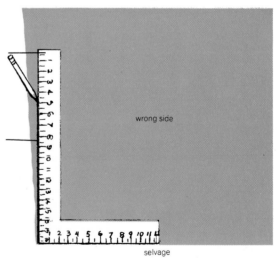

8. If your fabric is knit, place an L-shaped square near one crosswise edge of the fabric. Align one side of the square with a selvage edge.

9. Draw a chalk line along the crosswise grain of the fabric at a right angle to the selvage.

10. Cut along the chalk line from one selvage to the other.

11. Repeat Steps 8-10 at the opposite end of the fabric.

## B CHECKING THE ALIGNMENT OF CROSSWISE AND LENGTHWISE EDGES

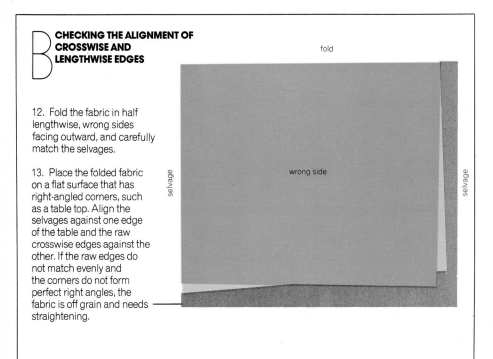

12. Fold the fabric in half lengthwise, wrong sides facing outward, and carefully match the selvages.

13. Place the folded fabric on a flat surface that has right-angled corners, such as a table top. Align the selvages against one edge of the table and the raw crosswise edges against the other. If the raw edges do not match evenly and the corners do not form perfect right angles, the fabric is off grain and needs straightening.

## C STRAIGHTENING THE FABRIC

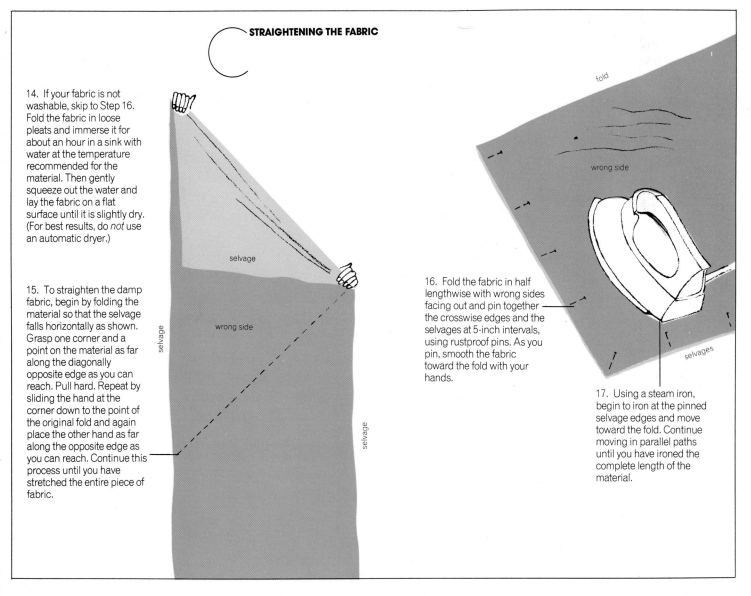

14. If your fabric is not washable, skip to Step 16. Fold the fabric in loose pleats and immerse it for about an hour in a sink with water at the temperature recommended for the material. Then gently squeeze out the water and lay the fabric on a flat surface until it is slightly dry. (For best results, do *not* use an automatic dryer.)

15. To straighten the damp fabric, begin by folding the material so that the selvage falls horizontally as shown. Grasp one corner and a point on the material as far along the diagonally opposite edge as you can reach. Pull hard. Repeat by sliding the hand at the corner down to the point of the original fold and again place the other hand as far along the opposite edge as you can reach. Continue this process until you have stretched the entire piece of fabric.

16. Fold the fabric in half lengthwise with wrong sides facing out and pin together the crosswise edges and the selvages at 5-inch intervals, using rustproof pins. As you pin, smooth the fabric toward the fold with your hands.

17. Using a steam iron, begin to iron at the pinned selvage edges and move toward the fold. Continue moving in parallel paths until you have ironed the complete length of the material.

# Humble instruments for precision cutting

The cutting and marking tools in use today are such a completely functional and ordinary part of everyday living that their heritage has long been forgotten. Consider the lowly pin—that indispensable adjunct to measurement, marking and cutting. Nowadays a packet of shiny, rustproof pins is as close as the nearest dime or department store. But until a century and a half ago, when a machine was invented that could spill them out by the thousands, pins were most uncommon and very valuable.

Today, pins are cut and shaped from a single piece of metal wire and automatically spewed into boxes or thrust into crimped papers in a single operation. When pins of iron and brass were made in England and France some six centuries ago, they were laboriously fashioned by hand with a strand of wire coiled around the top to form the head, which frequently fell off. But, imperfect as these early models were, they were such a luxury that for a long time well-to-do women were given "pin money" by their husbands to buy pins on special occasions. Picking up a stray pin was a matter of simple thrift and could for good measure, as the old Mother Goose rhyme promises, mean "All the day you'll have good luck."

So precious an object naturally required a place for safekeeping and what better or handier receptacle could be devised than pimpilowes, pimpilos, pimplos, pimploes or pyn-pillows, as pincushions were fancifully called. Unlike the ubiquitous and unimaginative felt "tomato" found in most sewing kits today, these early pincushions were works of art, lovingly hand sewn of fine materials, lavishly embroidered and decorated and frequently worn as ornaments at the waist. During the reign of Elizabeth I, no high-ranking woman was ever without a plump pincushion and even the queen received an elaborate pyn-pillow as a gift one New Year's Day. During the 18th Century, pin poppets, small cases hand wrought from ivory and other valuable materials, were widely popular and like the pincushions, became family heirlooms.

The vogue for keeping sewing equipment in handsome housing extended even to tape measures. These forerunners of modern tape measures were stored in exquisite little containers made of brass, wood, bone, ivory or mother-of-pearl with tiny spindles and ingenious gadgets for winding and unwinding them. The tape measures—ribbons with lines embroidered or inked a certain distance apart—were of haphazard lengths. Not until the early 19th Century did the 36-inch size become generally accepted as the standard length.

The length of the tape measure was by no means its only variable; the units of measurement themselves were not standardized until fairly recently. For centuries, measurements were almost totally arbitrary. In medieval England, for example, the length of hunting or battle arrows was long the measure of a yard of cloth. In the 12th Century, the yard was decreed to be the length of the king's arm. That gave an approximate 36 inches, but standard-makers capriciously threw in an extra inch—the length of the first joint of a thumb—for good measure. The king's foot-long foot was divided into 12 units, but each of these units was based on the equivalent of three barleycorns laid end to end. Since barleycorns come in various sizes, the three-barleycorn inch was clearly not the same size as the inch based on the king's thumb.

These confusing and unsatisfactory rule-of-royal-thumb measurements were superseded in the 16th Century, in an effort at standardization, by the ell, a 45-inch unit. The ell was customarily laid out on a wooden ruler marked with golden nails set 2 1/2 inches apart. The tape ribbons took their measurements from these nailed sticks, which were known as "meteyards." Eventually the ell and other arbitrary measures were replaced by units based on the length of actual "standards." At first these were carefully wrought pieces of metal preserved in government laboratories at constant temperatures to prevent contraction or expansion of the metal. Eventually, the standards came to be based on wavelengths of light that could be precisely gauged.

As tape measures evolved from elaborate if inexact *objets d'art* into plain but efficient tools, so did scissors. Modern scissors, forged of quality steel, are prized more for the keenness of their cutting blades than the artistry of their workmanship. But when steel scissors first appeared, exquisitely hand-wrought models encased in elegant protective sheaths were cherished for their beauty, and were rare and extremely expensive. These were upper-class tools, of course; ordinary folk had to make do with plain iron scissors until improvements in steelmaking technology in the late 19th Century began to put quality scissors within the range of even the poorest pocketbook.

Steel also considerably simplified techniques of marking fabric for sewing after workable patterns became widely available following the Civil War. The patterns, *Harper's Bazaar* advised its readers in 1875, "must be transformed to separate sheets of paper. This can be done with the greatest of ease by the newly invented Copying Wheel—a simple instrument, consisting of a small notched steel wheel, revolving on a pivot, and set in a rose-wood handle." By rolling the wheel over the pattern, the paper lying beneath was punctured so that pattern pieces could be cut from it.

Today, of course, the tracing wheel serves an entirely different function. It is used with the pattern and dressmaker's carbon to mark cutting or sewing lines directly on the fabric itself. But the wheel that *Harper's* endorsed has spawned another type of wheel. The notches that were so useful for pricking paper tend to snag on the knit fabrics so widely used today. A smooth-wheeled model now marks the lines on knits before stitching commences. Either way, *Harper's* Copying Wheel remains a simple but essential instrument, like the rest of today's cutting and marking tools.

# Using scissors and marking wheel

Three basic scissors will see you through every step of making most garments; left-handed as well as right-handed versions of these scissors are readily available. A simple tracing wheel is the basic tool for transferring pattern markings.

Cut out your fabric with 8- or 10-inch bent-handled dressmaker's shears; clip into curves and small areas with 6-inch scissors, which are small enough for maximum precision. Finish raw seam edges by trimming with pinking shears having zigzag teeth. Directions for all of these actions are illustrated at right.

To transfer pattern markings to fabric, run a saw-toothed wheel (*opposite*) over the markings after the pattern, the fabric and dressmaker's carbon paper have been assembled as shown on page 83. On knits and double knits a plain wheel is used, to prevent snags. The secret of accurate marking is never to reverse the wheel; run it firmly forward.

## CUTTING

### STRAIGHT LINES

Open the shears wide and take in fabric the whole length of the blades. Cut with one long steady closure for a smooth edge.

### CURVES

Open the shears halfway and never quite close them as you cut around a curve.

This will make an even arc instead of a series of jagged lines.

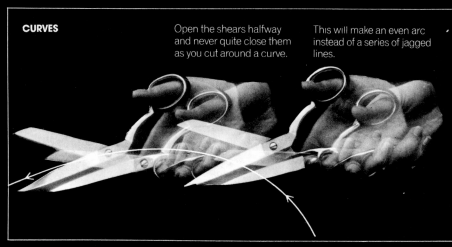

### RIGHT ANGLES

Cut two intersecting straight lines by cutting along one marked line, then pulling the shears out and cutting along the second line at the point at which the two meet. This produces a crisp, true angle instead of a swivel.

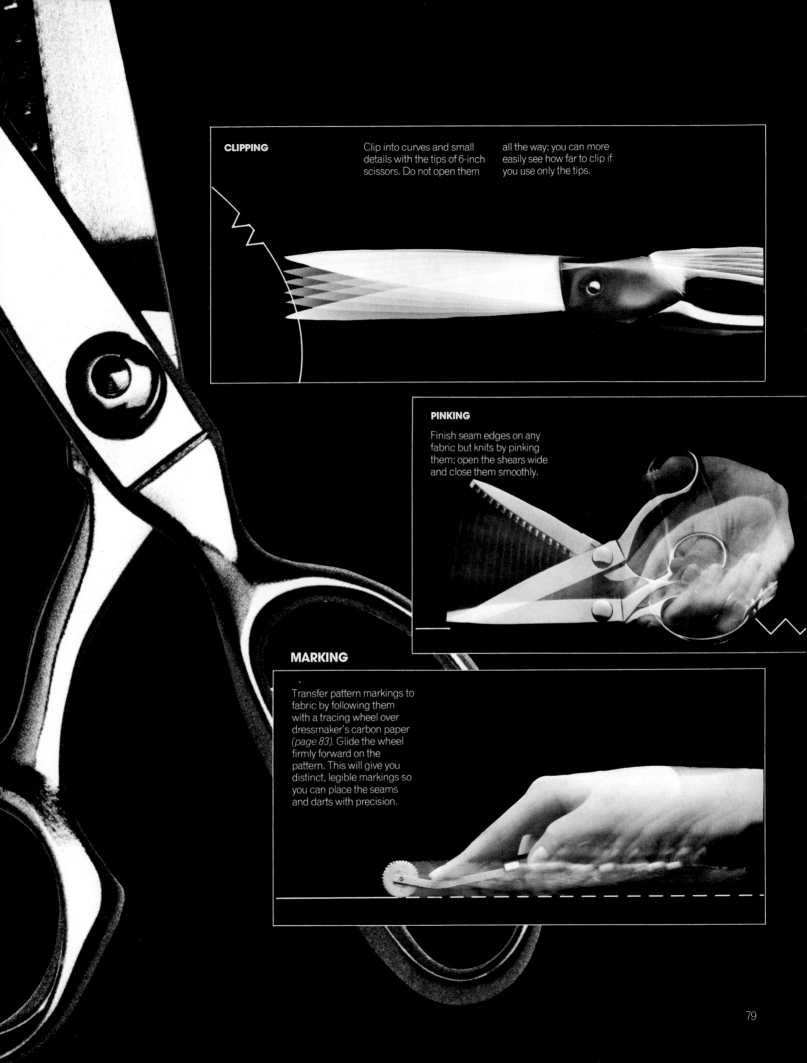

## CLIPPING

Clip into curves and small details with the tips of 6-inch scissors. Do not open them all the way; you can more easily see how far to clip if you use only the tips.

## PINKING

Finish seam edges on any fabric but knits by pinking them; open the shears wide and close them smoothly.

## MARKING

Transfer pattern markings to fabric by following them with a tracing wheel over dressmaker's carbon paper *(page 83)*. Glide the wheel firmly forward on the pattern. This will give you distinct, legible markings so you can place the seams and darts with precision.

# Arranging and cutting out pattern pieces

Find a flat, firm cutting surface large enough to hold the entire length of your fabric—a table or even the floor, if necessary—and spread out the material as shown at right. Pin and cut out the entire pattern without moving the fabric. To protect your cutting surface, use table pads or a dressmaker's cutting board.

Check the guide sheet that comes with your pattern; it will give several cutting guides—that is, diagrams showing how to arrange the pattern on the material according to its size and the width of the material.

If you are working with striped or checked fabric, use the numbered notches on your pattern pieces *(page 82)* to match the design at important seams. In matching, give priority where possible to front seams over back ones and to horizontal seams over vertical ones.

After cutting out your garment, transfer all pattern markings to the wrong side of the fabric before you remove the pattern. Use a tracing wheel *(page 79)* and dressmaker's carbon paper to do this job quickly and accurately.

## FOLDING THE FABRIC

### FOLDING SOLID FABRIC

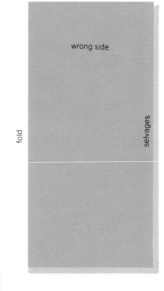

1. For most patterns, fold your fabric in half lengthwise so that it is wrong side out. This layout conserves fabric and enables you to position all at once as many pattern pieces as you need. Pin the selvages together at 1- to 2-inch intervals.

2. For pattern pieces that are too wide to be cut on fabric folded lengthwise, fold the fabric in half crosswise so that it is wrong side out.

3. If your cutting guide requires some pieces to be cut from a double and some from a single thickness of fabric, fold all the fabric as shown in Step 1 or 2, depending on the cutting guide instructions, and cut out all the pieces requiring double thicknesses. Then spread the rest of the material out in a single thickness, wrong side down.

## B FOLDING STRIPED OR CHECKED FABRIC

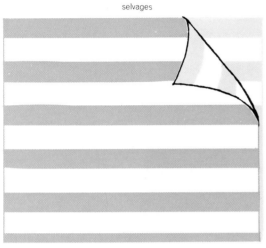

selvages

fold

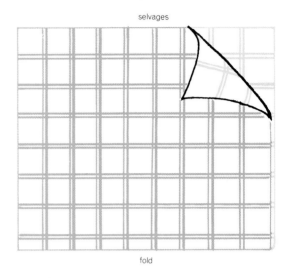

selvages

fold

4. If the fabric has stripes or checks of similar size, fold it so that the fold line falls exactly halfway through a stripe or check.

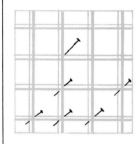

5. Starting near the fold and working to the selvages, stick pins through the top layer of fabric where check lines intersect (or at the edge of stripe lines).

6. Fold back the top layer and make sure that the pins bring together the two layers at points where the pattern matches exactly. If the pattern does not match, adjust the fabric.

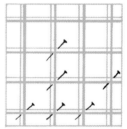

7. Catch the point of the pin to hold the layers together. Continue inserting pins in this manner at a number of points. Then pin the fabric together at the edges.

# USING THE PATTERN TO CUT OUT THE GARMENT

## A PINNING THE PATTERN TO A SOLID FABRIC

1. Separate all pattern pieces having a line marked "place on fold" and place them on the fabric so that the mark aligns with the fold of the fabric. Pin these pieces to the fabric along the fold.

2. Loosely arrange the other pieces according to the pattern cutting guide, with the printed grain-line arrows parallel to the fold and selvage edges.

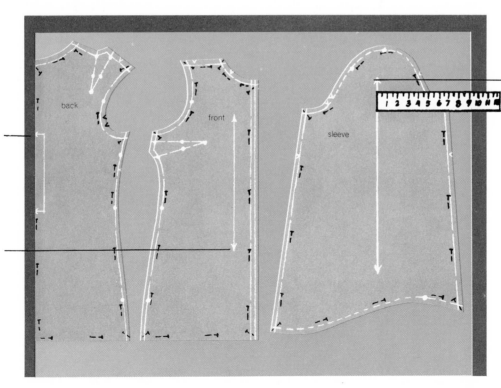

3. Measure from the fabric edge to both ends of the grain-line arrow on each pattern piece; make sure that the arrow is uniformly distant from the edge and therefore parallel to it.

4. Smooth each pattern piece to make sure it lies flat. Then pin each piece to the fabric, placing the pins diagonally at the corners and parallel to, and just inside, the cutting line.

continued

## PINNING THE PATTERN TO STRIPED OR CHECKED FABRIC

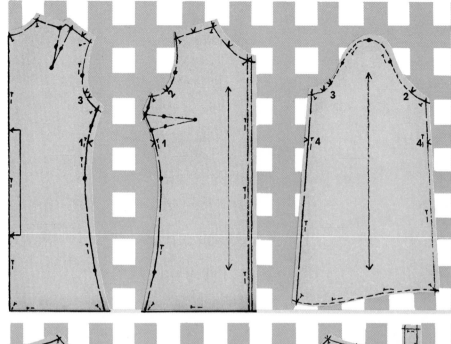

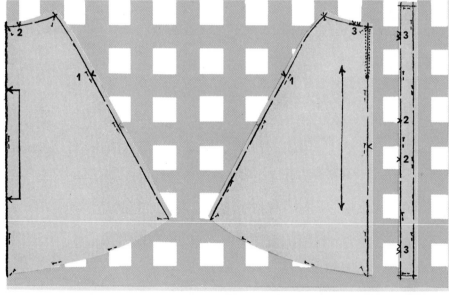

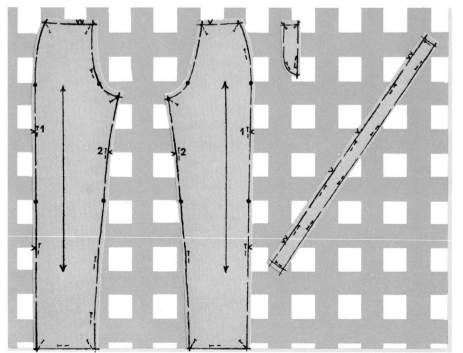

5. Loosely arrange the pattern pieces on the fabric according to the directions in the pattern layout guide. To make the design match where pieces must be seamed together, look for numbered notches on the patterns for those pieces; make sure that notches having the same numbers lie in exactly the same position relative to the checks or stripes.

6A. To match design along the most important seam lines of a dress, blouse or shirt, line up notches in the following order: side seams (notches marked 1 in this diagram), armhole and sleeve seams (notches 2 and 3), underarm sleeve seams (notch 4).

6B. To match seam lines of a skirt, line up the side seams (notches marked 1 in this drawing). The center front seam will match because both halves are cut out at once. If the waistband is cut parallel to the grain of the fabric, as in this example, line up the waistband with the waistline edge at the front (notch 2) and then the back (notch 3).

6C. To match seam lines of pants, line up the side seams (notches marked 1 in this drawing) and the inner leg seams (notch 2). If the waistband is cut on the bias, as in this example, the waistband is not matched to the waistline edge.

7. Pin at the notches.

8. Check to be sure that the grain line is parallel to the selvage, or lengthwise edge of the fabric, as in Step 3, and adjust where necessary.

9. Pin the entire pattern to the fabric, as in Step 4.

## C CUTTING OUT THE GARMENT

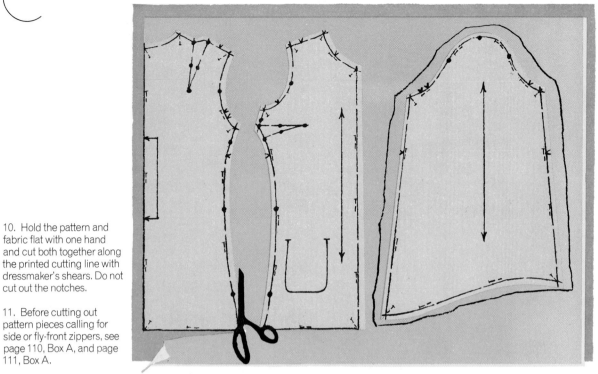

10. Hold the pattern and fabric flat with one hand and cut both together along the printed cutting line with dressmaker's shears. Do not cut out the notches.

11. Before cutting out pattern pieces calling for side or fly-front zippers, see page 110, Box A, and page 111, Box A.

12. For pattern pieces that are awkward to reach, cut loosely around the entire section, remove it and trim it separately at the cutting line.

## TRANSFERRING PATTERN MARKINGS

### A PREPARING TO MARK THE FABRIC

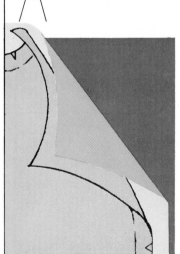

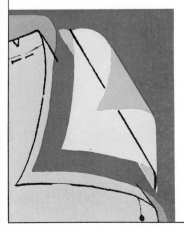

1. Working on one piece at a time, remove just enough pins—never all—to allow you to slip dressmaker's carbon paper between the layers of fabric and the pattern.

2. To mark two layers of fabric at once, first place one piece of carbon paper —carbon side up—under the bottom layer of fabric.

3. Place another piece of carbon paper—carbon side down—over the top layer of fabric.

4. Pin the pattern back into position.

5. To mark a single layer of fabric, place one piece of carbon paper—carbon side up—underneath the fabric.

### B MARKING THE FABRIC

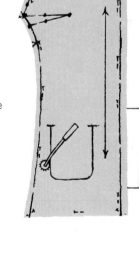

6. Run your tracing wheel along all stitching lines and dart lines, following the instructions on page 79. Use a straightedge ruler as a guide for straight lines and trace curves freehand.

7. Trace the notches with a dull pencil.

8. With the pencil, draw an X through the center of all circles and dots.

9. Remove the pattern from the fabric and baste along those markings that must show on both sides of the fabric: the center front line and the placement lines for pleats, buttonholes, pockets and trimmings.

# 4

## ASSEMBLING,
## FITTING
## BASIC SEWING
## STEPS
## SIMPLE PROJECTS

After all the preliminaries of dressmaking have been completed—the fabric and pattern selected, cutting and marking finished—the final stage of the sewing art is at hand. That is the actual sewing of the pieces into a garment, and its goal can be summed up in one word: fit.

No matter how distinctive the design, how luxurious the fabric, a garment can make you look well-dressed only if it con-

# THE SECRET OF CLOTHES THAT LOOK RIGHT — FIT

forms perfectly to your individual conformation—if it feels comfortable as you sit, stand and move about; hangs smoothly; conforms to bust and hips without pulling or bagging; buttons without gaps; lies smooth and neat around the neck and across the shoulder.

Perfect fit is achieved by assembling the separate pieces in the proper order and taking care to check each piece on your body before proceeding to the next step. Some people make the mistake of attempting shortcuts, of course. When putting together a skirt with patch pockets, for example, it is simpler to stitch the pockets on the fabric before completing the side seams and enclosing the skirt. Following that procedure, you can work with a flat, unclosed piece of fabric rather than one into which you have to reach to attach material; the technique is in fact recommended in instructions accompanying many patterns.

But that technique is not the best. The procedure detailed on page 137 takes longer, for you must baste the pockets to the skirt after you have placed the seams. But then you are able to make certain, by modeling the skirt in front of a full-length mirror, that the pockets are in the most becoming position, neither set too far off the center line nor placed too high or too low on the skirt. If necessary, you can make appropriate adjustments before proceeding to the final machine stitching.

Similarly, it is an unsound procedure—although fast, easy and frequently recommended—to stitch darts before putting in the seams. Following this method, final fit is then made simply by taking in or letting out the seams. But perfect fit over body contours requires a balance between darts and seams. To achieve that balance, you should first baste the darts and then the seams. Then you should try on the dress in front of your full-length mirror, and proceed to make adjustments to both darts and seams until that perfect balance you are in search of has been reached. Only then do you stitch in the darts, naturally putting the seams in second

because they have to pass over the darts.

You will, on the following pages, find other steps that seem unnecessary or superfluous. The instructions for assembling a dress on pages 93-94, for example, suggest basting a zipper in place before trying on the dress to check the fit of the neckline—a more time-consuming procedure than machine stitching the zipper to the dress in the first place. The zipper must be in place, of course, to check the fit, but if alterations are necessary and it is permanently attached, rather than basted in, you have the laborious task of removing the machine stitches. Or else you will have to make do with a less-than-perfect fit at the neckline.

Attention to good sewing techniques also helps to make your clothes last longer—an important consideration when working with classic styles. Since they never go out of fashion, classics should be wearable virtually forever. And they will last a long time if care is taken in the making.

Everything you do in sewing counts toward creating a better-fitting, better-looking, longer-wearing item of clothing—and even the smallest details, such as the making of items like pockets and buttonholes, are as important as, say, the fitting of a seam. These elements are subject to more than the normal amount of stress; they need to be built to take it. A pocket will quickly fray or collapse if it is not properly reinforced and stitched at the corners and edges and set firmly into the fabric. A buttonhole sloppily sewn or snipped will soon start to pull apart. And a button improperly placed or sewn without an adequate shank will never slip through its buttonhole with ease and could well pull the whole front of your otherwise carefully finished garment out of line. These may seem small things; nonetheless, they are essential to the durability and the final, finished look of any article of clothing.

# Distinctive ingredients of contemporary dress

In all clothes, there are certain basic elements that have come to be taken for granted—things like pockets and pleats or buttons and buttonholes.

But the fact is that not all of these have always been common. For centuries, men and women alike got along without pockets, for example; they made do instead with little pouches that hung around the waist. Not until the 16th Century did the first pocket appear inside the combination pants and hose most men wore. By the 19th Century men had become so attached to pockets they were put everywhere and at every angle—horizontally, vertically and diagonally. Women were not so fortunate. They got no pockets whatsoever until the 1800s and then hid them in skirt seams—apparently because no proper lady was supposed to carry anything with her—that was a task performed by a servant or gentleman escort.

Pleats came along more rapidly. They began to appear the moment fitted clothes introduced a need for garments that could billow neatly over body contours. At first pleats were tied or pinned in place, not stitched. The first fastened-down pleats were apparently those used around the waist of men's tunics; such permanent pleating nipped in the material at the waist without requiring a belt. As sewing techniques tried to keep up with fashion changes, pleats were used anywhere an excess of material needed to be concealed—atop a leg-of-mutton sleeve, for instance, or around the waist of a wide skirt. Such a pleated skirt was so wide it involved hours of hemming, and it eventually led to the development of a labor-saving device called a hemming bird (opposite) to hold long lengths of material.

What must be one of the oddest quirks in the history of clothes concerns the noninvention of the button and buttonhole. It would seem that such a simple fastening device would have been thought of at a very early stage. But no one got around to inventing buttons until clothes became too tight to pull over the head. Up until that time, along about the 14th Century, garments were held together by an assortment of ties and belts and girdles. There was also a gadget like a safety pin called a fibula. Fancy fibulae had decorative brooches or animal-shaped figures on top to conceal the real work that was going on underneath. But they proved too cumbersome once narrow waists and tight sleeves required a number of openings that had to be closed, and at last they were replaced by buttons and buttonholes.

By the 18th Century, buttons were everywhere; up and down waistcoats, up and down trousers. Even shoes did not escape. Some of these buttons were purely decorative, but a lot of them—a tiresome lot of them it seemed—actually worked.

The nuisance of fastening and unfastening endless rows of buttons inspired Whitcomb L. Judson of Chicago to hit upon the idea of the zipper in 1891. His arrangement—hooks and eyes mounted on a pair of small chains with a sliding clasp that fastened the hooks and eyes automatically—worked reasonably well. Judson did not, however, conceive of the name zipper. And despite efforts to promote his device—

he tried unsuccessfully to persuade Little Egypt to use a zipper-equipped skirt in her demure striptease at the Chicago World's Fair of 1893—his "C-Curity placket fastener" fastened few plackets aside from those on tobacco pouches and money belts. The final triumph did not come until 1923, when the B. F. Goodrich Company used a similar gadget on its new rubber galoshes and, so goes legend, the company president called for a name with "zip" in it.

Today, of course, zippers close not only galoshes but an extraordinarily wide range of garments. Sometimes, these mechanical fasteners are virtually invisible, unobtrusively tucked underneath a fold of fabric; some-

This fanciful "hemming bird" was a sewing-room aid in the first half of the 19th Century. Clamped to a table, it held the end of a swath of fabric in its beak. The seamstress, by pulling the fabric taut with one hand, could sew a seam or hem swiftly with the other. In an age when layers of skirting billowed out to hemlines that ran 50 or even 100 inches in circumference, the hemming bird was an eminently practical device.

times they dash boldly across articles of clothing, presenting as many zigs and zags as those rows of buttons of yore. Like skirts, they have their ups and downs on the fashion scene—and perhaps more than one woman, in view of fluctuating changes in skirt lengths from year to year *(right),* might have wished for a permanent, built-in C-Curity placket fastener at the hemline of every dress she owned.

# As hemlines go, so goes Wall Street

Two stereotypes in American humor are the tense investor checking the ups and downs of the stock market in *The Wall Street Journal* and the elegant socialite consulting *Vogue* to follow the ups and downs of hemlines. A look at the trends these two different types live by reveals an amusing correlation over the years. In general, whenever the Dow Jones stock index (graphed at the bottom of the picture at right) has risen, hems have also gone up. When stock prices have dipped, hems have too. Though dress designers are not commonly thought of as bulls and bears, they may express in fashion the same underlying cycles of optimism and pessimism that govern the market. Or could it be that when a woman raises her hemline, her husband feels cheerful and buys more stock?

Changes in skirt lengths—as shown on stars Joan Crawford (1925)

1945    1947    1966    1970

Claudette Colbert (1935), Kay Francis (1945) and three models—correspond to ups and downs of stock prices *(graph, bottom)*.

# Putting the elements together

Before immersing yourself in the specific construction details of a garment—its darts, zippers, pleats, pockets, etc., as shown on pages 100-143—it will help to get an overall picture of the order in which to tackle these details and consequently to assemble a dress, shirt or blouse, skirt and pants.

The assembling procedure is always a logical one: the body section of a blouse, for example, is fitted and sewn before the sleeve is attached, otherwise the armhole in which the sleeve is inserted might not have the proper dimensions. Similarly, buttonholes and buttons are positioned after the garment is otherwise completed, so the closures will be smooth and neat.

If you have chosen the right size pattern *(pages 58-61)* and adjusted it where necessary to your figure *(pages 62-67),* you should encounter very few fitting problems in assembling your garment. But even a perfectly proportioned figure might have some minor quirks: a protruding collarbone that makes a lower neckline desirable, for example, or a slight swayback that necessitates adjusting a waistband. By making such minor fitting adjustments at the points recommended on the following pages, you will ensure that your finished garment hangs properly and fits perfectly.

# THE CLASSIC DRESS

## A  BASTING THE DARTS AND SEAMS

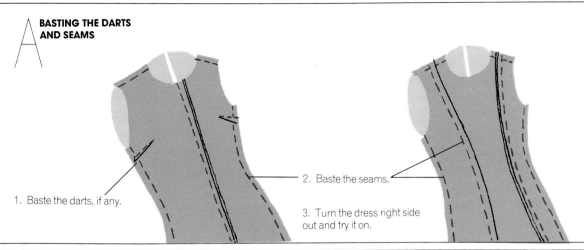

1. Baste the darts, if any.

2. Baste the seams.

3. Turn the dress right side out and try it on.

## B  ADJUSTING THE DARTS AND THE SEAMS

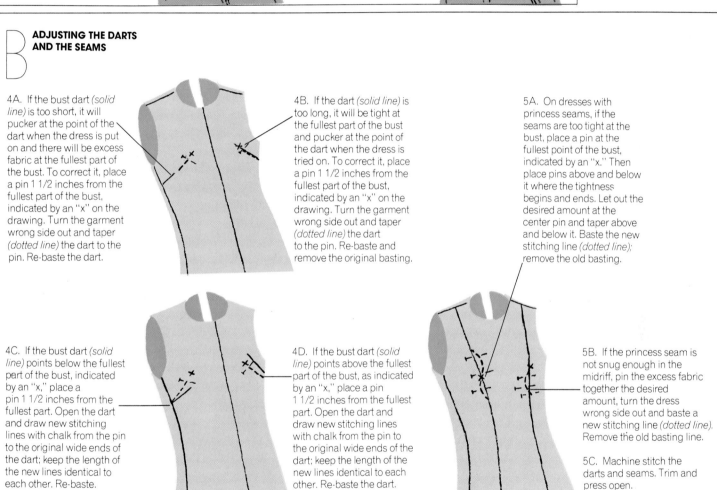

4A. If the bust dart (solid line) is too short, it will pucker at the point of the dart when the dress is put on and there will be excess fabric at the fullest part of the bust. To correct it, place a pin 1 1/2 inches from the fullest part of the bust, indicated by an "x" on the drawing. Turn the garment wrong side out and taper (dotted line) the dart to the pin. Re-baste the dart.

4B. If the dart (solid line) is too long, it will be tight at the fullest part of the bust and pucker at the point of the dart when the dress is tried on. To correct it, place a pin 1 1/2 inches from the fullest part of the bust, indicated by an "x" on the drawing. Turn the garment wrong side out and taper (dotted line) the dart to the pin. Re-baste and remove the original basting.

5A. On dresses with princess seams, if the seams are too tight at the bust, place a pin at the fullest point of the bust, indicated by an "x." Then place pins above and below it where the tightness begins and ends. Let out the desired amount at the center pin and taper above and below it. Baste the new stitching line (dotted line); remove the old basting.

4C. If the bust dart (solid line) points below the fullest part of the bust, indicated by an "x," place a pin 1 1/2 inches from the fullest part. Open the dart and draw new stitching lines with chalk from the pin to the original wide ends of the dart; keep the length of the new lines identical to each other. Re-baste.

4D. If the bust dart (solid line) points above the fullest part of the bust, as indicated by an "x," place a pin 1 1/2 inches from the fullest part. Open the dart and draw new stitching lines with chalk from the pin to the original wide ends of the dart; keep the length of the new lines identical to each other. Re-baste the dart.

5B. If the princess seam is not snug enough in the midriff, pin the excess fabric together the desired amount, turn the dress wrong side out and baste a new stitching line (dotted line). Remove the old basting line.

5C. Machine stitch the darts and seams. Trim and press open.

## C  ADJUSTING THE NECKLINE

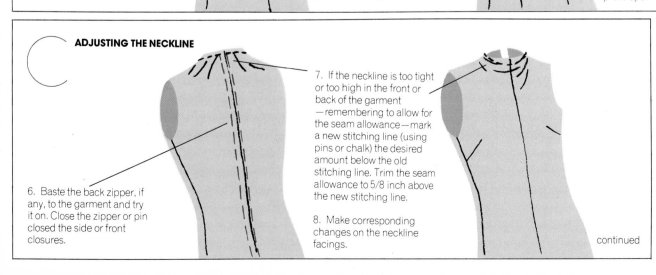

6. Baste the back zipper, if any, to the garment and try it on. Close the zipper or pin closed the side or front closures.

7. If the neckline is too tight or too high in the front or back of the garment —remembering to allow for the seam allowance—mark a new stitching line (using pins or chalk) the desired amount below the old stitching line. Trim the seam allowance to 5/8 inch above the new stitching line.

8. Make corresponding changes on the neckline facings.

continued

## D  FINISHING THE NECKLINE AND CLOSURES

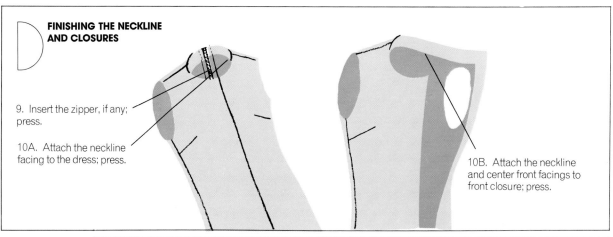

9. Insert the zipper, if any; press.

10A. Attach the neckline facing to the dress; press.

10B. Attach the neckline and center front facings to front closure; press.

## E  ARMHOLES AND SLEEVES

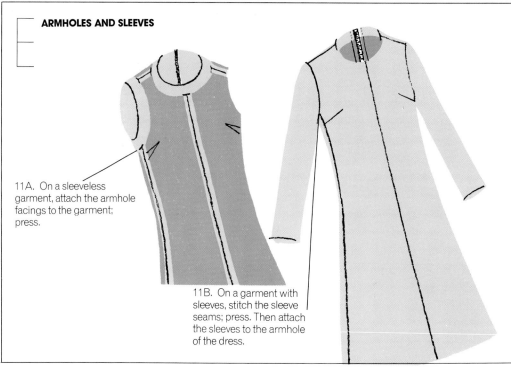

11A. On a sleeveless garment, attach the armhole facings to the garment; press.

11B. On a garment with sleeves, stitch the sleeve seams; press. Then attach the sleeves to the armhole of the dress.

## F  FINISHING TOUCHES

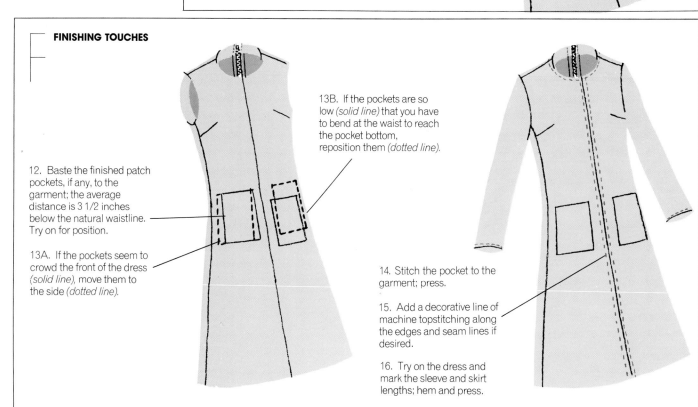

12. Baste the finished patch pockets, if any, to the garment; the average distance is 3 1/2 inches below the natural waistline. Try on for position.

13A. If the pockets seem to crowd the front of the dress *(solid line),* move them to the side *(dotted line).*

13B. If the pockets are so low *(solid line)* that you have to bend at the waist to reach the pocket bottom, reposition them *(dotted line).*

14. Stitch the pocket to the garment; press.

15. Add a decorative line of machine topstitching along the edges and seam lines if desired.

16. Try on the dress and mark the sleeve and skirt lengths; hem and press.

# THE CLASSIC SHIRT

## A — THE BODY SECTION

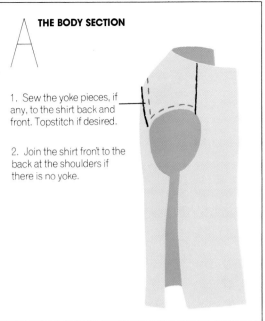

1. Sew the yoke pieces, if any, to the shirt back and front. Topstitch if desired.

2. Join the shirt front to the back at the shoulders if there is no yoke.

## B — SLEEVES AND SIDE SEAMS

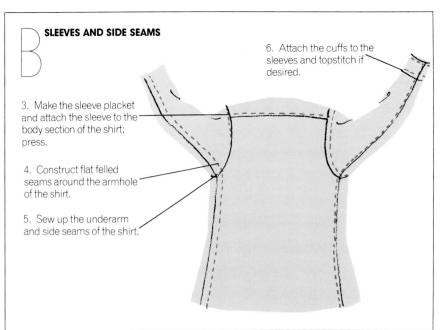

6. Attach the cuffs to the sleeves and topstitch if desired.

3. Make the sleeve placket and attach the sleeve to the body section of the shirt; press.

4. Construct flat felled seams around the armhole of the shirt.

5. Sew up the underarm and side seams of the shirt.

## C — COLLARS AND FACINGS

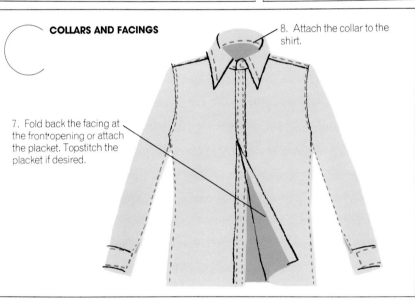

8. Attach the collar to the shirt.

7. Fold back the facing at the front opening or attach the placket. Topstitch the placket if desired.

## D — BUTTONHOLES AND BUTTONS

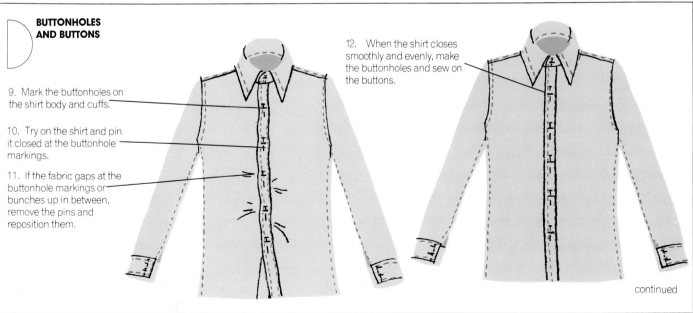

12. When the shirt closes smoothly and evenly, make the buttonholes and sew on the buttons.

9. Mark the buttonholes on the shirt body and cuffs.

10. Try on the shirt and pin it closed at the buttonhole markings.

11. If the fabric gaps at the buttonhole markings or bunches up in between, remove the pins and reposition them.

continued

## E ⌐ POCKETS

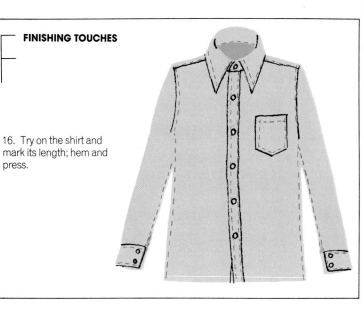

13. Baste the finished breast pocket or pockets to the shirt and try the shirt on for positioning.

14. If the pocket is so high that it comes close to the tip of the collar, and is uncomfortable to reach, reposition it *(dotted lines)* on the shirt.

15. Sew the pocket to the shirt; press.

## F ⌐ FINISHING TOUCHES

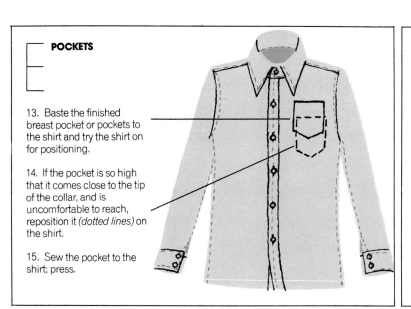

16. Try on the shirt and mark its length; hem and press.

## THE CLASSIC BLOUSE

### A BODY SECTION

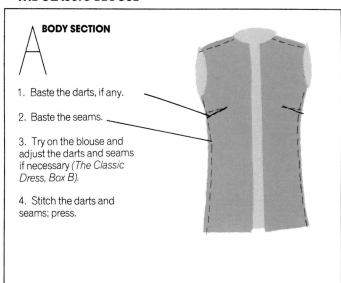

1. Baste the darts, if any.

2. Baste the seams.

3. Try on the blouse and adjust the darts and seams if necessary *(The Classic Dress, Box B).*

4. Stitch the darts and seams; press.

### B FACINGS AND COLLARS

6. Attach the collar to the neckline of the blouse; press.

5. Attach the facing or fold back the self-facing at the center front opening; press.

### C SLEEVES

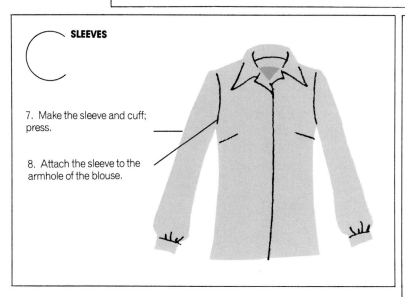

7. Make the sleeve and cuff; press.

8. Attach the sleeve to the armhole of the blouse.

### D FINISHING TOUCHES

11. Baste the finished breast pocket to the blouse and check its position *(The Classic Shirt, Box E, Step 14).*

9. Mark the buttonholes and try on the blouse for positioning *(The Classic Shirt, Box D).*

10. Sew the buttons on the blouse and cuff.

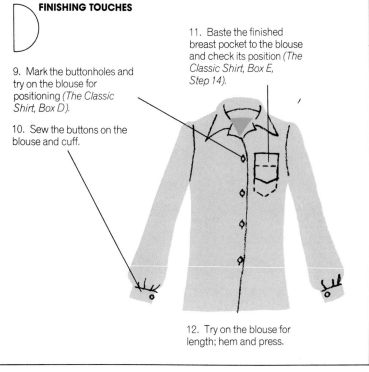

12. Try on the blouse for length; hem and press.

# THE CLASSIC SKIRT

## A — DARTS AND SEAMS ON PLEATED SKIRTS

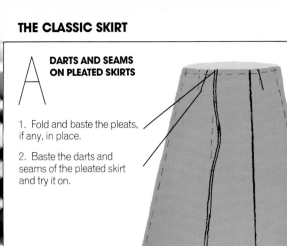

1. Fold and baste the pleats, if any, in place.

2. Baste the darts and seams of the pleated skirt and try it on.

3. If the pleat gapes or rolls open *(solid lines),* remove the basting at the waistline and lift the underlay of the pleat until it falls properly *(dotted lines).* Re-baste.

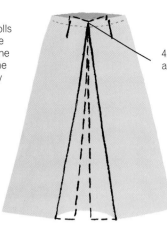

4. Stitch the darts, seams and pleats in place; press.

## B — DARTS AND SEAMS ON UNPLEATED SKIRTS

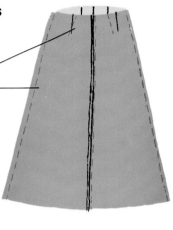

5. Baste the darts, if any.

6. Baste the seams.

7. Try on the skirt.

8A. If the dart points away from the fullest part of the hip or abdomen, indicated by an "x," place a pin 1 1/2 inches above the fullest part of the protrusion. Remove the dart bastings and draw new stitching lines from the pin, marking the new tip of the dart to the original wide ends of the dart; the lines must be the same length. Re-baste the dart.

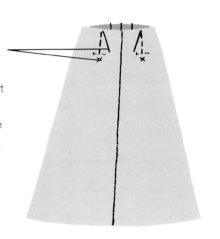

8B. If the waist dart is too short *(solid line),* it will pucker at the tip when tried on and the skirt will have excess fabric at the hip or abdomen. Correct it by placing a pin 1 1/2 inches above the fullest part of the upper hip or abdomen, indicated by an "x" on the drawing, and tapering the dart to the pin. Re-baste the dart.

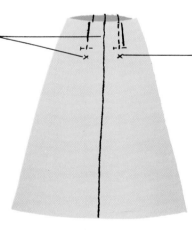

8C. If the dart is too long, the skirt will be tight over the upper hip or abdomen and the dart will pucker at the tip when tried on. Correct it by placing a pin 1 1/2 inches above the fullest part of the protrusion, indicated by an "x" on the drawing, tapering the dart to the pin, and re-basting.

9. Sew all darts and seams; press.

## C — ZIPPER AND WAISTBAND

10. Baste the zipper, if any, to the skirt.

11. Baste the waistband or waistline facing to the skirt.

12. Try on the skirt.

13. If the skirt below the waistband bulges because the band is too high on the back, mark a new stitching line with pins or chalk to the desired width. Remove the waistband; trim the skirt seam allowance to 5/8 inch above the new stitching line.

14. Insert the zipper, if any, to the skirt.

15. Attach the waistband or waistline facing to the skirt.

continued

## D FRONT CLOSURES

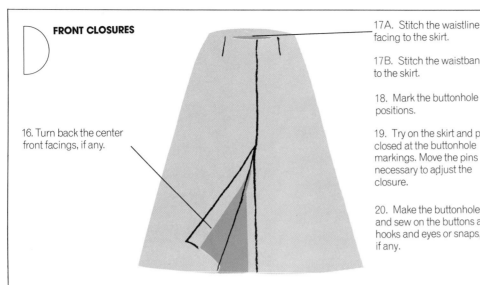

17A. Stitch the waistline facing to the skirt.

17B. Stitch the waistband to the skirt.

18. Mark the buttonhole positions.

16. Turn back the center front facings, if any.

19. Try on the skirt and pin closed at the buttonhole markings. Move the pins if necessary to adjust the closure.

20. Make the buttonholes and sew on the buttons and hooks and eyes or snaps, if any.

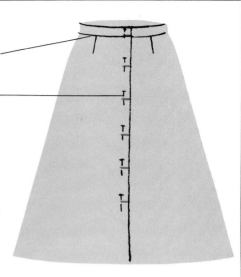

## E FINISHING TOUCHES

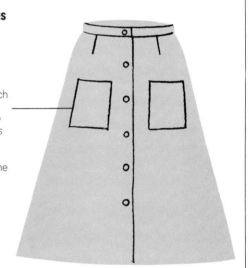

21. Baste the finished patch pockets, if any, to the skirt and try on for position (*The Classic Dress, Box F, Steps 12 and 13*).

22. Stitch the pockets to the skirt; press.

23. Try on the skirt and mark its length; hem and press.

## THE CLASSIC WOMEN'S PANTS

### A DARTS, SEAMS AND ZIPPERS

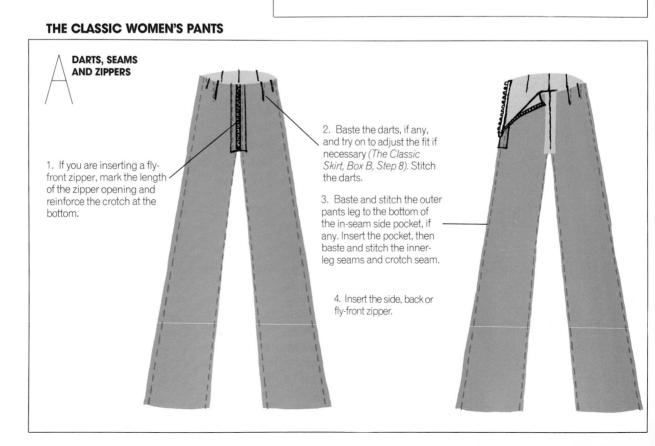

1. If you are inserting a fly-front zipper, mark the length of the zipper opening and reinforce the crotch at the bottom.

2. Baste the darts, if any, and try on to adjust the fit if necessary (*The Classic Skirt, Box B, Step 8*). Stitch the darts.

3. Baste and stitch the outer pants leg to the bottom of the in-seam side pocket, if any. Insert the pocket, then baste and stitch the inner-leg seams and crotch seam.

4. Insert the side, back or fly-front zipper.

## B  WAISTBAND OR WAISTLINE FACING

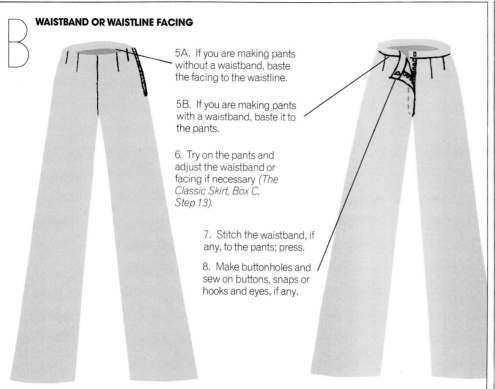

5A. If you are making pants without a waistband, baste the facing to the waistline.

5B. If you are making pants with a waistband, baste it to the pants.

6. Try on the pants and adjust the waistband or facing if necessary (*The Classic Skirt, Box C, Step 13*).

7. Stitch the waistband, if any, to the pants; press.

8. Make buttonholes and sew on buttons, snaps or hooks and eyes, if any.

## C  FINISHING TOUCHES

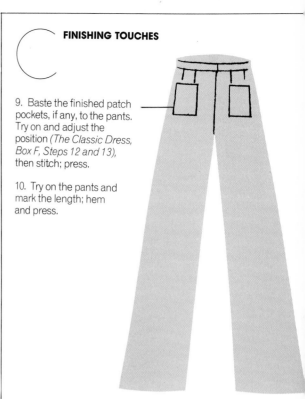

9. Baste the finished patch pockets, if any, to the pants. Try on and adjust the position (*The Classic Dress, Box F, Steps 12 and 13*), then stitch; press.

10. Try on the pants and mark the length; hem and press.

# THE CLASSIC MEN'S PANTS

## A  ZIPPER AND SEAMS

1. Insert the fly-front zipper.

2. Baste and stitch the outer-leg seams to the bottom of the in-seam side pocket, if any, then insert the pocket. Baste and stitch the inner-leg seams and crotch seam; press.

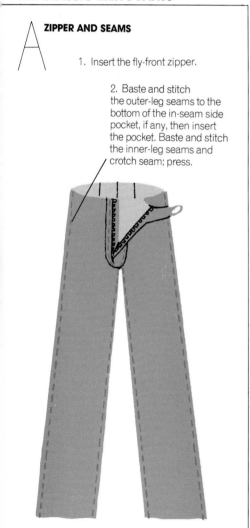

## B  WAISTBAND

3. Attach the waistband to the pants; press.

4. Make buttonholes or attach snaps or hooks and eyes to the belt.

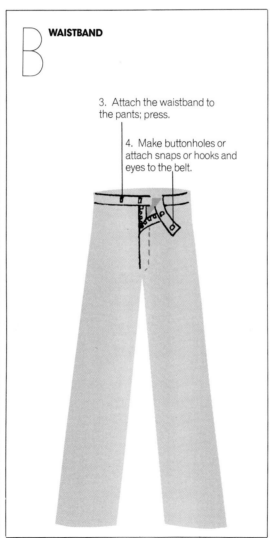

## C  FINISHING TOUCHES

5. Baste the finished patch pockets, if any, to the pants. Try on and adjust the position if necessary (*The Classic Dress, Box F, Steps 12 and 13*) and stitch; press.

6. Try on the pants and mark the length; hem and press.

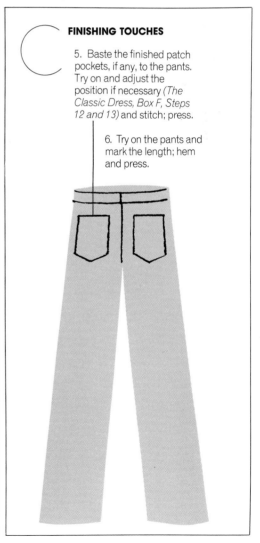

99

# Making strong, smooth seams

Seams not only hold pieces of a garment together—they are also the most obvious indicators of whether a garment is well or poorly made. With the techniques shown here, you can sew as flat, smooth and finished-looking a seam as any professional dressmaker might make.

There are various problems involved in making a basic "plain seam": getting two seams to intersect properly, "easing" a longer piece of fabric into the seam line of a smaller piece, working on curves, reducing bulkiness and finishing the raw edges. All of these are encountered as well in making other, more complicated types of seams, such as the strong seam used on men's shirts that is known as a flat felled seam—a double seam in which the raw edges of the seam are folded over and encased inside a second row of stitching *(page 32)*.

Essential to the success of all seams is careful marking and basting, followed by machine stitching with the proper needle, thread and stitch size for your fabric and garment *(page 28)*. Even more important is a smooth pressing of each seam as soon as it is completed; not even the most thorough pressing of the finished garment can substitute for pressing each seam as you go.

## THE PLAIN SEAM

### A  BASTING AND STITCHING THE PLAIN SEAM

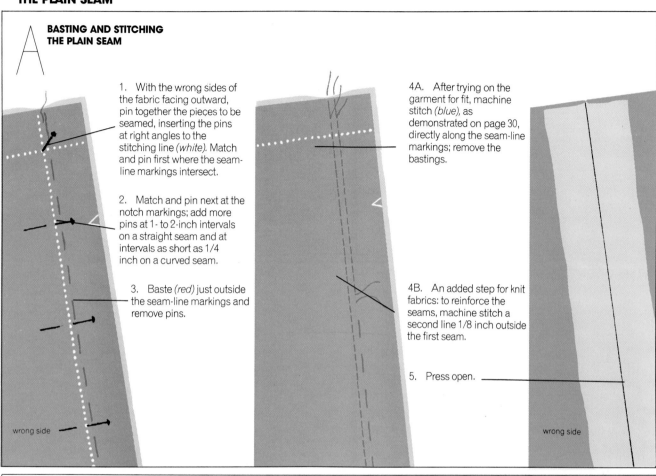

1. With the wrong sides of the fabric facing outward, pin together the pieces to be seamed, inserting the pins at right angles to the stitching line *(white)*. Match and pin first where the seam-line markings intersect.

2. Match and pin next at the notch markings; add more pins at 1- to 2-inch intervals on a straight seam and at intervals as short as 1/4 inch on a curved seam.

3. Baste *(red)* just outside the seam-line markings and remove pins.

wrong side

4A. After trying on the garment for fit, machine stitch *(blue)*, as demonstrated on page 30, directly along the seam-line markings; remove the bastings.

4B. An added step for knit fabrics: to reinforce the seams, machine stitch a second line 1/8 inch outside the first seam.

5. Press open.

wrong side

### B  FINISHING SEAM EDGES

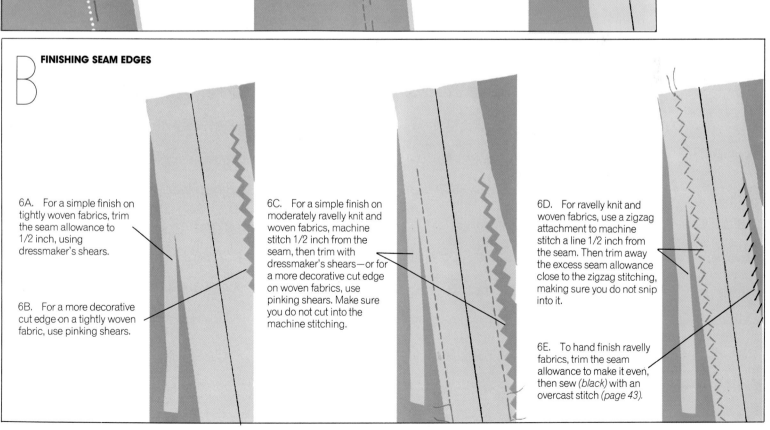

6A. For a simple finish on tightly woven fabrics, trim the seam allowance to 1/2 inch, using dressmaker's shears.

6B. For a more decorative cut edge on a tightly woven fabric, use pinking shears.

6C. For a simple finish on moderately ravelly knit and woven fabrics, machine stitch 1/2 inch from the seam, then trim with dressmaker's shears—or for a more decorative cut edge on woven fabrics, use pinking shears. Make sure you do not cut into the machine stitching.

6D. For ravelly knit and woven fabrics, use a zigzag attachment to machine stitch a line 1/2 inch from the seam. Then trim away the excess seam allowance close to the zigzag stitching, making sure you do not snip into it.

6E. To hand finish ravelly fabrics, trim the seam allowance to make it even, then sew *(black)* with an overcast stitch *(page 43)*.

## INTERSECTING SEAMS

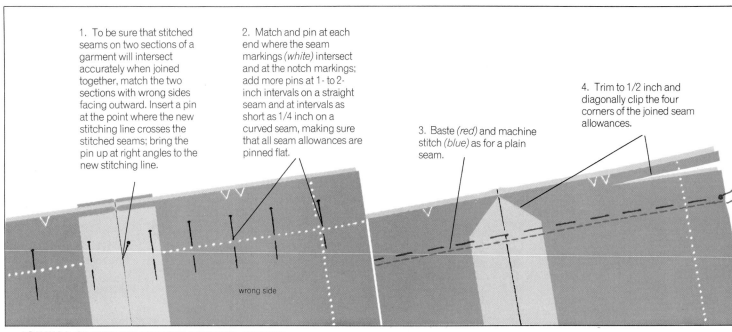

1. To be sure that stitched seams on two sections of a garment will intersect accurately when joined together, match the two sections with wrong sides facing outward. Insert a pin at the point where the new stitching line crosses the stitched seams; bring the pin up at right angles to the new stitching line.

2. Match and pin at each end where the seam markings (white) intersect and at the notch markings; add more pins at 1- to 2-inch intervals on a straight seam and at intervals as short as 1/4 inch on a curved seam, making sure that all seam allowances are pinned flat.

3. Baste (red) and machine stitch (blue) as for a plain seam.

4. Trim to 1/2 inch and diagonally clip the four corners of the joined seam allowances.

wrong side

## JOINING SEAMS OF UNEVEN LENGTH: EASING

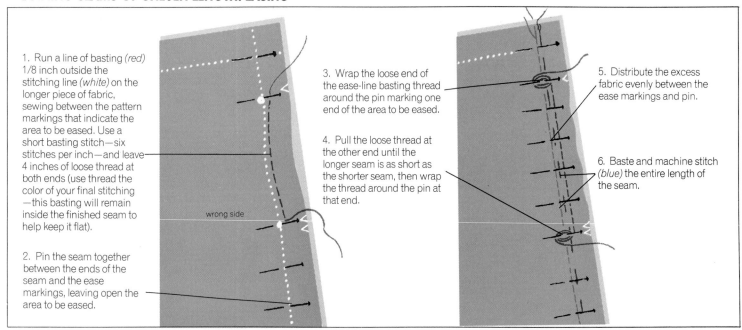

1. Run a line of basting (red) 1/8 inch outside the stitching line (white) on the longer piece of fabric, sewing between the pattern markings that indicate the area to be eased. Use a short basting stitch—six stitches per inch—and leave 4 inches of loose thread at both ends (use thread the color of your final stitching —this basting will remain inside the finished seam to help keep it flat).

2. Pin the seam together between the ends of the seam and the ease markings, leaving open the area to be eased.

3. Wrap the loose end of the ease-line basting thread around the pin marking one end of the area to be eased.

4. Pull the loose thread at the other end until the longer seam is as short as the shorter seam, then wrap the thread around the pin at that end.

5. Distribute the excess fabric evenly between the ease markings and pin.

6. Baste and machine stitch (blue) the entire length of the seam.

wrong side

## STITCHING CURVED SEAMS

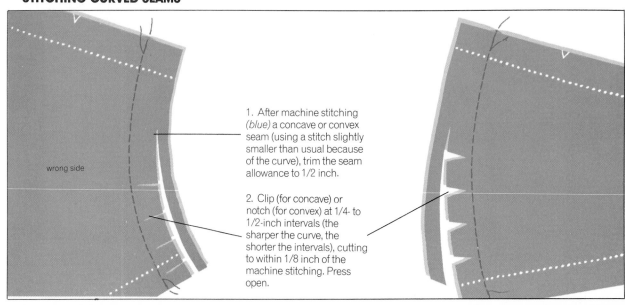

1. After machine stitching (blue) a concave or convex seam (using a stitch slightly smaller than usual because of the curve), trim the seam allowance to 1/2 inch.

2. Clip (for concave) or notch (for convex) at 1/4- to 1/2-inch intervals (the sharper the curve, the shorter the intervals), cutting to within 1/8 inch of the machine stitching. Press open.

wrong side

# TRIMMING ENCLOSED SEAMS

1. To reduce the bulk of seam allowances where there is a facing (a layer of fabric backing at garment edges) and an interfacing (a stiff fabric, shown here in dark gray, between the outside of the garment and the facing), trim the seam allowance of the interfacing to 1/16 of inch.

2. Trim the seam allowance of the facing to 1/8 inch.

3. Trim the seam allowance of the outer fabric to 1/4 inch.

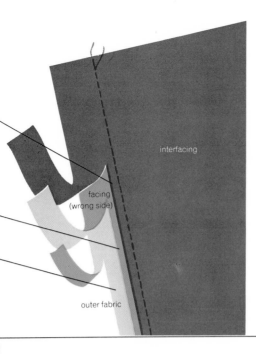

interfacing

facing (wrong side)

outer fabric

4. To reduce seam bulk at corners that have been faced and perhaps also interfaced, trim both sides of the corner, starting 1 1/2 inches from the corner on the outer fabric and cutting through all layers. Do not cut closer to the stitching line than 1/16 inch.

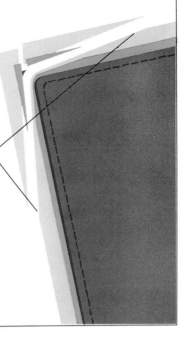

# THE FLAT FELLED SEAM

## A PREPARING TO MAKE THE FLAT FELLED SEAM

1. Make a plain seam, as shown in Box A, page 101, with either the right sides —the sides that will be visible in the completed garment—or the wrong sides of the fabric together, depending on your pattern. Press the seam open. Then fold and press both seam allowances in the direction indicated on your pattern.

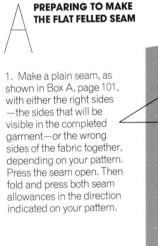

wrong side

2. Trim the underneath seam allowance to 1/8 inch.

3. Trim the top seam allowance to 1/2 inch.

## B FOLDING THE FLAT FELLED SEAM

4. Fold the top seam allowance over the underneath one, lining up the edge of the top seam allowance along the machine stitching (blue) of the original plain seam; this encloses the underneath seam allowance.

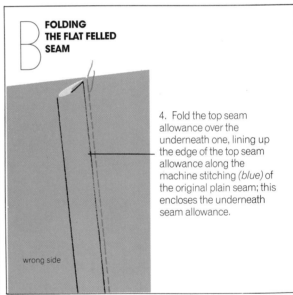

wrong side

## C BASTING AND STITCHING THE FLAT FELLED SEAM

5. Turn the fold to the side on which the felled seam should fall.

6. Pin the felled seam, inserting the pins from the folded edge toward the seam at right angles.

7. Baste (red) 1/8 inch from the folded edge.

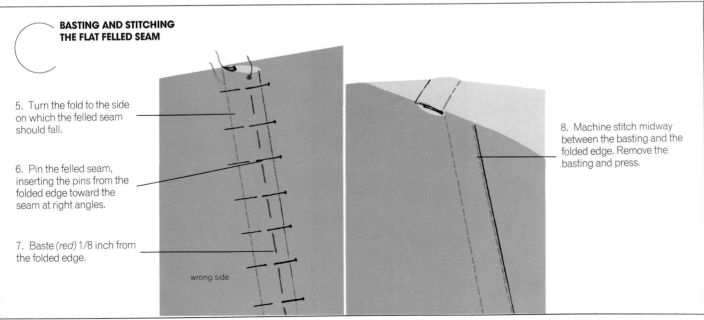

wrong side

8. Machine stitch midway between the basting and the folded edge. Remove the basting and press.

# Building shape with the dart

Darts, those stitched tapered folds that help to shape flat pieces of fabric to the curves and bumps of the human body, can also be used decoratively: their placement and manner of stitching often add to the design of a garment.

There are really only two kinds of darts, and both are based on triangular shapes. The most common type begins with the wide part of the fold at a seam and narrows to a point. This is the single-pointed dart and is placed at waist, bust, elbow or shoulder seams. The vertical double-pointed dart is less common; it is used to give contour to a waistless dress or long blouse or jacket.

As simple as darts are, making them look as smoothly perfect as the one in the picture at right requires careful adjustment to the figure (*pages 92-99*) and precise marking, stitching and pressing. You will find that it is worth the few extra minutes needed to make the extra markings recommended at right, which prevent an off-center or misplaced dart; in addition, a seemingly small step —sewing a few stitches off the fabric edge at the dart tip—can eliminate a puckered point.

# THE SINGLE AND DOUBLE DART

## A  GETTING READY TO MAKE DARTS

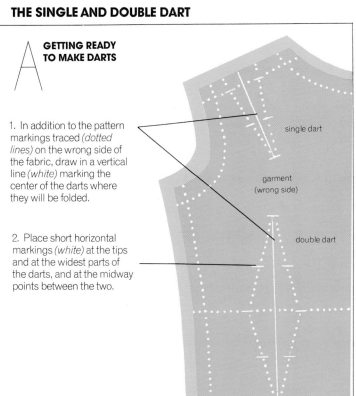

1. In addition to the pattern markings traced (dotted lines) on the wrong side of the fabric, draw in a vertical line (white) marking the center of the darts where they will be folded.

2. Place short horizontal markings (white) at the tips and at the widest parts of the darts, and at the midway points between the two.

single dart

garment (wrong side)

double dart

## B  PINNING THE DARTS

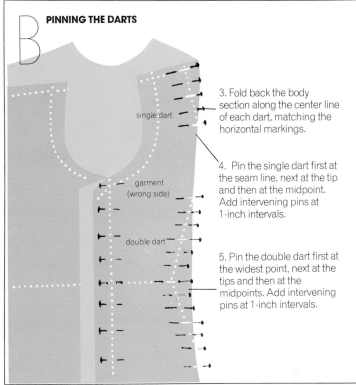

single dart

garment (wrong side)

double dart

3. Fold back the body section along the center line of each dart, matching the horizontal markings.

4. Pin the single dart first at the seam line, next at the tip and then at the midpoint. Add intervening pins at 1-inch intervals.

5. Pin the double dart first at the widest point, next at the tips and then at the midpoints. Add intervening pins at 1-inch intervals.

## C  BASTING AND FITTING

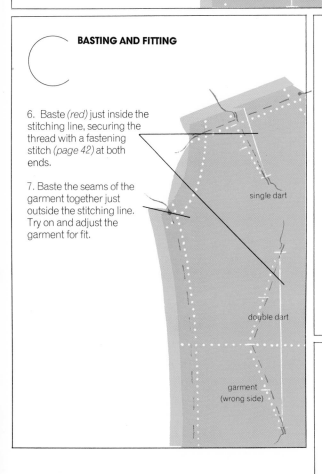

6. Baste (red) just inside the stitching line, securing the thread with a fastening stitch (page 42) at both ends.

7. Baste the seams of the garment together just outside the stitching line. Try on and adjust the garment for fit.

single dart

double dart

garment (wrong side)

## D  FINISHING THE SINGLE DART

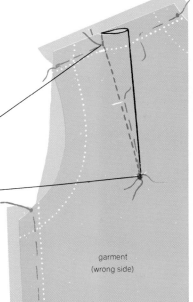

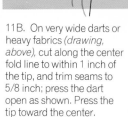

8. Remove only enough of the seam basting around the dart to permit you to stitch the dart.

9. Machine stitch (blue), beginning at the widest end.

10. Sew a few stitches off the edge of the fabric at the tip end. Then cut the thread and hand knot (page 29). Remove the dart bastings.

11A. Press average-sized darts on medium-weight fabric so that the fold is toward the center of the garment, except for the bust dart, which is pressed down.

garment (wrong side)

11B. On very wide darts or heavy fabrics (drawing, above), cut along the center fold line to within 1 inch of the tip, and trim seams to 5/8 inch; press the dart open as shown. Press the tip toward the center.

## E  FINISHING THE DOUBLE DART

12. Machine stitch, beginning at one tip, at the very edge of the fold; sew a few stitches off the fabric edge at the other tip, then cut the thread and hand knot the threads at both tips (page 29). Remove bastings.

13. Clip into the dart at 1-inch intervals to within 1/8 inch of the stitching line.

14. Press toward the center of the garment.

# Pleats for comfort and grace

The only secret to making a perfect pleat is to take the time to mark and fold it absolutely accurately—a small price to pay for the grace, movement and controlled fullness pleats can add to a garment.

The classic pleat is a straight pleat. It can be used singly or in a series in which each pleat is folded to lie in the same direction; it can also be used to form an inverted pleat, in which two pleats are turned toward each other to meet in the center. Pleats can be left unpressed, for a soft, draping effect, or firmly pressed along their folds for a crisp, tailored look. For an even more tailored look, pressed pleats can also be stitched on the side of the fabric that will be visible when the garment is completed, from the top edge to a point partway down the pleat.

The actual steps in making a pleat are few and simple. But to ensure evenly spaced, straight pleats, work on a flat surface large enough to lay out the entire piece to be pleated, and keep all basting stitches in until you reach the stage recommended in the instructions opposite.

# PLEATS

## A MARKING THE PLEATS

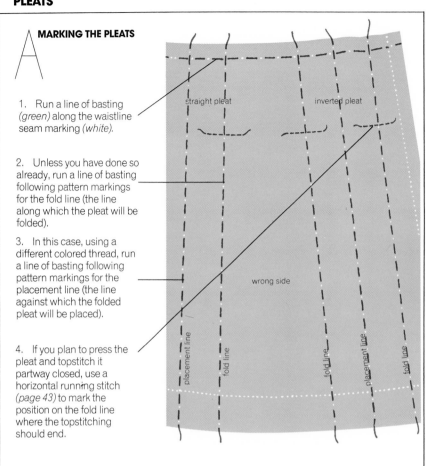

straight pleat    inverted pleat

wrong side

placement line    fold line    fold line    placement line    fold line

1.   Run a line of basting *(green)* along the waistline seam marking *(white)*.

2.   Unless you have done so already, run a line of basting following pattern markings for the fold line (the line along which the pleat will be folded).

3.   In this case, using a different colored thread, run a line of basting following pattern markings for the placement line (the line against which the folded pleat will be placed).

4.   If you plan to press the pleat and topstitch it partway closed, use a horizontal running stitch *(page 43)* to mark the position on the fold line where the topstitching should end.

## B CONSTRUCTING THE PLEATS

straight pleat    inverted pleat

5.   With the fabric wrong side down, fold each pleat on its fold line and pin it against its placement line. Begin to pin at the bottom to ensure an even hemline, and make sure to catch all layers of fabric. (The number of pleats and the direction in which they are folded will depend upon your pattern.)

6.   Baste *(red)* the folded pleats, stitching from the bottom of the garment to the top, 1/4 inch from the fold. Stitch through all layers of fabric.

7.   Machine stitch *(blue)* along the waistline seam, a fraction above the basted markings, to hold the pleats in place.

## C FINISHING THE PLEATS

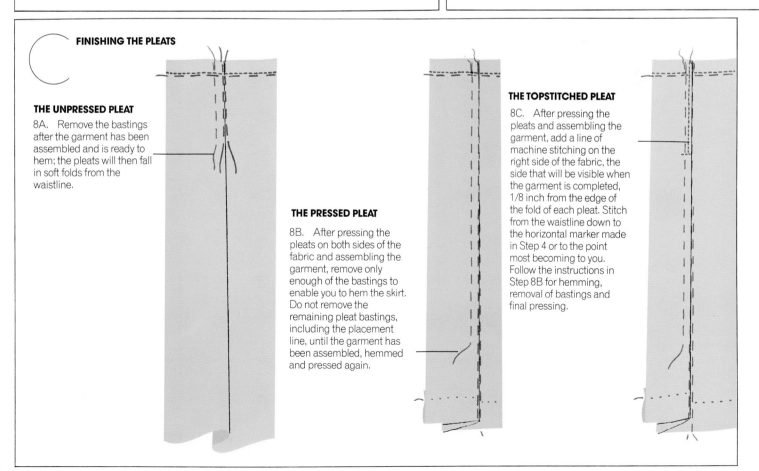

### THE UNPRESSED PLEAT

8A.   Remove the bastings after the garment has been assembled and is ready to hem; the pleats will then fall in soft folds from the waistline.

### THE PRESSED PLEAT

8B.   After pressing the pleats on both sides of the fabric and assembling the garment, remove only enough of the bastings to enable you to hem the skirt. Do not remove the remaining pleat bastings, including the placement line, until the garment has been assembled, hemmed and pressed again.

### THE TOPSTITCHED PLEAT

8C.   After pressing the pleats and assembling the garment, add a line of machine stitching on the right side of the fabric, the side that will be visible when the garment is completed, 1/8 inch from the edge of the fold of each pleat. Stitch from the waistline down to the horizontal marker made in Step 4 or to the point most becoming to you. Follow the instructions in Step 8B for hemming, removal of bastings and final pressing.

# Foolproof ways to insert zippers

Although zippers have intimidated the home sewer for years, it is perfectly possible to make a neat, smooth zipper with hardly an unsightly gap or bulge.

Resist the temptation to take shortcuts or to insert the zipper before the garment is assembled. Only by fitting the garment and making the necessary adjustments to darts and seams—including the zipper seam—before putting the zipper in will you ensure a perfect fit.

The most common way of inserting a zipper is the centered application, used in neckline and center back and front closings, in which the zipper is concealed under two flaps and has two rows of stitching visible. In the lapped application, used in side seam closings for skirts, women's pants and dresses, the zipper is concealed beneath a single wide lap, with only one line of stitching visible. The fly-front zipper, providing a wide lap of fabric over the zipper, is used on the front of men's and sometimes women's pants.

Select a zipper in the color of your fabric and the length specified on the pattern. One final tip: before inserting the zipper, press it flat.

## THE CENTERED ZIPPER

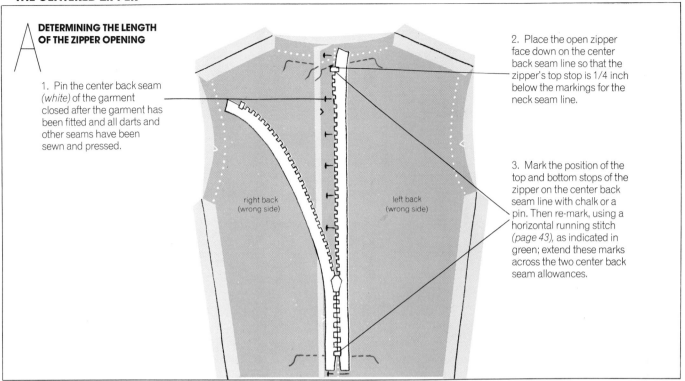

### A DETERMINING THE LENGTH OF THE ZIPPER OPENING

1. Pin the center back seam *(white)* of the garment closed after the garment has been fitted and all darts and other seams have been sewn and pressed.

2. Place the open zipper face down on the center back seam line so that the zipper's top stop is 1/4 inch below the markings for the neck seam line.

3. Mark the position of the top and bottom stops of the zipper on the center back seam line with chalk or a pin. Then re-mark, using a horizontal running stitch *(page 43),* as indicated in green; extend these marks across the two center back seam allowances.

right back (wrong side)

left back (wrong side)

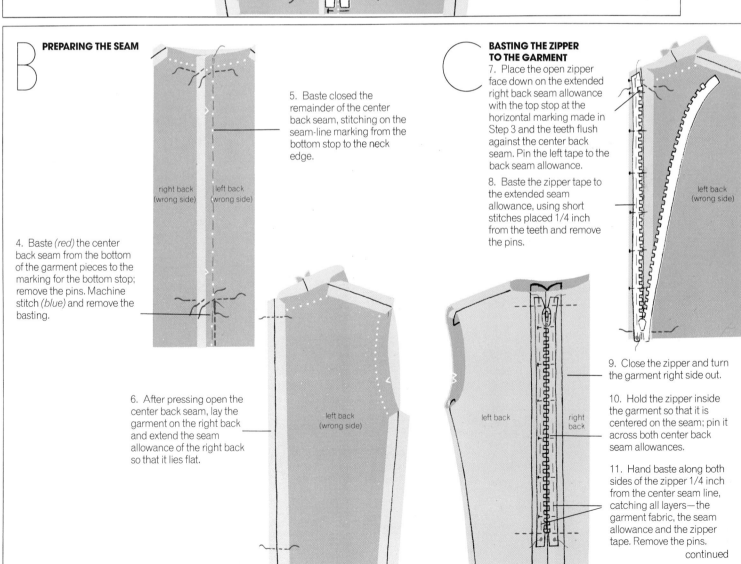

### B PREPARING THE SEAM

5. Baste closed the remainder of the center back seam, stitching on the seam-line marking from the bottom stop to the neck edge.

4. Baste *(red)* the center back seam from the bottom of the garment pieces to the marking for the bottom stop; remove the pins. Machine stitch *(blue)* and remove the basting.

right back (wrong side)  left back (wrong side)

6. After pressing open the center back seam, lay the garment on the right back and extend the seam allowance of the right back so that it lies flat.

left back (wrong side)

### C BASTING THE ZIPPER TO THE GARMENT

7. Place the open zipper face down on the extended right back seam allowance with the top stop at the horizontal marking made in Step 3 and the teeth flush against the center back seam. Pin the left tape to the back seam allowance.

8. Baste the zipper tape to the extended seam allowance, using short stitches placed 1/4 inch from the teeth and remove the pins.

left back (wrong side)

9. Close the zipper and turn the garment right side out.

10. Hold the zipper inside the garment so that it is centered on the seam; pin it across both center back seam allowances.

left back    right back

11. Hand baste along both sides of the zipper 1/4 inch from the center seam line, catching all layers—the garment fabric, the seam allowance and the zipper tape. Remove the pins.

continued

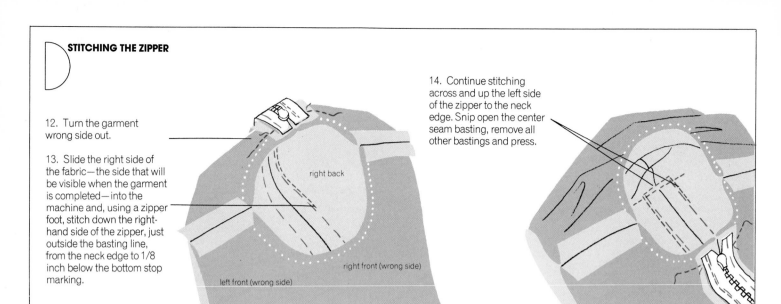

### STITCHING THE ZIPPER

12. Turn the garment wrong side out.

13. Slide the right side of the fabric—the side that will be visible when the garment is completed—into the machine and, using a zipper foot, stitch down the right-hand side of the zipper, just outside the basting line, from the neck edge to 1/8 inch below the bottom stop marking.

14. Continue stitching across and up the left side of the zipper to the neck edge. Snip open the center seam basting, remove all other bastings and press.

right back

right front (wrong side)

left front (wrong side)

## THE LAPPED ZIPPER

### A PREPARING THE SIDE SEAM FOR THE INSERTION OF THE ZIPPER

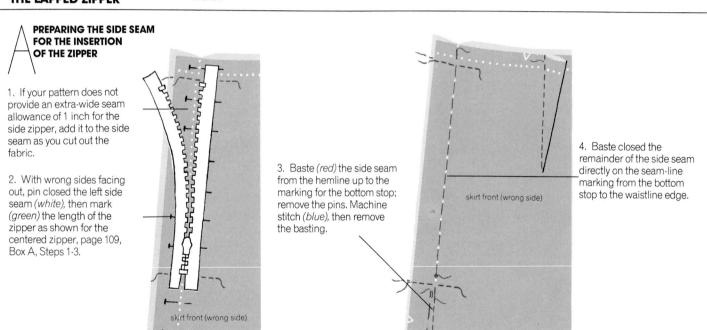

1. If your pattern does not provide an extra-wide seam allowance of 1 inch for the side zipper, add it to the side seam as you cut out the fabric.

2. With wrong sides facing out, pin closed the left side seam (white), then mark (green) the length of the zipper as shown for the centered zipper, page 109, Box A, Steps 1-3.

3. Baste (red) the side seam from the hemline up to the marking for the bottom stop; remove the pins. Machine stitch (blue), then remove the basting.

4. Baste closed the remainder of the side seam directly on the seam-line marking from the bottom stop to the waistline edge.

skirt front (wrong side)

skirt front (wrong side)

### B SEWING THE ZIPPER TO THE SKIRT BACK

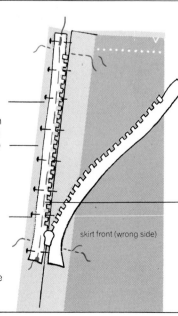
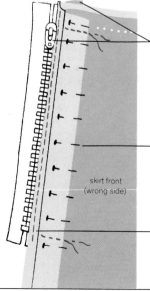

5. Press open the side seam.

6. Lay the garment down on the back section and extend the back seam allowance so that it lies flat.

7. Place the open zipper face down on the extended back seam allowance, with its top and bottom stops at the horizontal markings made in Box A, Step 2. The teeth should be flush against the closed side seam. Pin the left tape to the back seam allowance.

8. Baste the zipper tape to the extended back seam allowance close to the teeth. Work from the bottom of the zipper tape to the top, machine basting with a zipper foot or using short hand stitches. Remove the pins.

skirt front (wrong side)

9. Close the zipper and fold the back seam allowance under the garment along the line of basting made in Step 8, thus causing the zipper to flip up.

10. Pin together all layers of the fabric—the front seam allowance, the skirt front and back, and the back seam allowance.

skirt front (wrong side)

11. Using a zipper foot, machine stitch along the narrow strip of folded seam allowance from the bottom of the zipper tape to the top. Remove the pins.

## C   SEWING THE ZIPPER TO THE SKIRT FRONT

12. Turn the skirt right side out.

13. Hold the zipper inside the skirt so that it lies flat on the seam. Pin it in place across both seam allowances.

14. Hand baste 1/2 inch from the side seam up the skirt front from the bottom stop marking to the top edge, sewing through all layers—the skirt front, front seam allowance and the zipper tape. Remove pins.

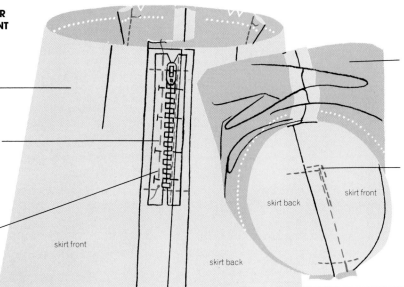

skirt front

skirt back

skirt back

15. Turn the skirt wrong side out.

16. Slide the skirt front, wrong side down, under the zipper foot. Beginning at the side seam and following a line 1/8 inch outside the marking for the bottom stop made in Box A, Step 2, page 110, stitch across the bottom and up the length of the zipper to the top edge of the garment. Then snip open the side seam basting, remove all other bastings and press.

skirt front

# WOMEN'S FLY-FRONT ZIPPER

## A   PREPARING THE PANTS FRONT

1. If your pattern does not include fly facings as part of the front sections, pin the fly pattern to the front section when laying the pattern on the fabric. Cut as if one piece.

2. Baste (green) along the center front seam-line marking (white) of the left front section, stitching the length of the fly facing.

3. Run a line of basting parallel to the basted line made in Step 2, and 1/4 inch in, toward the fly facing. This will become the fly fold line.

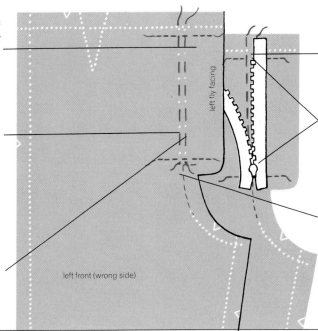

left fly facing

left front (wrong side)

4. Place the open zipper face down on the left center seam line, so that the zipper's top stop is 1/4 inch below the waist seam line.

5. Mark the position of the top and bottom stops with chalk or pins; re-mark with a horizontal running stitch (page 43).

6. To reinforce the crotch, machine stitch (blue) a line beginning at the left fly fold line 1/4 inch below the marking for the bottom stop. Stitch across from the fold line to the center seam line and then down 1 inch along the center seam line.

7. Repeat Steps 2-6 on the right front pants section.

## B   ASSEMBLING THE PANTS

8. To ensure the proper hang of the garment, assemble the pants in the following sequence: sew and press the darts, the outer leg seams and the inner leg seams. Then join the legs by sewing the center seam, beginning at the center back waistline and ending at the bottom stop marking on the center front seam line.

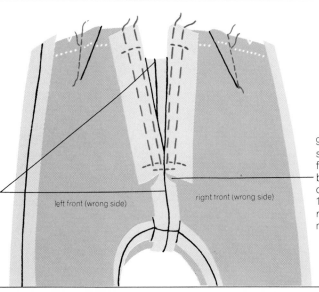

left front (wrong side)

right front (wrong side)

9. With the tips of a scissors, clip into the center front seam allowance at the base of the fly facing, cutting diagonally to within 1/16 inch of the line of reinforcement stitching made in Box A, Step 6.

continued

111

## SEWING THE ZIPPER TO THE RIGHT FLY FACING

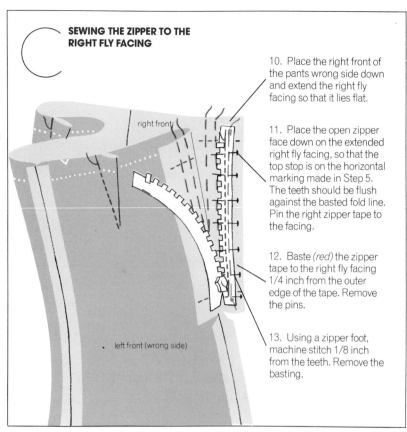

right front

left front (wrong side)

10. Place the right front of the pants wrong side down and extend the right fly facing so that it lies flat.

11. Place the open zipper face down on the extended right fly facing, so that the top stop is on the horizontal marking made in Step 5. The teeth should be flush against the basted fold line. Pin the right zipper tape to the facing.

12. Baste *(red)* the zipper tape to the right fly facing 1/4 inch from the outer edge of the tape. Remove the pins.

13. Using a zipper foot, machine stitch 1/8 inch from the teeth. Remove the basting.

## SEWING THE ZIPPER TO THE LEFT FRONT

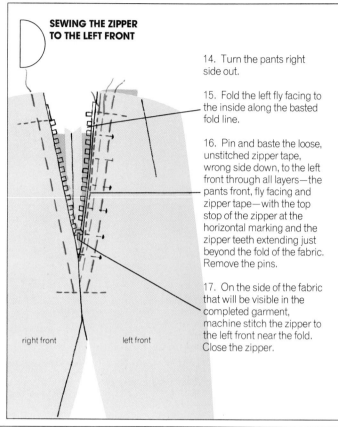

right front        left front

14. Turn the pants right side out.

15. Fold the left fly facing to the inside along the basted fold line.

16. Pin and baste the loose, unstitched zipper tape, wrong side down, to the left front through all layers—the pants front, fly facing and zipper tape—with the top stop of the zipper at the horizontal marking and the zipper teeth extending just beyond the fold of the fabric. Remove the pins.

17. On the side of the fabric that will be visible in the completed garment, machine stitch the zipper to the left front near the fold. Close the zipper.

## FINISHING THE FLY FRONT

18. Lap the right front over the zipper until the fabric lies flat, covers the teeth and meets the center seam line of the left front. Pin in place close to the folded edge.

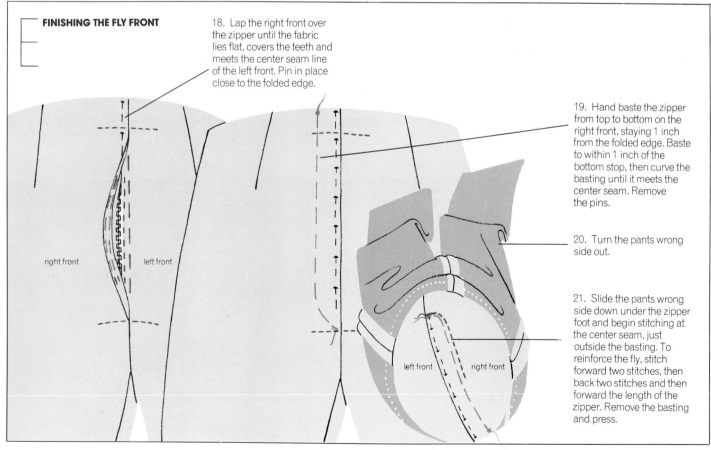

right front        left front

left front        right front

19. Hand baste the zipper from top to bottom on the right front, staying 1 inch from the folded edge. Baste to within 1 inch of the bottom stop, then curve the basting until it meets the center seam. Remove the pins.

20. Turn the pants wrong side out.

21. Slide the pants wrong side down under the zipper foot and begin stitching at the center seam, just outside the basting. To reinforce the fly, stitch forward two stitches, then back two stitches and then forward the length of the zipper. Remove the basting and press.

## MEN'S FLY-FRONT ZIPPER

### A PREPARING THE PANTS FRONT

1. If you have not already done so, run a line of basting (*green*) along the waist seam-line marking (*white*) of each front section so that it will show on both sides of the fabric.

2. On the right pants front, run a line of basting parallel to the center seam line and 1/4 inch outside it, extending from the waistline edge to the bottom of the fly opening marked on the pattern; this will become the fly fold line.

3. To reinforce the crotch on each front section, machine stitch (*blue*) along the center seam line, beginning 1 inch below the marking for the bottom of the fly opening and ending 1 inch above that point.

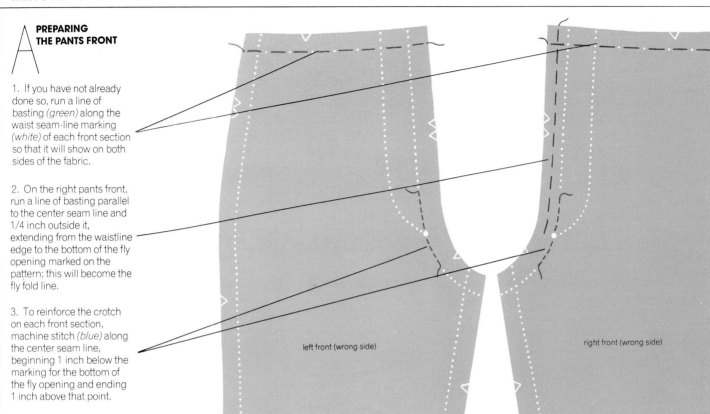

left front (wrong side)

right front (wrong side)

### B JOINING THE PANTS FRONT

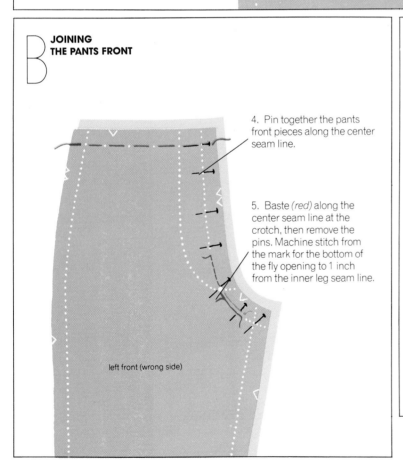

left front (wrong side)

4. Pin together the pants front pieces along the center seam line.

5. Baste (*red*) along the center seam line at the crotch, then remove the pins. Machine stitch from the mark for the bottom of the fly opening to 1 inch from the inner leg seam line.

### C MAKING THE LEFT FLY

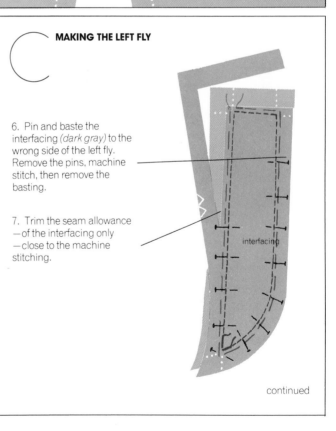

interfacing

6. Pin and baste the interfacing (*dark gray*) to the wrong side of the left fly. Remove the pins, machine stitch, then remove the basting.

7. Trim the seam allowance —of the interfacing only —close to the machine stitching.

continued

## D ATTACHING THE LEFT FLY TO THE LEFT PANTS FRONT

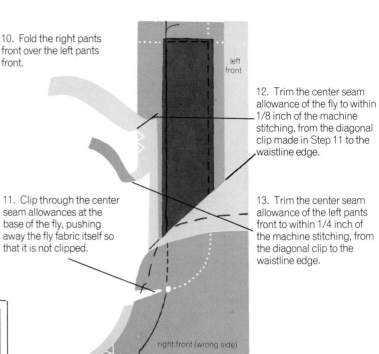

8. With the wrong sides of the fabric facing outward, pin the left fly to the left pants front along the center seam line, making sure that the markings for the seam intersections and notches match.

9. Baste the left fly to the left pants front along the center seam line, starting at the top edge of the pants and ending at the bottom of the fly opening. Remove the pins, machine stitch and remove the bastings.

10. Fold the right pants front over the left pants front.

11. Clip through the center seam allowances at the base of the fly, pushing away the fly fabric itself so that it is not clipped.

12. Trim the center seam allowance of the fly to within 1/8 inch of the machine stitching, from the diagonal clip made in Step 11 to the waistline edge.

13. Trim the center seam allowance of the left pants front to within 1/4 inch of the machine stitching, from the diagonal clip to the waistline edge.

## E ATTACHING THE ZIPPER TO THE LEFT FLY

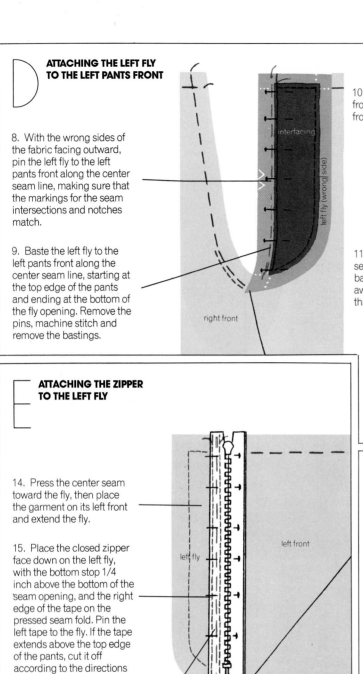

14. Press the center seam toward the fly, then place the garment on its left front and extend the fly.

15. Place the closed zipper face down on the left fly, with the bottom stop 1/4 inch above the bottom of the seam opening, and the right edge of the tape on the pressed seam fold. Pin the left tape to the fly. If the tape extends above the top edge of the pants, cut it off according to the directions given on the zipper package.

16. Baste the zipper tape to the left fly 1/4 inch from the teeth. Remove the pins.

17. Using a zipper foot, attach the zipper to the left fly with two rows of machine stitching, one row along the left edge of the basted tape and a second row close to the teeth.

## F FINISHING THE LEFT FLY FRONT

18. With the pants wrong side down, fold under the left fly, causing the zipper to flip up. Pin the fly to the left front fabric at 1-inch intervals so that it lies flat.

19. Hand baste the left fly to the left front in a line 1 1/2 inches from the folded edge. When you come to within 1 1/2 inches of the bottom of the fly opening, curve the basting in to meet the center seam at the bottom of the opening. Do not catch the unstitched bottom end of the zipper tape in the stitches. Remove the pins.

20. Machine stitch the left fly to the left front, starting at the bottom curve just outside the basting. To reinforce the fly front, stitch forward two stitches, then back two stitches, and then forward to the waist. Remove all basting.

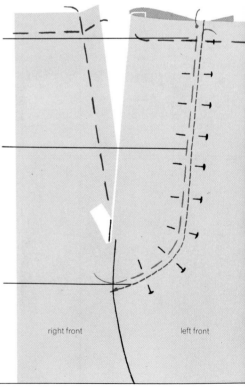

## G  BASTING THE ZIPPER TO THE RIGHT FRONT

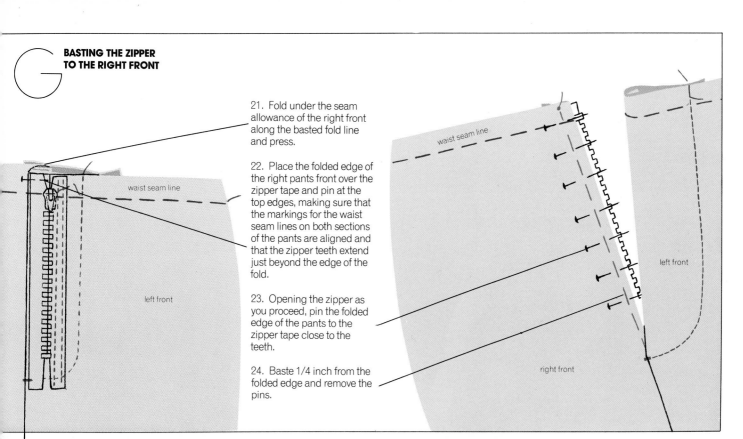

waist seam line

left front

21. Fold under the seam allowance of the right front along the basted fold line and press.

22. Place the folded edge of the right pants front over the zipper tape and pin at the top edges, making sure that the markings for the waist seam lines on both sections of the pants are aligned and that the zipper teeth extend just beyond the edge of the fold.

23. Opening the zipper as you proceed, pin the folded edge of the pants to the zipper tape close to the teeth.

24. Baste 1/4 inch from the folded edge and remove the pins.

waist seam line

left front

right front

## H  MAKING THE RIGHT FLY

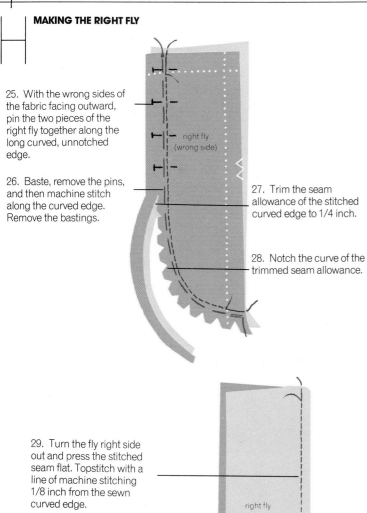

25. With the wrong sides of the fabric facing outward, pin the two pieces of the right fly together along the long curved, unnotched edge.

26. Baste, remove the pins, and then machine stitch along the curved edge. Remove the bastings.

right fly (wrong side)

27. Trim the seam allowance of the stitched curved edge to 1/4 inch.

28. Notch the curve of the trimmed seam allowance.

29. Turn the fly right side out and press the stitched seam flat. Topstitch with a line of machine stitching 1/8 inch from the sewn curved edge.

right fly

## ATTACHING THE RIGHT FLY TO THE RIGHT PANTS FRONT

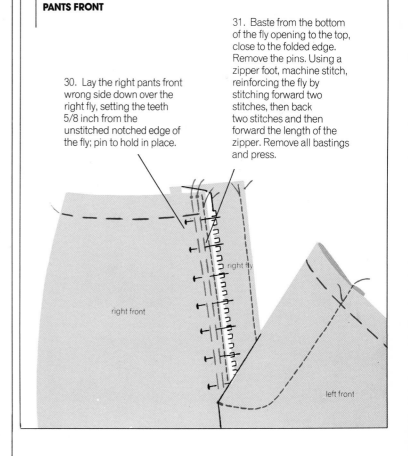

30. Lay the right pants front wrong side down over the right fly, setting the teeth 5/8 inch from the unstitched notched edge of the fly; pin to hold in place.

31. Baste from the bottom of the fly opening to the top, close to the folded edge. Remove the pins. Using a zipper foot, machine stitch, reinforcing the fly by stitching forward two stitches, then back two stitches and then forward the length of the zipper. Remove all bastings and press.

right front

right fly

left front

# Hints for a trim waistband

There are two marks of a well-made waistband: it lies flat without wrinkling or buckling, like the one at left; and it has a soft, rolled edge at the top. The secret to this look is in the way you handle the interfacing. Properly attached, by means of the method shown at right, the waistband should not crumple even when you move actively. And cutting and stitching above, rather than along, the center fold line gives the top edge a soft, professional finish.

Waistbands are fastened by hooks and eyes or buttons (pages 140-143) that are attached to an extension of the band called the lap. Many patterns call for an extension that overlaps at least 3/4 inch across the opening of the pants or skirt. Some patterns, however, have an extension that underlaps the opening; the visible edge of the opening runs then in a straight line all the way up to the top of the waistband. The basic method of construction remains the same for both.

# THE WAISTBAND

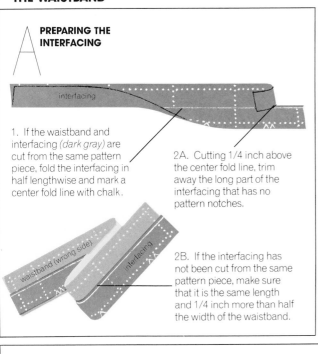

## A PREPARING THE INTERFACING

1. If the waistband and interfacing *(dark gray)* are cut from the same pattern piece, fold the interfacing in half lengthwise and mark a center fold line with chalk.

2A. Cutting 1/4 inch above the center fold line, trim away the long part of the interfacing that has no pattern notches.

2B. If the interfacing has not been cut from the same pattern piece, make sure that it is the same length and 1/4 inch more than half the width of the waistband.

## B ATTACHING THE INTERFACING

3. Place the interfacing on the wrong side of the waistband, lining it up with the notched edge. Pin together, matching the notches and pattern markings *(white)*.

4. Baste *(red)* the interfacing to the waistband along the notched side and both ends. Remove the pins.

5. Hand stitch *(black)* the interfacing to the waistband 1/8 inch above the center fold line, using thread the same color as the fabric. Make 1/2-inch stitches on the interfacing side but do not stitch through the waistband material; pick up only a thread of the waistband fabric.

6. Trim the interfacing close to the bastings along the three outer edges. Do not trim along the center fold line.

## C SEWING THE WAISTBAND

7. Fold the waistband in half lengthwise, wrong side out.

8. Pin along the seam markings around the corner of the waistband, from the lap line to the folded edge. Then baste and remove the pins.

9. Machine stitch *(blue)* along the seam markings, from the lap line around the corner to the folded edge.

12. Clip into the seam allowance diagonally at the lap line, cutting close to but not into the stitching.

13. At the lapped end, trim the seam allowance to 1/4 inch and trim both corners diagonally.

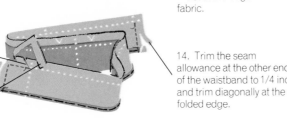

10. Pin the other end of the waistband together. Then baste along the end seam markings and remove the pins.

11. Machine stitch along the end seam markings, beginning at the corner where the end and long seam markings intersect —not at the edge of the fabric.

14. Trim the seam allowance at the other end of the waistband to 1/4 inch and trim diagonally at the folded edge.

## D SEWING THE WAISTBAND TO THE GARMENT

15. Turn the waistband and the garment right sides out.

16. Pin the long notched edge of the waistband to the garment along the waist seam-line markings, matching notches and seams. Be sure the sides of the waistband and garment fabric that will be visible in the finished garment are facing each other.

17. Baste along the waist seam-line markings. Remove the pins, and then machine stitch.

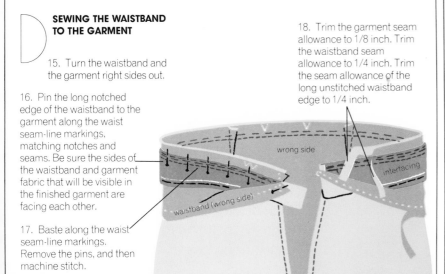

18. Trim the garment seam allowance to 1/8 inch. Trim the waistband seam allowance to 1/4 inch. Trim the seam allowance of the long unstitched waistband edge to 1/4 inch.

## E THE FINAL TOUCHES

19. Turn over the long unstitched edge of the waistband to the inside of the garment.

20. Fold under the unstitched edge along the seam markings and pin it to the garment, then baste and remove the pins.

21. Hand stitch the folded edge of the waistband to the garment with a slip stitch *(page 45)*. Do not stitch into the garment fabric but pick up only a few threads of the seam allowance. Remove all bastings and press.

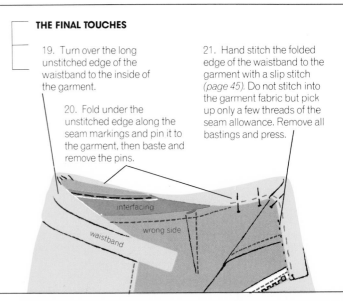

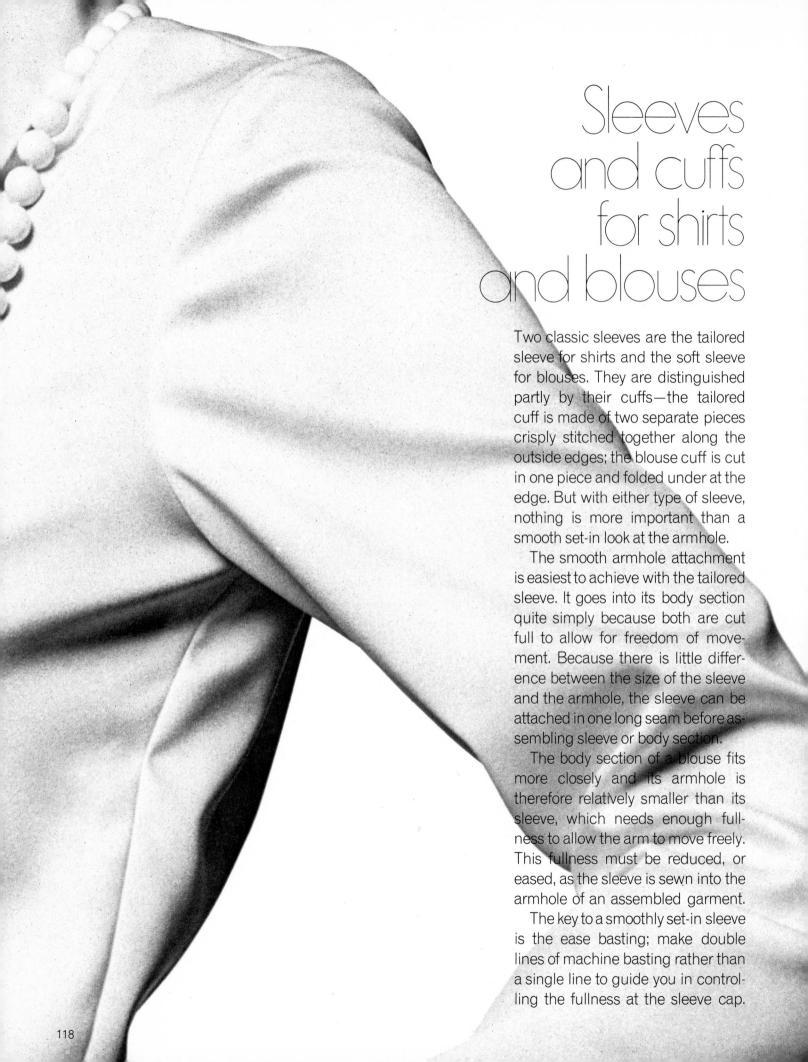

# Sleeves and cuffs for shirts and blouses

Two classic sleeves are the tailored sleeve for shirts and the soft sleeve for blouses. They are distinguished partly by their cuffs—the tailored cuff is made of two separate pieces crisply stitched together along the outside edges; the blouse cuff is cut in one piece and folded under at the edge. But with either type of sleeve, nothing is more important than a smooth set-in look at the armhole.

The smooth armhole attachment is easiest to achieve with the tailored sleeve. It goes into its body section quite simply because both are cut full to allow for freedom of movement. Because there is little difference between the size of the sleeve and the armhole, the sleeve can be attached in one long seam before assembling sleeve or body section.

The body section of a blouse fits more closely and its armhole is therefore relatively smaller than its sleeve, which needs enough fullness to allow the arm to move freely. This fullness must be reduced, or eased, as the sleeve is sewn into the armhole of an assembled garment.

The key to a smoothly set-in sleeve is the ease basting; make double lines of machine basting rather than a single line to guide you in controlling the fullness at the sleeve cap.

# MAKING A SLEEVE FOR A TAILORED SHIRT

## A | PREPARING THE CUFF OPENING

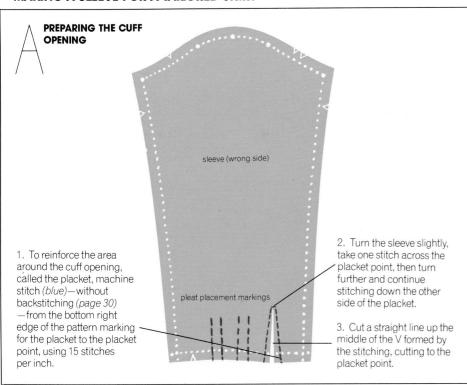

sleeve (wrong side)

pleat placement markings

1. To reinforce the area around the cuff opening, called the placket, machine stitch (blue)—without backstitching (page 30) —from the bottom right edge of the pattern marking for the placket to the placket point, using 15 stitches per inch.

2. Turn the sleeve slightly, take one stitch across the placket point, then turn further and continue stitching down the other side of the placket.

3. Cut a straight line up the middle of the V formed by the stitching, cutting to the placket point.

## B | ATTACHING THE STRIP OF FABRIC TO THE PLACKET

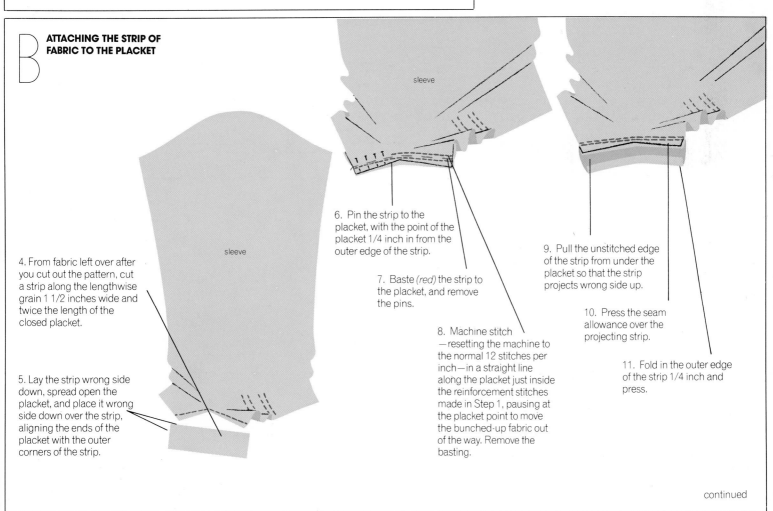

sleeve

sleeve

4. From fabric left over after you cut out the pattern, cut a strip along the lengthwise grain 1 1/2 inches wide and twice the length of the closed placket.

5. Lay the strip wrong side down, spread open the placket, and place it wrong side down over the strip, aligning the ends of the placket with the outer corners of the strip.

6. Pin the strip to the placket, with the point of the placket 1/4 inch in from the outer edge of the strip.

7. Baste (red) the strip to the placket, and remove the pins.

8. Machine stitch —resetting the machine to the normal 12 stitches per inch—in a straight line along the placket just inside the reinforcement stitches made in Step 1, pausing at the placket point to move the bunched-up fabric out of the way. Remove the basting.

9. Pull the unstitched edge of the strip from under the placket so that the strip projects wrong side up.

10. Press the seam allowance over the projecting strip.

11. Fold in the outer edge of the strip 1/4 inch and press.

continued

## ENCLOSING THE PLACKET

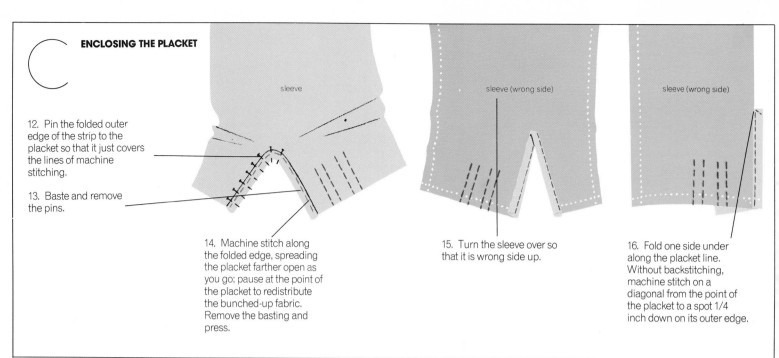

12. Pin the folded outer edge of the strip to the placket so that it just covers the lines of machine stitching.

13. Baste and remove the pins.

14. Machine stitch along the folded edge, spreading the placket farther open as you go; pause at the point of the placket to redistribute the bunched-up fabric. Remove the basting and press.

15. Turn the sleeve over so that it is wrong side up.

16. Fold one side under along the placket line. Without backstitching, machine stitch on a diagonal from the point of the placket to a spot 1/4 inch down on its outer edge.

## PLEATING THE BOTTOM OF THE SLEEVE

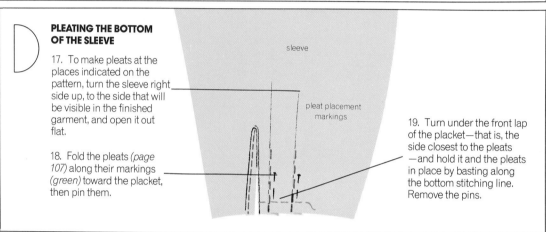

17. To make pleats at the places indicated on the pattern, turn the sleeve right side up, to the side that will be visible in the finished garment, and open it out flat.

18. Fold the pleats (page 107) along their markings (green) toward the placket, then pin them.

19. Turn under the front lap of the placket—that is, the side closest to the pleats—and hold it and the pleats in place by basting along the bottom stitching line. Remove the pins.

## ATTACHING THE SLEEVE TO THE BODY SECTION

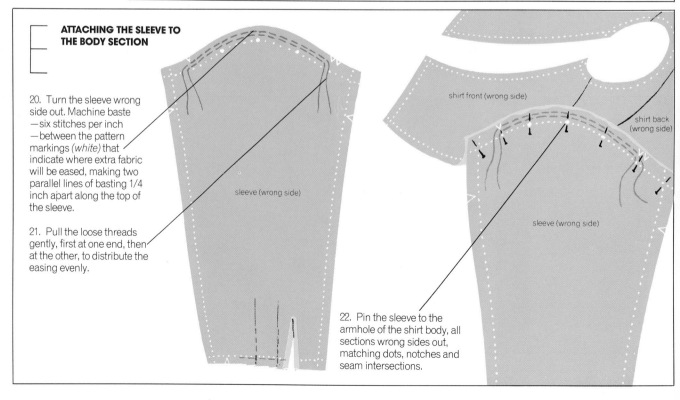

20. Turn the sleeve wrong side out. Machine baste—six stitches per inch—between the pattern markings (white) that indicate where extra fabric will be eased, making two parallel lines of basting 1/4 inch apart along the top of the sleeve.

21. Pull the loose threads gently, first at one end, then at the other, to distribute the easing evenly.

22. Pin the sleeve to the armhole of the shirt body, all sections wrong sides out, matching dots, notches and seam intersections.

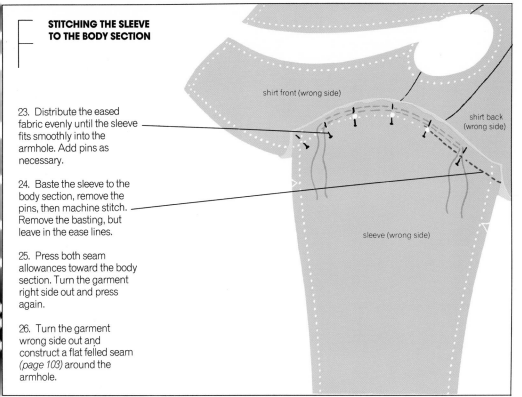

## F STITCHING THE SLEEVE TO THE BODY SECTION

shirt front (wrong side)

shirt back (wrong side)

sleeve (wrong side)

23. Distribute the eased fabric evenly until the sleeve fits smoothly into the armhole. Add pins as necessary.

24. Baste the sleeve to the body section, remove the pins, then machine stitch. Remove the basting, but leave in the ease lines.

25. Press both seam allowances toward the body section. Turn the garment right side out and press again.

26. Turn the garment wrong side out and construct a flat felled seam *(page 103)* around the armhole.

## G MAKING THE SIDE SEAM

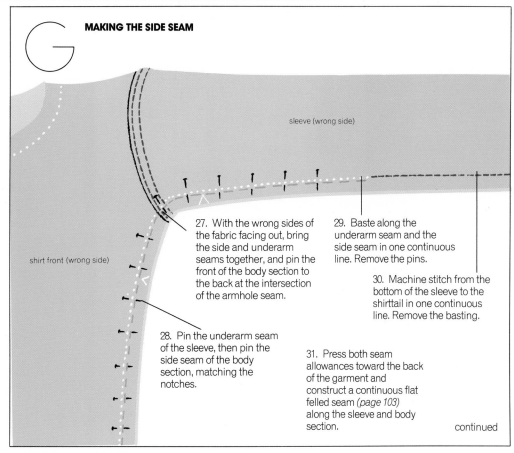

sleeve (wrong side)

shirt front (wrong side)

27. With the wrong sides of the fabric facing out, bring the side and underarm seams together, and pin the front of the body section to the back at the intersection of the armhole seam.

28. Pin the underarm seam of the sleeve, then pin the side seam of the body section, matching the notches.

29. Baste along the underarm seam and the side seam in one continuous line. Remove the pins.

30. Machine stitch from the bottom of the sleeve to the shirttail in one continuous line. Remove the basting.

31. Press both seam allowances toward the back of the garment and construct a continuous flat felled seam *(page 103)* along the sleeve and body section.

continued

121

## ATTACHING THE INTERFACING AND FACING TO THE CUFF

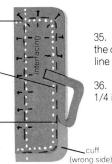

32. Lay the cuff down wrong side up. Place the interfacing (*dark gray*) on top and pin together.

33. Baste just outside the stitching line. Remove the pins.

34. Trim away the interfacing all around the basting.

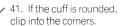

cuff (wrong side)

35. Fold in the top edge of the cuff along the stitching line and press.

36. Trim the folded edge to 1/4 inch.

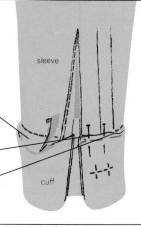

37. Place the cuff facing wrong side down and cover with the interfaced cuff wrong side up. Pin together.

38. Baste along the three outer sides, leaving the folded edge open. Remove the pins.

39. Machine stitch along the three basted sides.

facing

40. Trim the seam allowance to 1/4 inch around the three stitched sides; the facing will extend on the fourth side of the cuff. Remove the basting.

41. If the cuff is rounded, clip into the corners.

42. Turn the cuff right side out and press it and its extended facing flat.

cuff

facing (wrong side)

## ATTACHING THE CUFF TO THE SLEEVE

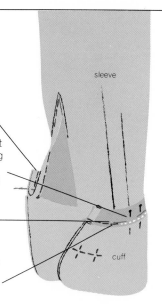

sleeve

43. Turn the sleeve right side out and curl up the bottom edge.

44. Holding the cuff so that the wrong side of the facing is toward you, pin the extension of the cuff facing to the curled-up bottom of the sleeve. Match notches.

45. Hand baste the cuff facing to the sleeve, then remove the pins.

46. Machine stitch the facing to the sleeve, following the stitching line. Remove the basting.

cuff

## COMPLETING THE CUFF

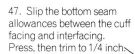

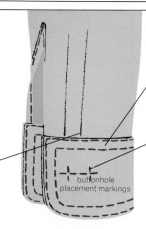

sleeve

cuff

47. Slip the bottom seam allowances between the cuff facing and interfacing. Press, then trim to 1/4 inch.

48. Pin the folded edge of the cuff just over the stitching line of the sleeve.

49. Hand baste, then remove the pins.

50. Machine stitch along the folded edge (*Edge Stitching, page 32*), sewing at the top of the cuff from one edge of the placket to the other. Then pivot the cuff in the machine and stitch all along the outer edge of the cuff. When you reach the top edge of the cuff again, secure the last stitches by backstitching. Remove the basting.

buttonhole placement markings

51. Machine stitch a second line all around the cuff 1/4 inch in from the stitching line made in Step 50 (*Topstitching, page 32*).

52. Following the basted pattern markings for buttonhole positions, make buttonholes and attach buttons (*pages 141-143*).

53. Repeat the preceding steps on the other sleeve.

# MAKING A SLEEVE FOR A WOMAN'S BLOUSE

## A PREPARING THE CUFF OPENING

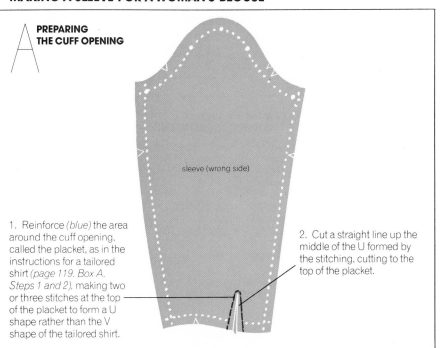

sleeve (wrong side)

1. Reinforce *(blue)* the area around the cuff opening, called the placket, as in the instructions for a tailored shirt *(page 119. Box A. Steps 1 and 2)*, making two or three stitches at the top of the placket to form a U shape rather than the V shape of the tailored shirt.

2. Cut a straight line up the middle of the U formed by the stitching, cutting to the top of the placket.

## B ATTACHING THE STRIP OF FABRIC TO THE PLACKET

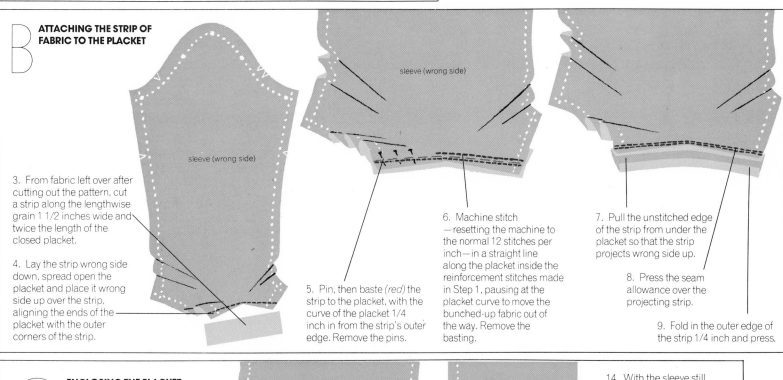

sleeve (wrong side)

sleeve (wrong side)

sleeve (wrong side)

3. From fabric left over after cutting out the pattern, cut a strip along the lengthwise grain 1 1/2 inches wide and twice the length of the closed placket.

4. Lay the strip wrong side down, spread open the placket and place it wrong side up over the strip, aligning the ends of the placket with the outer corners of the strip.

5. Pin, then baste *(red)* the strip to the placket, with the curve of the placket 1/4 inch in from the strip's outer edge. Remove the pins.

6. Machine stitch —resetting the machine to the normal 12 stitches per inch—in a straight line along the placket inside the reinforcement stitches made in Step 1, pausing at the placket curve to move the bunched-up fabric out of the way. Remove the basting.

7. Pull the unstitched edge of the strip from under the placket so that the strip projects wrong side up.

8. Press the seam allowance over the projecting strip.

9. Fold in the outer edge of the strip 1/4 inch and press.

## C ENCLOSING THE PLACKET

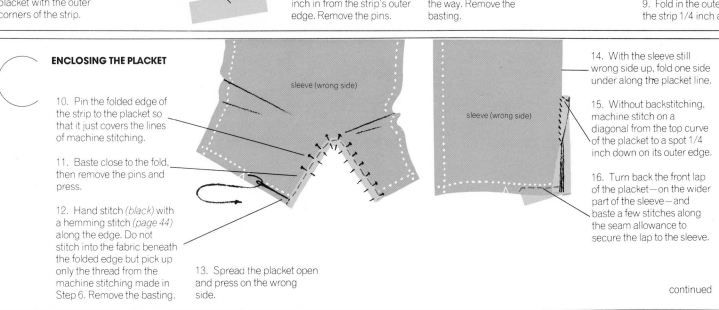

sleeve (wrong side)

sleeve (wrong side)

10. Pin the folded edge of the strip to the placket so that it just covers the lines of machine stitching.

11. Baste close to the fold, then remove the pins and press.

12. Hand stitch *(black)* with a hemming stitch *(page 44)* along the edge. Do not stitch into the fabric beneath the folded edge but pick up only the thread from the machine stitching made in Step 6. Remove the basting.

13. Spread the placket open and press on the wrong side.

14. With the sleeve still wrong side up, fold one side under along the placket line.

15. Without backstitching, machine stitch on a diagonal from the top curve of the placket to a spot 1/4 inch down on its outer edge.

16. Turn back the front lap of the placket—on the wider part of the sleeve—and baste a few stitches along the seam allowance to secure the lap to the sleeve.

continued

## MAKING THE SLEEVE SEAM

17. Open the sleeve out flat, wrong side up, and machine baste—six stitches per inch—between the pattern markings (*white*) used to indicate the area where extra fabric will be eased, making two parallel lines 1/4 inch apart along the top of the sleeve.

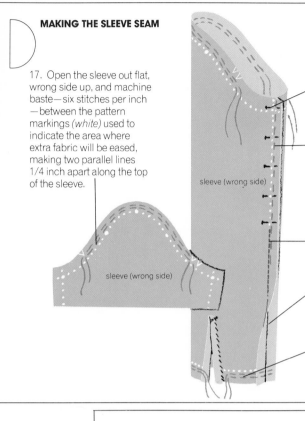

sleeve (wrong side)

sleeve (wrong side)

18. Fold the sleeve in half, wrong sides out, and pin along the underarm seam, matching and pinning first at the seam intersection, next at the notches, then at any other pattern markings. Add more pins at 1- to 2-inch intervals.

19. Baste from the armhole to the end of the sleeve, then remove the pins.

20. Machine stitch—resetting the machine to the normal 12 stitches per inch—from the armhole to the end of the sleeve, then remove the basting.

21. Press the seam open on a sleeve board.

22. Make two parallel ease lines 1/4 inch apart, as in Step 17, in the seam allowance at the bottom of the sleeve, starting and ending 1/2 inch from the placket.

## ATTACHING THE INTERFACING TO THE CUFF

23. Lay the cuff down, wrong side up. Place the interfacing (*dark gray*) on top and pin the two together on the three outer sides, matching notches or other pattern markings. Leave the inside edge open.

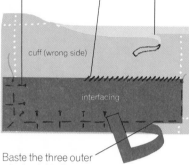

cuff (wrong side)

interfacing

24. Baste the three outer sides just outside the stitching line. Remove the pins, and trim the interfacing.

25. Attach the open edge of the interfacing to the cuff using a hemming stitch (*page 44*).

26. On the half of the cuff that has no interfacing, fold in the outer edge along the stitching line. Press, and trim the folded edge to 1/4 inch.

## ATTACHING THE CUFF TO THE SLEEVE

cuff (wrong side)

interfacing

sleeve (wrong side)

27. With the sleeve wrong side out, gently pull the loose ease threads sewn in Step 22 to begin adjusting the ease.

28. Turn up the bottom of the interfaced half of the cuff.

29. Pin the sleeve to the cuff along its turned-up edge, matching notches.

30. Align the stitching lines of the cuff edges with the outer edges of the placket; if your pattern calls for the cuff to extend beyond the placket, disregard the cuff stitching lines on the extension and match notches and other pattern markings.

31. To ease the sleeve into the cuff, pull the loose ease threads, first at one end, then at the other, gradually distributing the easing until the sleeve fits the cuff. Secure with additional pins at 1/2-inch intervals.

32. Hand baste just below the ease lines. Remove the pins and machine stitch.

33. Trim the two layers of the seam allowance—sleeve and cuff—1/4 inch from the stitching line. Remove the basting, then press the trimmed seam allowance toward the cuff.

## G STITCHING THE ENDS OF THE CUFF

34. Turn the sleeve right side out. Fold the cuff in half along its fold line so that it is wrong side out.

35. Pin the open ends of the cuff together and baste. Remove the pins.

36. Machine stitch the ends together, sewing a few stitches off the edge of the fabric. Tie off the threads.

37. Trim the seam allowances to 1/4 inch and remove the basting.

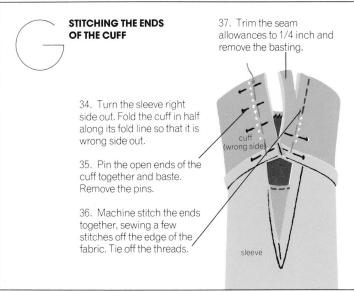

## H COMPLETING THE CUFF

38. Turn the sleeve wrong side out. Turn the cuff right side out.

39. Pin the edge of the cuff over the stitching line of the sleeve and baste. Remove the pins.

40. Stitch the cuff to the sleeve with a hemming stitch (page 44) along the edge. Do not stitch into the fabric beneath the folded edge but pick up only the thread from the machine stitching made in Step 32. Remove the basting.

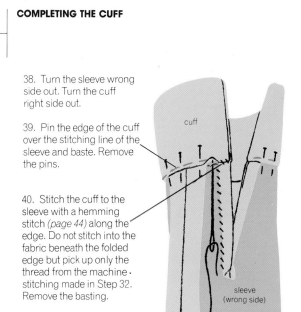

## INSERTING THE SLEEVE INTO THE ARMHOLE

41. Pull the ease lines made in Step 17 at the top of the sleeve, distributing the easing evenly.

42. Turn the sleeve right side out and slip it into the armhole of the body section of the blouse, which should be wrong side out.

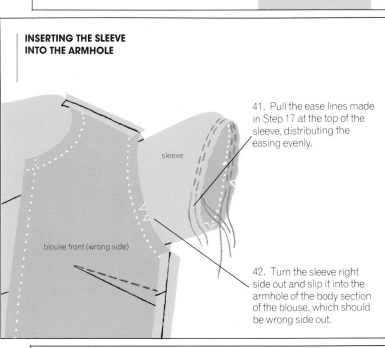

## J CONNECTING THE SLEEVE TO THE ARMHOLE

43. Roll the top of the sleeve over the armhole of the body section, and pin, matching the center marking at the top of the sleeve to the shoulder seam, and aligning the seams under the arm, the notches and other pattern markings.

44. With the two layers of fabric rolled over your forefingers, redistribute the extra fabric of the sleeve.

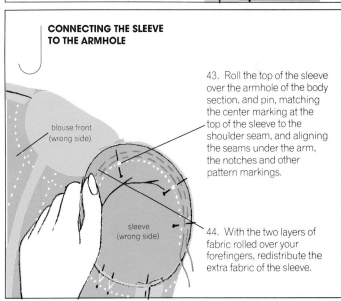

## K STITCHING THE SLEEVE TO THE ARMHOLE

45. With the wrong side of the sleeve rolled over the shoulder, pin and baste all around the armhole, starting at the underarm seam. Remove the pins.

46. Machine stitch and remove the basting. Press.

47. Trim the seam allowance to 1/2 inch except under the arm, where it should be tapered to 1/4 inch. Press.

48. Following the pattern markings on the cuff for buttonhole positions, make buttonholes and attach buttons to the cuff (pages 141-143).

49. Repeat the preceding steps on the other sleeve.

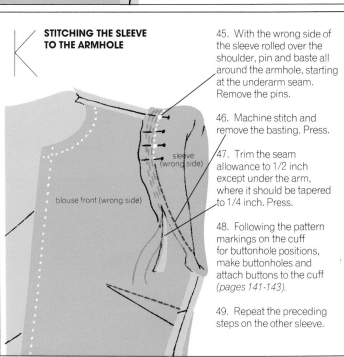

# How to construct and attach collars

There are two classic collars. One is the familiar man's shirt collar, described on the pattern envelopes as "man's two-piece stand collar." In fact it is constructed with six pieces: the collar and the undercollar, with interfacing between, and outer and inner neckbands, with interfacing. The man's collar is often worn by women on their tailored shirts and shirtwaist dresses.

The second classic collar, seen at left, is designed for more casual wear, open. It is sometimes called the Italian collar, or, on pattern envelopes, the "convertible collar." It is constructed with only three pieces, the collar and the undercollar and interfacing. It attaches to the garment without an intervening neckband.

Here is a hint to avoid puckers as you stitch together the layers of the assembled collar: in basting any of the sections together, do not turn corners with the same thread. Stop at each corner and leave 2 or 3 inches of thread loose; begin again in the next direction with a new thread.

# THE SHIRT COLLAR

## A INTERFACING THE COLLAR

1. Assemble the pieces you will need to interface the collar: the piece that will be visible, called simply the collar; the under part of the collar known as the undercollar; and the interfacing that will be stitched between the two to provide stiffening.

2. Pin and baste (red) the collar interfacing to the wrong side of the collar, matching the pattern markings (white). Remove the pins.

3. Trim the interfacing just above the basting along the neckline only.

4. Turn the collar over so that the interfacing lies on the table and the right side of the collar, the side that will be visible in the finished garment, faces up.

5. Place the undercollar, wrong side up, on top of the collar. Pin together, matching the pattern markings.

6. Baste the undercollar to the collar along the two ends and the curved bottom edge. Leave the upper neck edge open. Remove the pins.

7. Machine stitch (blue) alongside the basting, following the instructions on page 30. Remove the basting.

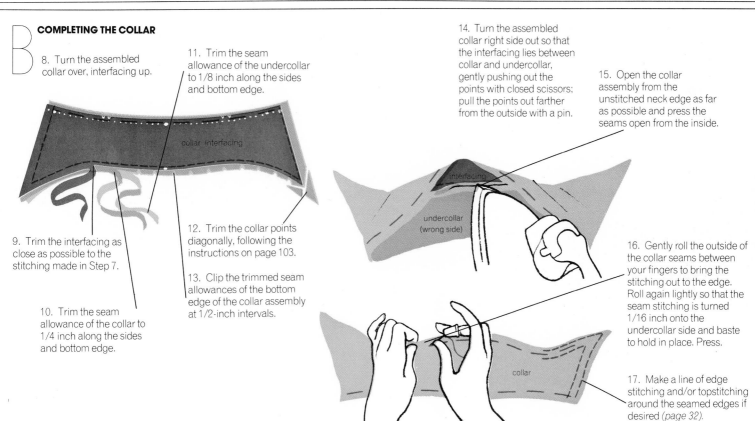

## B COMPLETING THE COLLAR

8. Turn the assembled collar over, interfacing up.

9. Trim the interfacing as close as possible to the stitching made in Step 7.

10. Trim the seam allowance of the collar to 1/4 inch along the sides and bottom edge.

11. Trim the seam allowance of the undercollar to 1/8 inch along the sides and bottom edge.

12. Trim the collar points diagonally, following the instructions on page 103.

13. Clip the trimmed seam allowances of the bottom edge of the collar assembly at 1/2-inch intervals.

14. Turn the assembled collar right side out so that the interfacing lies between collar and undercollar, gently pushing out the points with closed scissors; pull the points out farther from the outside with a pin.

15. Open the collar assembly from the unstitched neck edge as far as possible and press the seams open from the inside.

16. Gently roll the outside of the collar seams between your fingers to bring the stitching out to the edge. Roll again lightly so that the seam stitching is turned 1/16 inch onto the undercollar side and baste to hold in place. Press.

17. Make a line of edge stitching and/or topstitching around the seamed edges if desired (page 32).

## C INTERFACING THE NECKBAND

18. Lay out the pieces you will need to attach the collar to the neckband—the assembled interfaced collar (just completed), the outer neckband, the inner neckband and the interfacing that will be stitched between them to stiffen the neckband.

19. Pin and baste the neckband interfacing to the wrong side of the outer neckband, matching the pattern markings. Remove the pins.

20. Trim the interfacing close to the basting along the straighter edge (bottom edge in drawing).

21. Trim the outer neckband along the straighter edge, 1/4 inch from the trimmed interfacing.

22. Turn up the straighter edge of the outer neckband along the seam line, and baste it against the interfacing. Press.

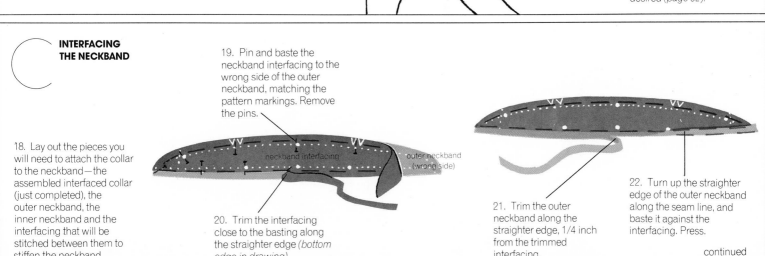

continued

## D ATTACHING THE OUTER NECKBAND TO THE COLLAR

23. Place the collar assembly on your table so that the undercollar faces up and the neck edge is at top. Lay the outer neckband on top of it with the interfacing up so that the edge with curved ends is at top.

24. Pin the neck edge of the collar assembly to the edge of the inner neckband having curved ends; match the pattern markings. Begin pinning in the center of the collar assembly and work toward each side. Baste, and remove the pins.

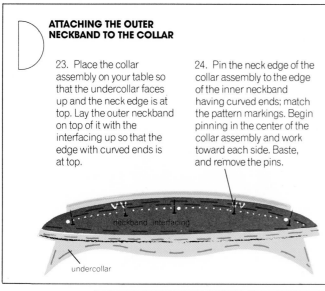

## E ATTACHING THE INNER NECKBAND TO THE COLLAR

25. Turn the collar assembly and outer neckband over so that the undercollar part of the assembled collar faces down and the outer neckband, wrong side up, is hidden underneath it.

26. Then place the inner neckband, wrong side up, on the collar. Pin and baste the curved-end edge of the inner neckband (at top in the drawing) to the unstitched neck edge of the collar, matching the pattern markings. Remove the pins.

27. Machine stitch alongside the basting, then remove all bastings.

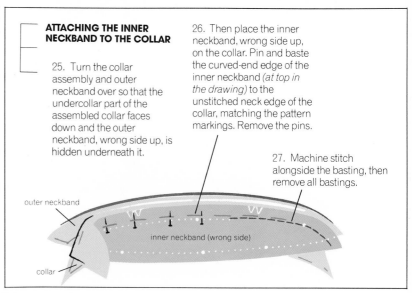

## F COMPLETING THE COLLAR AND NECKBAND

28. Turn the collar over so that the undercollar and neckband interfacing face up.

29. Trim the seam allowance of the interfacing close to the stitching line.

30. Trim the collar assembly seam allowances to 1/8 inch.

32. Clip all the trimmed seam allowances at 1/2 inch intervals along the middle and notch at 1/2 inch intervals along the ends, where the curve is more pronounced.

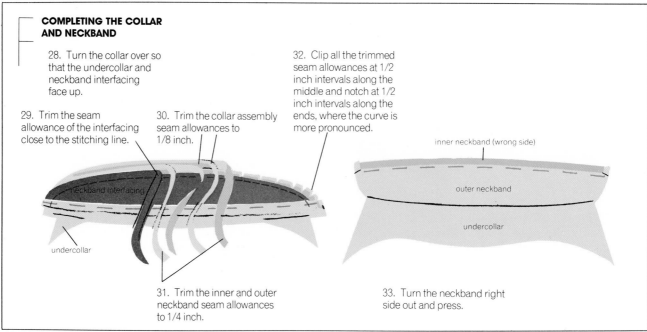

31. Trim the inner and outer neckband seam allowances to 1/4 inch.

33. Turn the neckband right side out and press.

## G SEWING THE NECKBAND TO THE GARMENT

34. Open the garment out flat, wrong side up with the neck edge at top. Clip the seam allowance of the neck edge of the garment at 1/2 inch intervals close to the stay stitching (page 102).

35. Spread the neckband open. Pin the inner neckband to the wrong side of the garment's neck edge. Begin pinning on the center of the neckband and work toward each side, matching the pattern markings. Baste and remove the pins.

36. Machine stitch and remove the basting.

37. Trim the inner neckband seam allowance to 1/8 inch.

38. Trim the garment neck edge seam allowance to 1/4 inch.

39. Turn the garment right side out. Press the garment neck edge and inner neckband seam allowances inside the neckband up toward the collar.

40. Pin and baste the outer neckband to the garment, covering the stitches made in Step 35. Remove the pins.

41. Machine stitch as close to the bottom edges of the neckband as possible from one end to the other. Remove the basting.

42. Run a line of decorative edge stitching and/or topstitching on the outer neckband if desired.

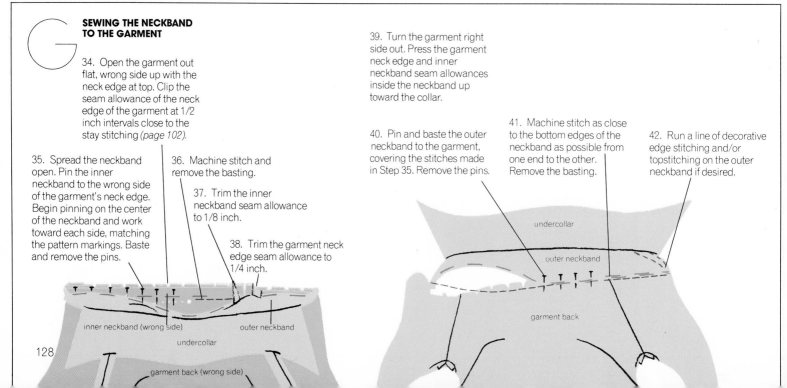

# THE CONVERTIBLE COLLAR

## A   MAKING THE COLLAR

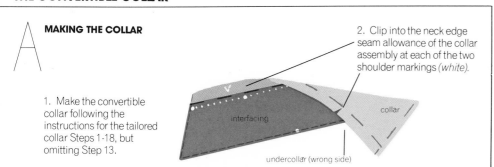

1. Make the convertible collar following the instructions for the tailored collar Steps 1-18, but omitting Step 13.

2. Clip into the neck edge seam allowance of the collar assembly at each of the two shoulder markings *(white)*.

*(labels: interfacing, collar, undercollar (wrong side))*

## B   ATTACHING THE COLLAR TO THE GARMENT

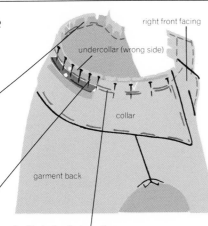

*(labels: right front facing, undercollar (wrong side), collar, garment back)*

3. Clip the seam allowance around the neck edge of the garment at 1/2 inch intervals, cutting close to the stay stitching as shown in blue *(page 102)*.

4. Pin the collar assembly to the outside of the garment at the neck edge, matching center back, shoulder and center front seam markings. Begin pinning in the center of the undercollar and work toward each side. Do not pin the collar seam allowance between the shoulder markings or the front facings.

5. Baste *(red)* along the neck edge from one front edge of the collar to the clip marking at the shoulder. At the clipped shoulder marking, fold down the seam allowance of the collar. Then continue to baste across to the other edge; do not catch the loose seam allowance of the collar when basting between the two shoulder seams. Remove the pins.

6. Fold both front facings of the garment back along the fold lines and pin and baste the facings to the collar, matching pattern markings. Remove the pins.

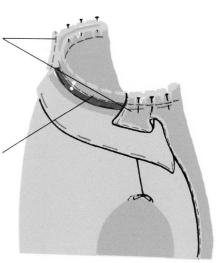

7. Machine stitch the entire length of the neck edge. Be sure not to catch the loose seam allowance of the collar when stitching between the shoulder seams. Remove the basting.

8. Spread apart the seam allowances of the facing and garment neck edge, then trim the collar assembly seam allowance to 1/8 inch. Be careful not to cut the folded down section of collar seam allowance.

9. Trim the facings and garment neck edge to 1/4 inch.

10. Trim the seam allowance of the unstitched portion of the collar between the shoulders to 1/4 inch.

## C   FINISHING THE COLLAR

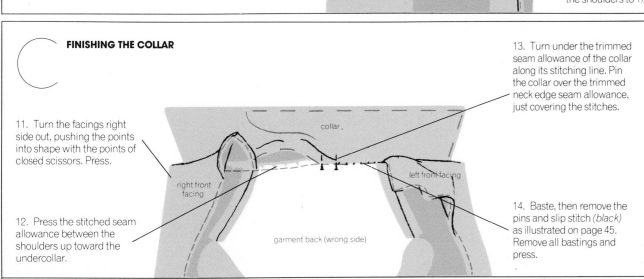

*(labels: collar, right front facing, left front facing, garment back (wrong side))*

11. Turn the facings right side out, pushing the points into shape with the points of closed scissors. Press.

12. Press the stitched seam allowance between the shoulders up toward the undercollar.

13. Turn under the trimmed seam allowance of the collar along its stitching line. Pin the collar over the trimmed neck edge seam allowance, just covering the stitches.

14. Baste, then remove the pins and slip stitch *(black)* as illustrated on page 45. Remove all bastings and press.

# Adding the facings and hems

Facings and hems finish and conceal raw edges by turning them inside the garment as shown on the open tunic on this page. The most important thing to remember about facings is that if the garment has been altered in the area where a facing will be stitched, the facing, and interfacing if there is any, should be altered in precisely the same way to ensure a proper fit.

Hemming is the last step in constructing trouser legs and sleeves that do not have cuffs, as well as dresses. Legs and sleeves are fairly easy: try the garment on before a mirror and pin up one or two places by eye. Take the garment off, measure the distance between the pin and the raw edge, turn the edge under evenly all around, and sew it as shown in the drawings opposite.

Hemming a dress is somewhat more involved. First, hang it up overnight. Next day, whether someone is pinning for you or you are using a chalk marker, stand on the floor (not a deep carpet) in a natural posture and measure from the floor up. Pin or make a chalk mark every 3 inches around the bottom edge. Then construct the hem as shown on the following pages. To guide you in determining the depth of the hem, the general rule is: the heavier the fabric or the more flared the skirt, the narrower the hem should be.

# MAKING A PLAIN HEM

## A TURNING UP THE HEM

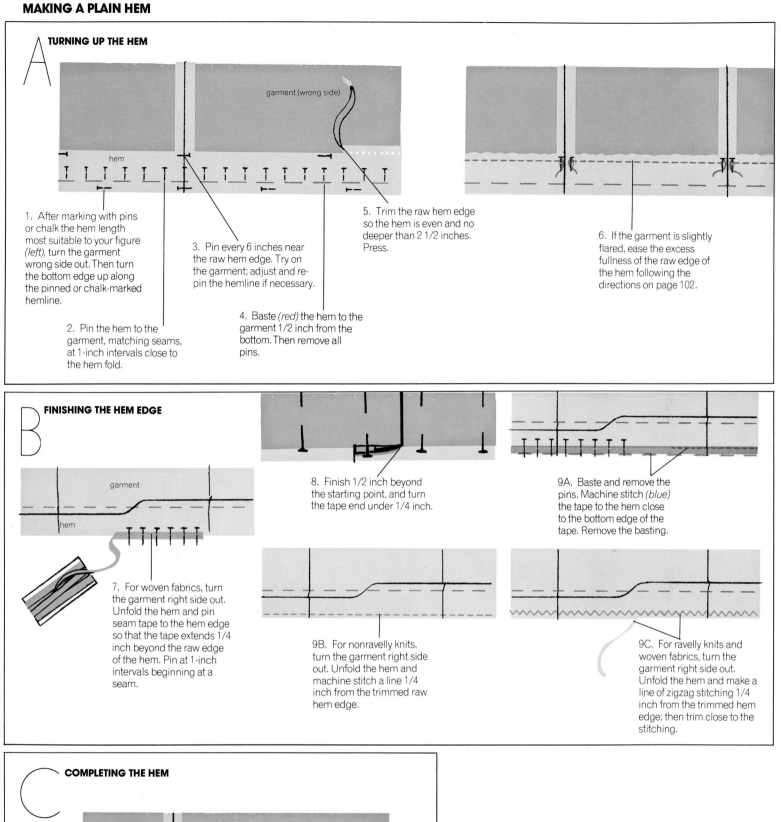

garment (wrong side)

hem

1. After marking with pins or chalk the hem length most suitable to your figure *(left)*, turn the garment wrong side out. Then turn the bottom edge up along the pinned or chalk-marked hemline.

2. Pin the hem to the garment, matching seams, at 1-inch intervals close to the hem fold.

3. Pin every 6 inches near the raw hem edge. Try on the garment; adjust and re-pin the hemline if necessary.

4. Baste *(red)* the hem to the garment 1/2 inch from the bottom. Then remove all pins.

5. Trim the raw hem edge so the hem is even and no deeper than 2 1/2 inches. Press.

6. If the garment is slightly flared, ease the excess fullness of the raw edge of the hem following the directions on page 102.

## B FINISHING THE HEM EDGE

garment

hem

7. For woven fabrics, turn the garment right side out. Unfold the hem and pin seam tape to the hem edge so that the tape extends 1/4 inch beyond the raw edge of the hem. Pin at 1-inch intervals beginning at a seam.

8. Finish 1/2 inch beyond the starting point, and turn the tape end under 1/4 inch.

9A. Baste and remove the pins. Machine stitch *(blue)* the tape to the hem close to the bottom edge of the tape. Remove the basting.

9B. For nonravelly knits, turn the garment right side out. Unfold the hem and machine stitch a line 1/4 inch from the trimmed raw hem edge.

9C. For ravelly knits and woven fabrics, turn the garment right side out. Unfold the hem and make a line of zigzag stitching 1/4 inch from the trimmed hem edge; then trim close to the stitching.

## C COMPLETING THE HEM

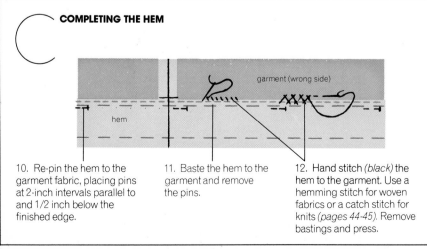

garment (wrong side)

hem

10. Re-pin the hem to the garment fabric, placing pins at 2-inch intervals parallel to and 1/2 inch below the finished edge.

11. Baste the hem to the garment and remove the pins.

12. Hand stitch *(black)* the hem to the garment. Use a hemming stitch for woven fabrics or a catch stitch for knits *(pages 44-45)*. Remove bastings and press.

131

## MAKING A HEM WITH AN OPEN-FACED CORNER

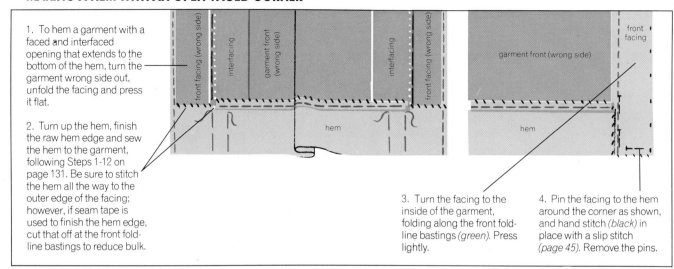

1. To hem a garment with a faced and interfaced opening that extends to the bottom of the hem, turn the garment wrong side out, unfold the facing and press it flat.

2. Turn up the hem, finish the raw hem edge and sew the hem to the garment, following Steps 1-12 on page 131. Be sure to stitch the hem all the way to the outer edge of the facing; however, if seam tape is used to finish the hem edge, cut that off at the front fold-line bastings to reduce bulk.

3. Turn the facing to the inside of the garment, folding along the front fold-line bastings (green). Press lightly.

4. Pin the facing to the hem around the corner as shown, and hand stitch (black) in place with a slip stitch (page 45). Remove the pins.

## MAKING A NARROW HEM FOR SHIRTS AND BLOUSES

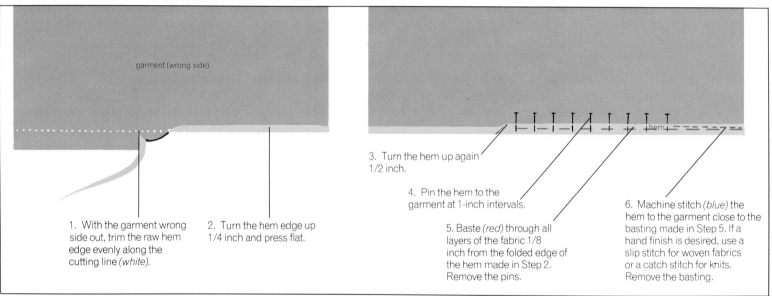

1. With the garment wrong side out, trim the raw hem edge evenly along the cutting line (white).

2. Turn the hem edge up 1/4 inch and press flat.

3. Turn the hem up again 1/2 inch.

4. Pin the hem to the garment at 1-inch intervals.

5. Baste (red) through all layers of the fabric 1/8 inch from the folded edge of the hem made in Step 2. Remove the pins.

6. Machine stitch (blue) the hem to the garment close to the basting made in Step 5. If a hand finish is desired, use a slip stitch for woven fabrics or a catch stitch for knits. Remove the basting.

## FACING A ROUND NECKLINE

### A PREPARING THE GARMENT

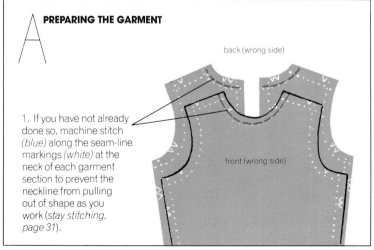

1. If you have not already done so, machine stitch (blue) along the seam-line markings (white) at the neck of each garment section to prevent the neckline from pulling out of shape as you work (stay stitching, page 31).

### B PREPARING THE INTERFACING

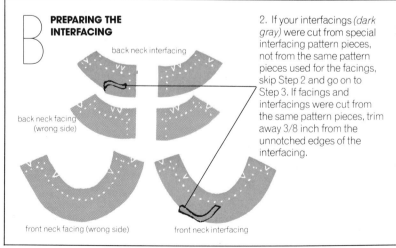

2. If your interfacings (dark gray) were cut from special interfacing pattern pieces, not from the same pattern pieces used for the facings, skip Step 2 and go on to Step 3. If facings and interfacings were cut from the same pattern pieces, trim away 3/8 inch from the unnotched edges of the interfacing.

**BASTING THE INTERFACING TO THE GARMENT**

3. Adjust your garment for fit, and make corresponding adjustments to your interfacing.

4. Pin the interfacing pieces to the wrong sides of the garment sections along the neck seam-line markings, matching notches and shoulder seam lines.

5. Baste (red) the interfacings to the garment outside the neck seam line; begin and end at the neck and shoulder seam intersections. Do not sew to the ends of the interfacings. Remove the pins.

6. Trim the interfacing around the neckline close to the bastings.

7. Pin and baste the shoulder seams along the seam-line markings. Remove the pins, machine stitch and remove the bastings.

8. Trim the interfacing ends along the shoulder seams 1/8 inch from the stitching.

9. Press open the shoulder seams; trim to 1/2 inch.

10. Insert the zipper (Centered Zipper, pages 109-110).

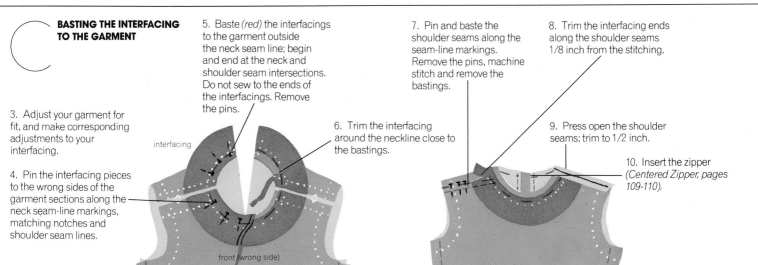

interfacing

front (wrong side)

**PREPARING THE FACING**

11. With the wrong sides of the fabric facing out, pin and baste together the back and front neck facing pieces along the shoulder seam markings. Remove the pins, machine stitch the shoulder seams and remove the basting.

12. Press open the seams and trim to 1/2 inch.

13. Trim the unnotched curved edge of the facing to make an even curve.

14. Finish the unnotched edge as you would any seam (page 101), or turn the edge under 1/4 inch, press flat and machine stitch 1/8 inch from the fold.

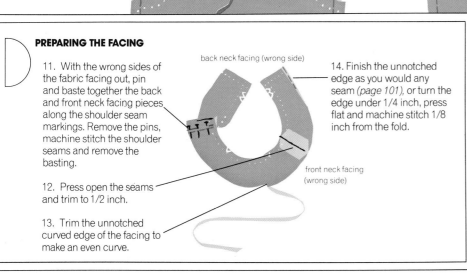

back neck facing (wrong side)

front neck facing (wrong side)

**ATTACHING THE FACING TO THE GARMENT**

15. Turn the garment right side out and pin the facing wrong side out to it along the neck seam-line markings. Make notches and shoulder seams on the facing align with those on the garment. Pin first at notches and seam intersections, then at 1/2 inch intervals in between.

16. Baste the facing to the garment along the neck seam line. Remove the pins, machine stitch the neck seam. Remove all neckline bastings.

17. Trim the facing seam allowance around the neckline to 1/8 inch.

18. Trim the garment seam allowance around the neckline to 1/4 inch.

19. Clip into all neckline seam allowances every 1/2 inch around the curve. Cut close to but not into the line of stitching.

20. Turn the garment wrong side out. Lift the facing so it extends away from the garment and press the neckline seam allowances toward the facing.

21. Slide the facing, wrong side down, under the sewing machine presser foot and make a line of stitching—called understitching—close to the neckline seam. Be sure the understitching catches the seam allowances beneath the facing fabric.

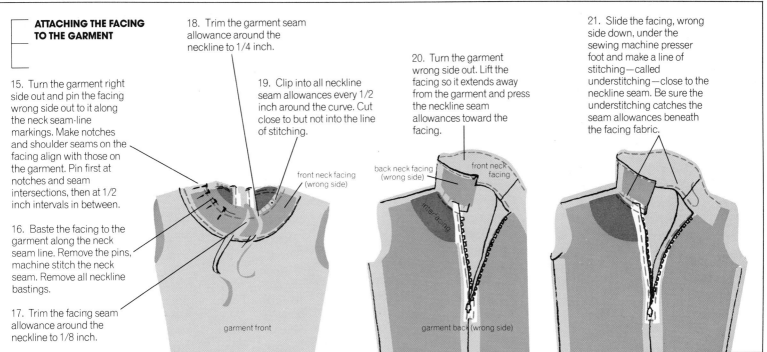

front neck facing (wrong side)

back neck facing (wrong side)

front neck facing

interfacing

garment front

garment back (wrong side)

## FINISHING THE FACING

22. Turn the facing down over the wrong side of the garment and press flat.

23. Pin the facing to the garment at the shoulder seams and attach it there with a slip stitch (page 45) shown in black. Remove the pins.

24. Fold under the center back ends of the facing so that they clear the zipper teeth. Pin and sew the fold with a slip stitch. Remove the pins and press.

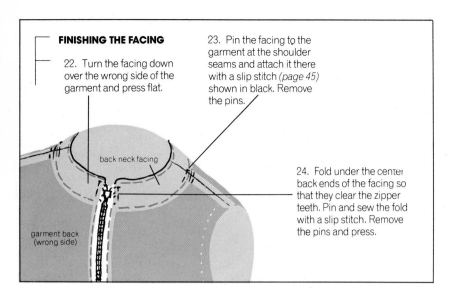

back neck facing

garment back (wrong side)

## THE ARMHOLE FACING

### PREPARING THE FACING

1. Cut and mark the front and back armhole facing pieces. With the wrong sides facing out, pin together the front and back facing pieces along the underarm and the shoulder seam markings (white). Baste (red), remove the pins and machine stitch (blue) the shoulder and underarm seams. Remove the basting.

2. Press open both seams and trim to 1/2 inch.

3. Finish the unnotched edge of the facing as you would any seam (page 101), or turn the edge over 1/4 inch and press flat. Then machine stitch 1/8 inch from the fold.

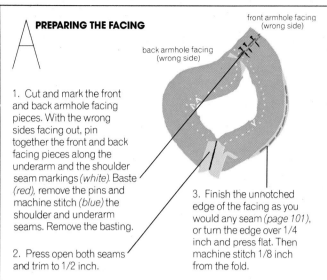

front armhole facing (wrong side)

back armhole facing (wrong side)

### B ATTACHING THE FACING TO THE GARMENT

4. Turn the garment right side out and pin the facing —wrong side out—to it along the armhole seam markings. Pin at notches and seam intersections, then at 1/2-inch intervals. Baste and remove the pins.

5. Machine stitch along seam markings, beginning and ending at the intersection between the underarm and armhole seams. Remove the basting.

6. Trim the facing armhole seam allowance to 1/8 inch.

7. Trim the garment armhole seam allowance to 1/4 inch.

8. Clip into both armhole seam allowances at 1/2-inch intervals, cutting close to but not into the stitching.

9. Turn the garment wrong side out.

10. Turn the facing up so that it extends away from the garment and press the armhole seam allowances toward the facing.

11. Understitch the facing and seam allowances as shown for the round neck facing, Step 21. Begin and end at the underarm seam.

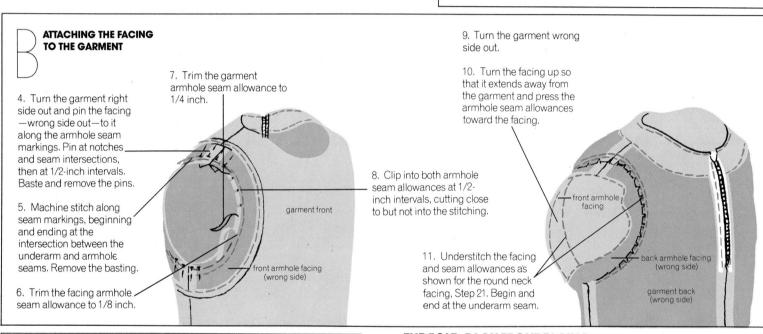

garment front

front armhole facing (wrong side)

front armhole facing

back armhole facing (wrong side)

garment back (wrong side)

### C HAND FINISHING THE FACING

12. Turn the facing down over the wrong side of the garment and press flat.

13. Pin the facing to the garment at the shoulder and underarm seams as shown and attach the facing to those seam allowances with a slip stitch (black). Remove the pins and press.

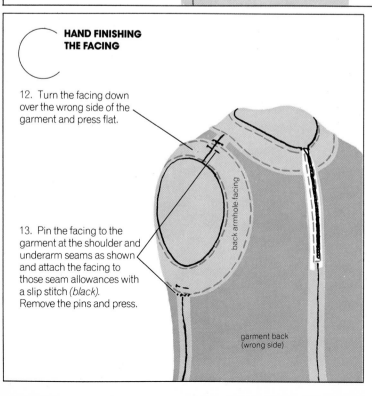

back armhole facing

garment back (wrong side)

## THE FOLD-BACK FRONT FACING

### PREPARING THE GARMENT AND INTERFACING

1. If you have not already done so, reinforce (blue) the neckline. Re-mark the center front and front fold lines (white) with basting (green).

2. Trim the interfacings (dark gray), following the instructions for facing a round neckline, Box B, Step 2.

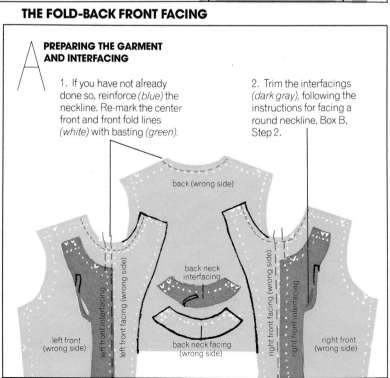

back (wrong side)

back neck interfacing

left front (wrong side)

left front interfacing

left front facing (wrong side)

back neck facing (wrong side)

right front facing (wrong side)

right front interfacing

right front (wrong side)

## B ATTACHING THE INTERFACING TO THE GARMENT

3. Adjust the garment for fit and make corresponding adjustments on the interfacing.

4. Pin and baste (red) all interfacings to the front and back sections of the garment at the neck along the neck seam-line markings. Be sure to baste only between the seam intersections, not all the way to the ends of the interfacing. Remove the pins.

5. Pin the left and right front interfacings to the corresponding front sections 1/8 inch outside the center front fold line. Baste along the pinned line with thread the same color as the fabric. Make long stitches on the interfacing side but do not stitch through the garment fabric; pick up only a thread of the garment fabric. Begin the basting at the neck seam line and end at the bottom of the garment. Remove the pins.

6. Trim the interfacing around the neckline close to the bastings. Do not trim along the front fold lines.

7. With the wrong sides of the fabric facing out, pin and baste the shoulder seams of the garment. Remove the pins, machine stitch along the seam markings, and remove the basting.

8. Trim all interfacings along the shoulder seams 1/8 inch from the stitching.

9. Press the shoulder seams open and trim to 1/2 inch.

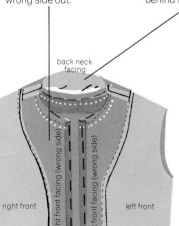

## C ATTACHING THE BACK NECK FACING TO THE GARMENT

10. Pin and baste the back neck facing to the front facings along the shoulder seam markings. Remove the pins, machine stitch along the seam markings and remove the basting.

11. Press the seams open and trim to 1/2 inch.

12. Finish the unnotched edge of the facing as you would any seam (Finishes for Seams, page 101), or fold it over 1/4 inch and press. Machine stitch 1/8 inch from the folded edge.

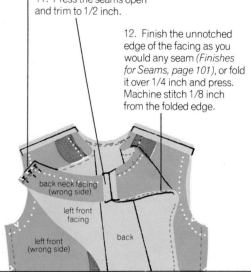

## D STITCHING THE FACING AND GARMENT TOGETHER

13. Turn the garment right side out. Then fold back the front facings along the front fold lines so that they are wrong side out.

14. Slide the back neck facing, wrong side out, behind the garment back.

15. Pin all facings to the garment along the neck seam line. Match and pin at notches and seam intersections, then at 1/2-inch intervals in between.

16. Baste along the neck seam line and remove the pins. Machine stitch the neck seam, and remove the basting.

17. Trim the center front corners diagonally, cutting to within 1/8 inch of the stitching.

18. Trim the facings around the neckline to within 1/8 inch of the neckline seam and trim the garment seam to within 1/4 inch of the neckline.

19. Clip into all seam allowances at 1/2-inch intervals around the neck, cutting close but not into the stitching.

20. Turn the garment wrong side out.

21. Extend the facing away from the garment and press the neckline seam allowances toward the facing.

22. Understitch the facing and seam allowances around the neck as shown for the round neck facing, Step 21. Begin and end the understitching 1 inch from the corners as shown.

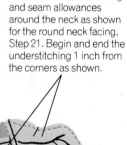

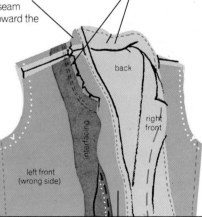

left front facing (wrong side)

## E HAND FINISHING THE FACING

23. Fold the facing over the wrong side of the garment and press flat.

24. Pin the facing to the garment at the shoulder seams as shown and hand stitch to the shoulder seam allowances with a slip stitch (black). Remove the pins.

25. Remove any remaining bastings and press again.

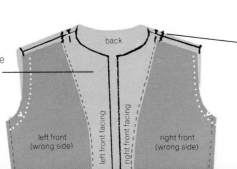

135

# Pockets to show and to hide

Two of the most common types of pockets are patch and in-seam —one in plain view *(right)*, the other concealed. The patch pocket may vary widely in shape, depending on the pattern, but it is simply a piece of fabric—usually the same that is used for the garment—stitched along three sides to the outside of the garment *(opposite)*. The in-seam pocket—stitched, as its name implies, inside the garment seams—is made of lining fabric, which is thin enough to avoid a telltale bulge. It must be made as a complete unit and then fastened to the side and waistline seams *(pages 138-139)*.

Even though the patch pocket is the easiest kind to make, it requires care in positioning. After you have put the pattern markings for the pocket on the body of the garment, try it on to make sure it is conveniently and attractively placed. On a skirt, for instance, the pocket may be too low for you to put your hand in comfortably. Or it may be so far to the side that it overemphasizes the hip.

The in-seam pocket offers no options in placement, but if you have let in or taken out the area where the pocket will be inserted, be sure to make a corresponding alteration to the pocket pattern piece.

# MAKING PATCH POCKETS

## A PREPARING THE POCKET SECTION

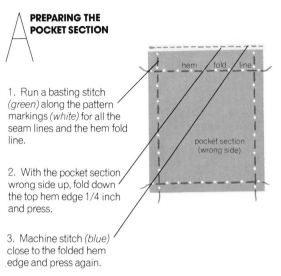

1. Run a basting stitch *(green)* along the pattern markings *(white)* for all the seam lines and the hem fold line.

2. With the pocket section wrong side up, fold down the top hem edge 1/4 inch and press.

3. Machine stitch *(blue)* close to the folded hem edge and press again.

## B FINISHING THE HEM EDGE

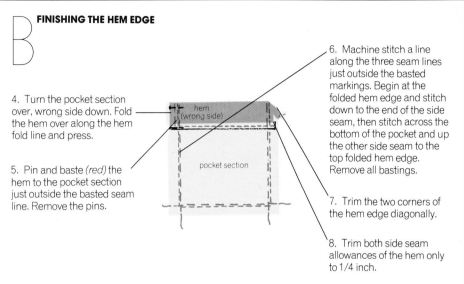

4. Turn the pocket section over, wrong side down. Fold the hem over along the hem fold line and press.

5. Pin and baste *(red)* the hem to the pocket section just outside the basted seam line. Remove the pins.

6. Machine stitch a line along the three seam lines just outside the basted markings. Begin at the folded hem edge and stitch down to the end of the side seam, then stitch across the bottom of the pocket and up the other side seam to the top folded hem edge. Remove all bastings.

7. Trim the two corners of the hem edge diagonally.

8. Trim both side seam allowances of the hem only to 1/4 inch.

## C COMPLETING THE POCKET SECTION

### STRAIGHT POCKETS

9A. On pockets with straight bottoms, turn the pocket section wrong side up, turn over the hem and press. Then fold in the side seam allowances just beyond the line of machine stitching made in Step 6 and press. Fold up the bottom seam allowance and press.

### POINTED POCKETS

9B. On pockets with pointed bottoms, turn the pocket section wrong side up, turn over the hem and press. Then fold up the two bottom seam allowances that form the point just beyond the line of machine stitching made in Step 6; press. Fold in the side seam allowances and press.

### ROUNDED POCKETS

9C. On pockets with rounded bottoms, turn the pocket section wrong side up, turn over the hem and press. Notch the curves at 1/2-inch intervals. Fold in the seam allowances just beyond the machine stitching made in Step 6 and press. Overlap the notched segments where necessary.

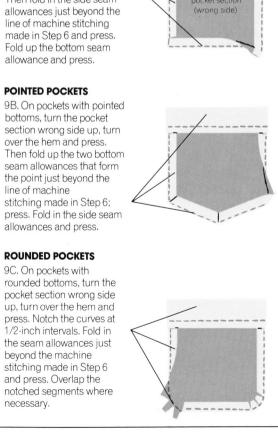

## D STITCHING THE POCKET TO THE GARMENT

10. Place the pocket, wrong side down, on the right side of the garment—the side that will be visible when the garment is completed. Align the edges of the pocket with the basted placement lines on the garment that were made when the pattern was cut out *(page 83)*.

11. Pin the pocket to the garment at each corner and at 1-inch intervals.

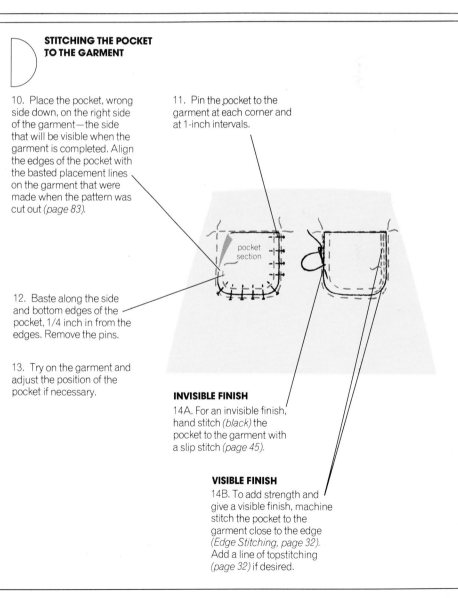

12. Baste along the side and bottom edges of the pocket, 1/4 inch in from the edges. Remove the pins.

13. Try on the garment and adjust the position of the pocket if necessary.

### INVISIBLE FINISH

14A. For an invisible finish, hand stitch *(black)* the pocket to the garment with a slip stitch *(page 45)*.

### VISIBLE FINISH

14B. To add strength and give a visible finish, machine stitch the pocket to the garment close to the edge *(Edge Stitching, page 32)*. Add a line of topstitching *(page 32)* if desired.

# MAKING THE IN-SEAM POCKET FOR PANTS

## A PREPARING THE POCKET SECTION

1. On the right-hand pocket section—cut out of lining, not garment, fabric—run a line of basting stitches *(green)* along the pattern markings *(white)* for the seam and placement lines.

2. If your pattern includes a marking at the waistline for aligning the pocket with the pants, re-mark it with a vertical running stitch *(page 43)*.

3. Re-mark with a horizontal running stitch the pattern markings for the bottom of the pocket opening.

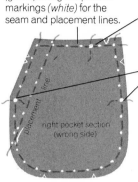

right pocket section (wrong side)

placement line

## B PREPARING THE FACINGS

4. Cut a right-hand pocket facing from the garment fabric, using the facing pattern piece, and run a line of basting stitches along the pattern markings for the seam lines.

5. If your pattern includes a marking at the waistline for aligning the pocket with the pants, re-mark it with a vertical running stitch.

6. Re-mark with a horizontal running stitch the pattern markings for the bottom of the pocket opening.

right facing (wrong side)

7. Fold over the long unnotched edge of the facing along the basted seam line and press.

8. Trim the pressed edge to 1/4 inch and trim the excess fabric from the bottom corner. Remove the basting from the pressed edge.

9. Cut a rectangular facing strip from the garment fabric, according to the measurements on your pattern guide sheet.

10. With the facing strip wrong side up, fold over one long edge 1/4 inch and press.

right facing strip (wrong side)

## C STITCHING THE FACINGS TO THE POCKET

11. Place the right-hand pocket section wrong side down and lay the facing, wrong side down, on it. Pin the facing to the pocket section along the basted seam line, matching the notches and the running-stitch markings.

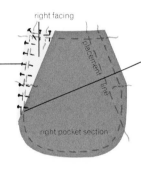

right facing

placement line

right pocket section

12. Baste the facing to the pocket section 1/4 inch outside the seam markings. Remove the pins.

13. Pin and baste the facing to the pocket along the folded edge made in Step 7. Remove the pins.

14. Machine stitch close to the folded edge. Remove the basting from the folded edge only.

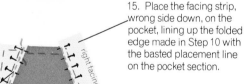

right facing strip

15. Place the facing strip, wrong side down, on the pocket, lining up the folded edge made in Step 10 with the basted placement line on the pocket section.

16. Pin and baste the facing strip to the pocket section along the folded edge. Remove the pins.

17. Machine stitch close to the folded edge. Remove the bastings from the folded edge.

18. Turn the pocket section over, wrong side up, and pin the pocket section to the facing strip along the outer seam-line markings.

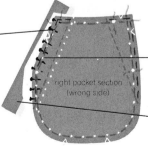

right pocket section (wrong side)

19. Baste 1/4 inch outside the seam markings. Remove the pins.

20. Trim the facing strip so that it is even with the pocket section around all edges.

## D SEWING THE POCKET

21. Fold the pocket in half lengthwise, wrong sides together, matching pattern markings and the horizontal running stitches marking the pocket opening.

22. Pin and baste the pocket together along the basted seam line from the horizontal running stitch that marks the bottom of the pocket opening *(Step 6)* to the bottom of the folded edge. Remove the pins.

right pocket section

23. Machine stitch the basted seam 1/4 inch outside the seam markings.

24. Clip into the seam allowances at the horizontal markings for the bottom of the pocket opening, cutting to the stitching line.

25. Trim the seam allowances to 1/8 inch, cutting from the bottom fold to the clip made in Step 24.

26. Notch around the curve. Then remove all basting from the stitched seam.

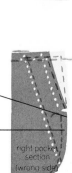

27. Turn the pocket wrong side out and press the stitched seam flat.

28. Machine stitch on the seam markings from the clip to the bottom folded edge. Reinforce the seam at the clip by going forward three stitches, back three, then forward to the seam end.

right pocket section (wrong side)

## ATTACHING THE POCKET TO THE PANTS

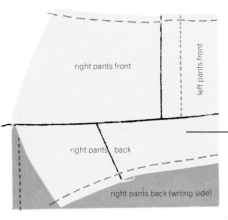

29. Complete the pants up to the point at which both front sections have been stitched together at the crotch, the zipper has been inserted and the outer pants leg seams have been stitched up to the pattern markings for the pocket opening.

30. Lay the pants front wrong side down and lay over it the back section wrong side up. Then fold down the upper portion of the pants back as far as the bottom of the pocket opening.

31. With the right-hand pocket wrong side out, lay it down on the right-hand pants front, matching the notches of the open side edges. The number of notches on the upper part of the pocket (two in this diagram) will correspond to the number of notches on the pants front opening.

32. Push the underneath side of the pocket out of the way.

33. Pin only the upper side of the pocket to the pants front along the side seam line. Insert the first pin at the very bottom of the seam opening. Pin next at the notches and at the intersection of the side seam line with the waist seam line, then at 1/2-inch intervals in between.

34. Baste the pocket to the pants just outside the side seam line and remove the pins. Then machine stitch along the seam line. Remove the basting.

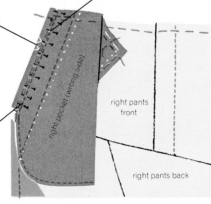

35. Press open the seam to the bottom of the pocket opening.

36. Fold the pocket over so that it lies outside the pants, and lift up the folded-down pants back.

37. Pin the remaining unstitched side of the pocket to the open portion of the pants back along the side seam line. Pin first at the very bottom of the opening, then at the notches and the intersection of the side seam line with the waist seam line, and finally at 1/2-inch intervals in between.

38. Baste the pocket to the pants back along the seam line. Remove the pins.

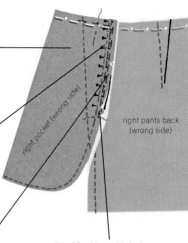

39. Machine stitch the seam. Remove all bastings except the basted marking along the waist seam line. Press open the stitched seam.

## FINISHING THE POCKET

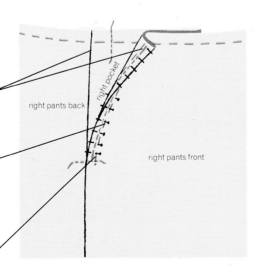

40. Open the right pants section so it lies flat, wrong side down, and turn the pocket toward the pants front. Press the front pocket seam flat.

41. Pin along the pressed seam to hold it flat, and baste 3/8 inch from the edge.

42. Pushing the rest of the pocket and the pants back fabric out of the way, place the pants front under the machine presser foot. Topstitch (page 32) the front pocket opening seam 1/4 inch in from the folded edge, from the waist to the bottom of the pocket opening.

43. Pull the threads to the inside of the pocket and tie them off (page 29). Remove the basting.

44. At the waistline, align the front edge of the pocket with the vertical running stitch and pin.

45. Pin the pants front to the folded pocket along the waist seam-line markings, then baste just outside the seam-line markings. Remove the pins.

46. Reinforce the bottom of the pocket opening by machine stitching at right angles to the side seam through all layers of the fabric from the end of the topstitching made in Step 42 to just beyond the side seam. Stitch forward, then backward, then forward again, then pull the threads through to the wrong side of the garment and tie them off (page 29). Press.

47. Repeat Steps 1-46 on the left pocket section, facing and strip.

139

# Buttons, buttonholes, snaps, hooks

Buttons, snaps, hooks and eyes are the final professional touch, to be added only after a garment is otherwise finished. Buttons are decorative as well as functional; select them with an eye to the fabric as well as the size of the wearer; for example, small pearl buttons would be inappropriate on a checked tweed dress, and large metallic buttons might overwhelm a tiny figure.

Horizontal buttonholes should be used on close-fitting garments, where there is some stress, vertical buttonholes where there is less strain, such as on a shirt. Once you have adjusted your pattern, reposition buttonholes as shown on pages 141 and 142. But first make a test run with the same fabric and the same number of layers with which you will be working on your garment. For knits, interface *(pages 134-135)* the area on which buttonholes will be placed or the fabric will stretch.

Hooks and eyes are best used as hidden fasteners for overlapping edges, such as the waistbands of skirts or pants. Snaps have little holding power and are used to tack down edges invisibly in conjunction with other fasteners.

These instructions are intended for women's garments, which close with the right-hand side over the left. For men's garments, reverse the directions in the instructions.

## MEASURING THE BUTTON

To find the size of your buttonholes, first measure the buttons to be attached. For a flat, thin button, measure its diameter and add 1/8 inch. For a thicker button, measure its diameter and add 1/4 inch. For a mounded or ball button, place a thin strip of paper across the mound or ball, pin it tightly in place, slide the paper off, flatten it, then measure it and add 1/4 inch.

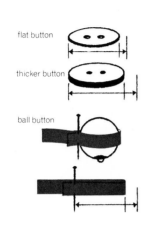

flat button

thicker button

ball button

## HORIZONTAL BUTTONHOLES

### A DETERMINING POSITION

1. To determine the outer placement line for your buttonholes, run basting stitches parallel to and 1/8 inch outside the center front line on the right front of the garment. Use thread of a different color to distinguish this placement line from other basted markings.

2. To determine the inner placement line for your buttonholes, measure in from the outside placement line a distance equal to the size of your buttonhole as established in the box at left. Then make a line of basting stitches parallel to the outer placement line.

center front line

3. To space buttonholes, begin at the top. Measure down a distance equal to 1 1/2 times the diameter of your button. Mark with a pin through all layers.

4. To determine the bottom placement line for your buttonholes, measure up from the hemline the distance specified on your pattern. Mark with a pin through all layers.

5. Using pins, space all the intervening buttonholes at equal intervals. Then mark the positions for all the buttonholes with horizontal running stitches *(page 43)* through all layers. To be sure each mark is straight, follow a horizontal grain line in the fabric. If the grain line is difficult to establish, as it would be in tightly woven or synthetic material, mark at right angles to the center front line. The marks should extend about 1/2 inch beyond either side of the placement lines. Remove the pins.

### B MAKING THE BUTTONHOLE

6. To make a buttonhole entirely by machine, follow the instructions provided with your particular model. To make a buttonhole without a special accessory, begin halfway between the placement lines and sew tiny machine stitches 1/16 inch outside the running stitches that mark the buttonhole position. The stitches should be continuous, pivoting at the corners *(page 30)*.

7. With a small pointed scissors, cut the buttonhole along the running stitches, starting in the middle and cutting to each placement line.

8. Sew the buttonhole edges with overcast stitches *(page 43)*, shown in black, to protect them from fraying.

9. Work the overcast edges with a buttonhole stitch *(page 45)*, beginning on the top edge of the buttonhole at the inner placement line.

10. At the outer placement line, make five to seven long buttonhole stitches, fanning out about 1/16 inch beyond the line. Then turn the garment around and repeat for the lower edge. End with a straight vertical stitch at the inner placement line.

11. To finish off the inner edge of the buttonhole with a reinforcement called a bar tack, make three long stitches, side by side, from the top to the bottom edge of the completed rows of buttonhole stitches. These stitches should extend 1/16 inch beyond the inner placement line.

12. At the bottom edge of the buttonhole, insert the needle horizontally under the three straight stitches made in Step 11, catching the top layer of the fabric underneath. Then pull the needle through, keeping the thread under the needle.

13. Continue to make small stitches across the three long stitches the full depth of the buttonhole.

14. End with two small fastening stitches *(page 42)*.

### C PLACING THE BUTTONS

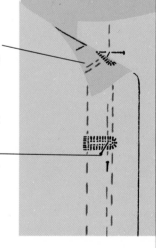

15. Pin the right side of the garment over the left, matching the neck edges of both sides and lining up the basting stitches marking the center front lines.

16. To determine the correct position for the center of each button, insert a pin through each buttonhole at the center front line; the pin should continue through the center front line of the left side of the garment.

17. Mark the position with another pin.

## VERTICAL BUTTONHOLES

### A DETERMINING POSITION

1. To find the size of your buttonholes, first measure the buttons to be attached, following the instructions on page 141.

2. To space your buttonholes begin at the top. Find the upper end of the first buttonhole by measuring down a distance equal to 1 1/2 times the diameter of your button. Mark with a pin through all layers.

3. To find the bottom end of the first buttonhole, measure down from the first pin a distance equal to the size of your buttonhole. Mark with a second pin through all layers.

4. To determine the bottom end of the last buttonhole, measure up from the hemline the distance specified on your pattern. Mark with a pin through all layers.

5. To determine the top end of the last buttonhole, measure up from the first pin a distance equal to the size of your buttonhole. Mark with a pin through all layers.

6. Using pins, space intervening buttonholes at equal intervals. Mark the positions for all the buttonholes with horizontal running stitches (page 43), as indicated in green, through all layers of the garment. The marks should extend about 1/2 inch on either side of the center front line. Remove the pins.

*wrong side*

### B MAKING A VERTICAL BUTTONHOLE

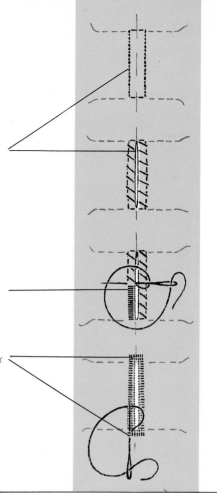

7. To make a buttonhole entirely by machine, follow the instructions provided with your particular model. To make a buttonhole without a special accessory, machine stitch, cut and overcast (*black*) the edges as for the horizontal buttonhole, Box B, Steps 6-8.

8. Work the overcast edges with a buttonhole stitch (*page 45*), beginning at the bottom of the inner edge.

9. After completing the inner edge, make a bar tack (*Horizontal Buttonholes, Box B, Steps 11-13*) and continue along the outer edge, finishing off with another bar tack.

10. End with two small fastening stitches (*page 42*).

### C PLACING BUTTONS

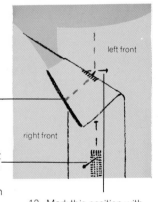

*left front*

*right front*

11. Pin the right side of the garment over the left, matching the neck edges and lining up the basting stitches marking the center front lines.

12. To determine the correct position for the center of each button, insert a pin 1/8 inch below the top end of each buttonhole; the pin should continue through the center front line of the garment's left side.

13. Mark this position with another pin.

## SEWING ON BUTTONS HAVING HOLES

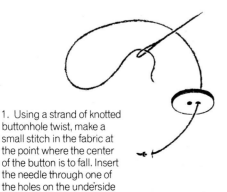

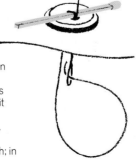

1. Using a strand of knotted buttonhole twist, make a small stitch in the fabric at the point where the center of the button is to fall. Insert the needle through one of the holes on the underside of the button and pull the thread through.

2. Hold a wooden kitchen match or a toothpick between the button holes and pull the thread over it as you point the needle down into the other hole. Then make two or three stitches across the match; in the case of a four-hole button, make two rows of parallel stitches across the match.

3. Remove the match and pull the button up, away from the fabric, to the top of the threads.

4. Wind the thread five or six times, tightly, around the loose threads below the button to create a thread shank.

5. End by making a fastening stitch (*page 42*) in the thread shank.

## SEWING ON BUTTONS HAVING SHANKS

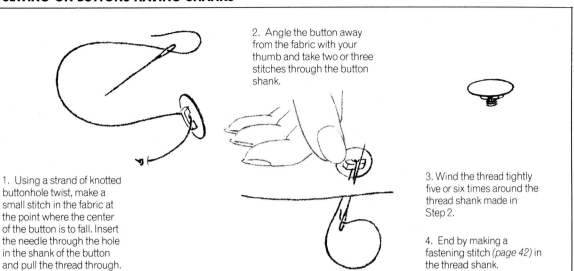

1. Using a strand of knotted buttonhole twist, make a small stitch in the fabric at the point where the center of the button is to fall. Insert the needle through the hole in the shank of the button and pull the thread through.

2. Angle the button away from the fabric with your thumb and take two or three stitches through the button shank.

3. Wind the thread tightly five or six times around the thread shank made in Step 2.

4. End by making a fastening stitch (*page 42*) in the thread shank.

## SEWING ON SNAPS

1. Place the half of the snap having a prong or ball in its center on the wrong side of the overlapping part of the garment.

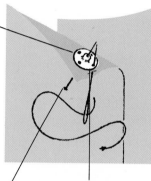

2. Hold the pronged half in place by putting it at the point of closure and about 1/8 inch from the edge to be held in place and inserting a straight pin through the tiny hole inside the prong.

3. Using a double strand of knotted thread, take a small stitch—catching only the inside layer of fabric —through one of the holes and then around the edge of the snap. Tuck the knot under the snap.

4. Take a second stitch at the first hole, then slide the needle under the snap and up through another hole. Repeat until all the holes are completed, and end with two small fastening stitches (*page 42*) at one edge under the snap.

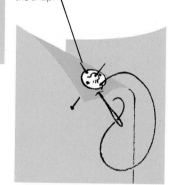

5. Place the overlap so that the straight pin holding the pronged half in place goes through the underlap. Insert a second pin through the underlap to mark the spot pierced by the first pin.

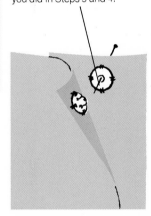

6. Slide the socket half of the snap onto the second pin and sew it in place as you did in Steps 3 and 4.

## SEWING ON HOOKS WITH ROUNDED EYES

1. When edges meet on the back of garments, place the hook at the left-hand side of the closure, 1/8 inch from the fabric edge. Using a double strand of knotted thread, stitch around each metal ring, catching only the inside fabric layer.

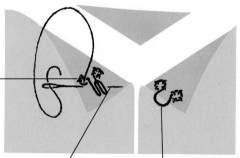

2. Continue by sliding the needle under the hook and take a few stitches over the hook, under the bend. End with a fastening stitch (*page 42*) through the inside layer of fabric.

3. Place the round eye on the right-hand side of the closure so that it protrudes just beyond the edge and the garment edges meet exactly. Sew around each metal ring as in Step 1. End with a fastening stitch (*page 42*).

## SEWING ON HOOKS WITH STRAIGHT EYES

1. On garments where the edges overlap, attach the hook to the overlapping side of the closure, as in Steps 1 and 2 in the box at left.

2. Place the overlap so that the bend of the hook falls where the straight eye is to be positioned. Sew the eye in place by stitching around the two metal rings, this time catching all layers of fabric.

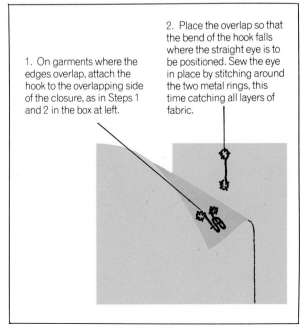

# Valued accessories from modest efforts

There are many moments when either the spirit is not willing or time will not allow major undertakings—the creation, for example, of a pair of black-velvet evening trousers topped by a creamy satin shirt. Those are the times for smaller, more modest enterprises. On the following pages are two good ideas for putting small pieces of fabric and small chunks of time to good use. Both of them, a scarf and a man's tie, are relatively easy to make. An afternoon's work, perhaps, with the finishing stitches applied as you relax in the evening.

Today, of course, both can be casual, simple complements to costumes. But there was a time when both, particularly the scarf, were utilitarian. The scarf reached a fashion high point in the early 19th Century after Napoleon's campaign in Egypt. He had sent home by warship a collection of cashmere shawls, close relatives of modern scarves, as presents for the Empress Josephine. Josephine at first loathed them, but after her forceful husband returned from the wars, she was seen wearing them regularly. The ladies of Napoleon's court, shivering in palaces lacking central heating in some of the most daring bare-shouldered dresses ever seen, quickly seized upon the imperial fancy, and the scarf became an adjunct to every woman's wardrobe.

The tie, too, is associated with royalty. Louis XIV, so the story goes, was attracted to the loose neck ornaments—Croats —worn by Croatian men in what is now part of Yugoslavia. He adopted *le Croat,* which eventually became *cravate,* as a royal emblem and used it to designate certain of the king's regiments. As time went on, the cravat even came to be associated with different life styles *(opposite).*

The charm of both accessories lies not only in how quickly you can finish them —both require simple techniques and stitches with which you are already familiar —but in how economical they can be. Anyone who sews at all has odd, seemingly useless lengths of material left over from past projects that generally are stuffed into a drawer in the hope that someday something useful can be made from them. The uses are rarely found, but such odds and ends are suitable for both ties and scarves, which can be made from a number of different fabrics in many sizes.

For a narrow tie, a small print or check is good. So is a printed tie-silk or a challis with a small Paisley design, or even blue denim or plain-colored raw silk.

For a wider tie, let your imagination run equally wide—depending, of course, on the taste of the intended recipient. Consider a large checked gingham in bright red or blue, for instance, or a colorful printed silk. If the market will bear it, you might even try a patchwork design constructed out of scraps from your own hoard. And, for a striking effect, here certainly is the place to try a wide, colorful stripe.

A scarf offers even more possibilities, both in terms of fabric and size. Whether small neckerchiefs or long trailing rectangles, all take the same degree of skill and the same relatively simple technique; the difference lies only in the dimensions of the individual scarf. However, one of the crucial points to remember with scarves is that the fabric should lean toward the pliant rather than stiff side. Otherwise the scarf will not fold and drape as it should.

Given this limitation, choices can run from fine cottons to handsome heavy silks.

Do not overlook the calico print from which you have made a child's pinafore or the brightly colored polyester left over from last season's favorite dress. Border prints and sheer embroidered cottons are also good bets. It is surprising how many of the designs you liked for other reasons will look just as pretty in a scarf. Even if you don't need one yourself, a scarf makes an attractive gift for a friend.

If your storehouse of small pieces of fabric doesn't inspire you, there is always the remnant section of your favorite fabric store. Here's an opportunity to make use of a yard or so of an interesting fabric that you would otherwise pass by.

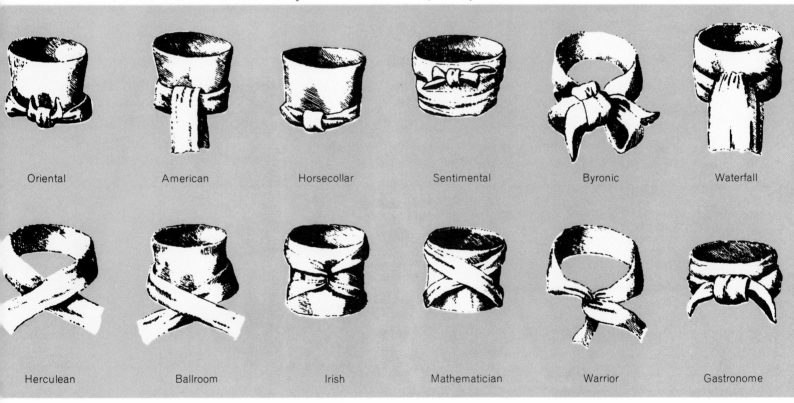

Oriental    American    Horsecollar    Sentimental    Byronic    Waterfall

Herculean    Ballroom    Irish    Mathematician    Warrior    Gastronome

The way one small accessory can epitomize the wearer's style, and even his vocation, was demonstrated whimsically in these cartoons from a Milan newspaper of 1827, when dandies cultivated the fine art of tying a cravat. The artist's captions, obscure now but comical then, celebrated such different styles as the no-nonsense American tie *(top, second from left)* and the loose bow *(fifth from left)* sported by Byron, the Romantic poet.

# Expert tricks for men's ties

The secrets to making a perfect tie lie in the initial cutting, the insertion of appropriate interfacing and in the final folding. You will need a commercial pattern to provide full-sized pieces as a cutting guide. These patterns, however, produce ties of varying lengths—anywhere from 40 to 60 inches—that may be too long or too short for the intended recipient. To tailor a tie to his dimensions, take the two halves of the pattern and lay them together where they will be joined at the neck seam. Place a tie that fits him on top and adjust the length at the narrow ends of each half. If the pattern is short, extend with paper at the narrow ends; if it is too long, cut off the ends. In either case, follow the taper of the pattern.

Tack the fabric to a piece of cardboard as shown below at left to prevent the material from shifting, so that you can cut it on the true bias.

Use interfacing fabric made especially for ties to provide the weight needed for a good knot. If the tie is made of a lightweight material, such as silk, use two layers of interfacing. To give the tie soft, rolled edges, cut out a cardboard form and use it to press your fold (below).

## TIPS FOR CUTTING AND SHAPING

### PINNING THE FABRIC AND PATTERN

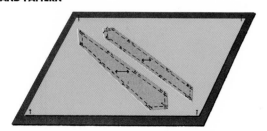

1. Make sure that the grain of the fabric is straight by pulling out one lengthwise thread (page 74).

2. Place the fabric wrong side down on cardboard. Tack the fabric at the corners with pins. Pin the pattern to the fabric so that the printed grain arrows are parallel to the fabric grain.

3. Remove the fabric and attached pattern pieces, cut out the tie, join the pieces and line and interface them following the pattern.

### SHAPING THE TIE WITH A CARDBOARD FORM

4. Turn in the edges of the pattern pieces along the inner fold lines and pin the pieces to cardboard.

5. Cut out cardboard forms that follow the shape of the tie.

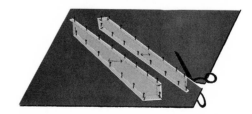

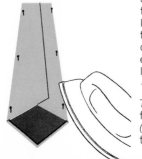

6. Center these cardboard forms on the inside of the lined, interfaced tie. Fold in the tie edges over the cardboard. Tack down the edges with pins, and press lightly with a steam iron —barely touching the fabric.

7. Remove the cardboard forms and use a slip stitch (page 45) to sew the edges together, closing the tie.

Two simple steps can turn a remnant or a yard or two of distinctive and unusual material into a scarf with a designer look. Before you cut, make certain your scarf will be perfectly symmetrical—and therefore hang properly—by drawing out two threads *(page 74)*. This will guarantee that the grain of the fabric will be absolutely straight. Then, using a T square *(diagram, opposite)*, draw lines at right angles to the two drawn threads.

Finish the edges with a rolled-hem stitch *(page 44)*, turning the corners as shown opposite. Use lightweight fabrics, avoiding diagonal weaves, and thread of a slightly darker color than the scarf—silk thread for silk material and cotton for other fabrics.

# Edges that make a scarf look right

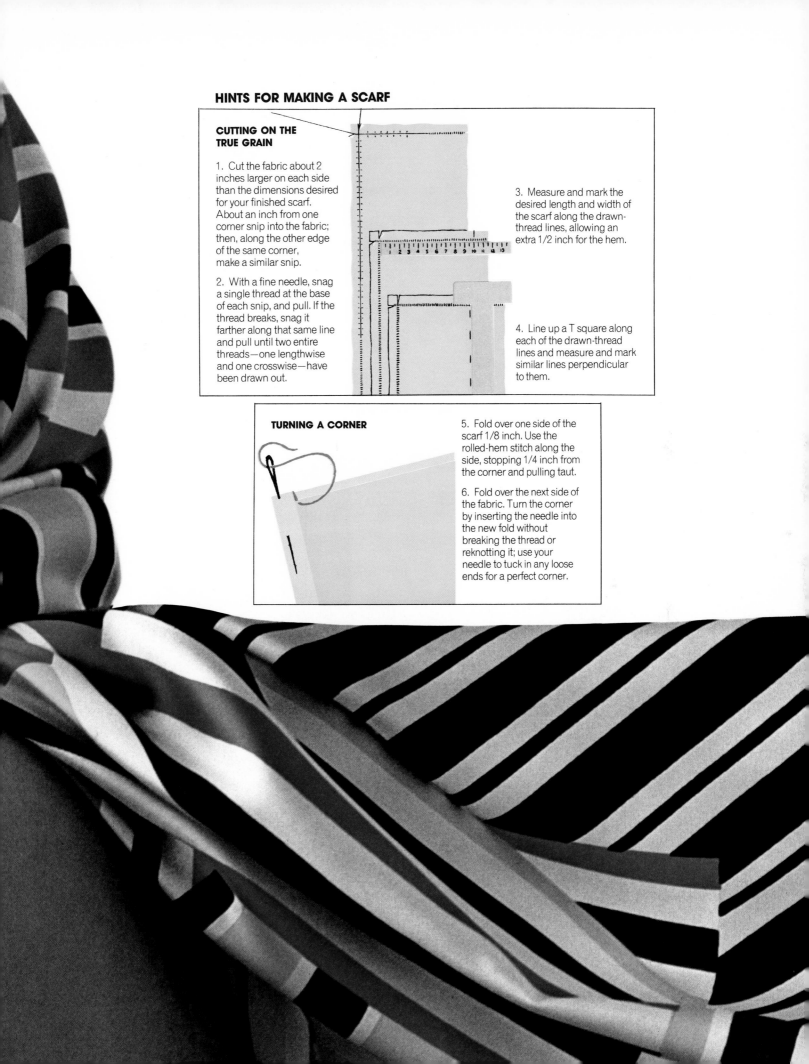

## HINTS FOR MAKING A SCARF

### CUTTING ON THE TRUE GRAIN

1. Cut the fabric about 2 inches larger on each side than the dimensions desired for your finished scarf. About an inch from one corner snip into the fabric; then, along the other edge of the same corner, make a similar snip.

2. With a fine needle, snag a single thread at the base of each snip, and pull. If the thread breaks, snag it farther along that same line and pull until two entire threads—one lengthwise and one crosswise—have been drawn out.

3. Measure and mark the desired length and width of the scarf along the drawn-thread lines, allowing an extra 1/2 inch for the hem.

4. Line up a T square along each of the drawn-thread lines and measure and mark similar lines perpendicular to them.

### TURNING A CORNER

5. Fold over one side of the scarf 1/8 inch. Use the rolled-hem stitch along the side, stopping 1/4 inch from the corner and pulling taut.

6. Fold over the next side of the fabric. Turn the corner by inserting the needle into the new fold without breaking the thread or reknotting it; use your needle to tuck in any loose ends for a perfect corner.

5

EMBROIDERY

From behind glass at the Hermitage museum in Leningrad, a mustached barbarian stares out with dark, intense eyes. Some identify him as a Hun. Others are less specific, but he is clearly a rough-and-ready nomad of some Eastern tribe.

He is also one of the world's oldest surviving works of embroidery, and a surprising, stirring introduction to that ancient craft. This rakish character's 6-by-12-inch

# PICTURES PAINTED WITH A NEEDLE

portrait, discovered in Noin-Ula, Mongolian People's Republic, was embroidered on wool rep 2,000 years ago.

Embroidery, which is the embellishment of fabric with a design in thread, ranks as something more than a craft. Generally, other needlecrafts originate in the need for clothing and shelter. Embroidery springs from the desire to record or decorate. It has been called painting with a needle.

As an art, embroidery historically has

been concerned with serious men and events, and with the most important symbols of ancient cultures. The emperors of China wore rich blue silk robes, high at the neck and fastening down the side, which were embroidered with 12 special ornaments, among them the sun with a three-legged bird, the moon with a hare, and mountains under stars. But the most striking imperial symbol was the five-toed dragon (common dragons had only four toes).

Royal vestments of this type, despite their range of design, were all embroidered in variations of a single stitch. The emperors' embroideries use the satin stitch, one of the small but versatile repertory of classic types of stitches employed all over the world.

Idest of the classic stitches is probably the chain stitch, which Egyptian mariners embroidered on their sails from the earliest times. The decorated sails have not survived intact, but hieroglyphics and mural carvings testify to their appearance.

The Orient was the birthplace of embroidery, and remains the art's natural home to this day. One reason might be that Oriental clothing, whether the high-necked, tailored Chinese style or the folded-and-draped, untailored Indian mode, admits of only subtle variations in line and form. So the decoration of the fabric is the garment's most important individual distinction.

For many centuries the most accomplished embroiderers in the world have probably been the Muslims of Benares. Benares (now officially called Varanasi) is the holy city on the river Ganges in India. Every sari displayed in the teeming arcades of Benares for the admiration of wealthy pilgrims is an identically sized length of silk. But the variation in border designs, embroidered in twisted thread of silver and gold, in Paisleys and peacocks, is endless. The motifs originate in Hindu mythology.

The art of embroidery was carried from the East to Europe in the course of two historic developments seemingly far removed from art and the crafts: the Islamic conquest of Spain, and the beginning of the spice trade between Europe and the Orient.

In the early Middle Ages, Europe wove little but plain cloth. The craft of weaving or printing patterned cloth, brocades and the like remained chiefly an Oriental trade. But when embroidery was imported, Europeans could study it and apply the lessons to their own work, using native worsted yarns to create designs on linen fabric.

The preeminent midpoint between the Orient and Europe, where embroidery was transmitted along with a host of other goods and skills, was Constantinople, capital of the Eastern Empire of Byzantium. There traders from Europe were introduced to the incredibly elaborate embroidery of Byzantine Church vestments.

Among the most important of these vestments were tunics with short, wide sleeves, called *sacci*. Such tunics were worn by the church patriarchs, according to tradition in remembrance of the purple cloak thrown around Christ's shoulders in mockery by his scourgers before the Crucifixion.

One of these *sacci,* embroidered in Constantinople in the 14th Century, is preserved today in the Vatican Treasury. It was embroidered in gold and silver threads, on a background of dark blue silk. On the back the embroidery shows Christ leading three of his Apostles up to a mountain crest, where he appears transfigured before them in his divinity. The front of the vestment depicts Christ's Second Coming, at the end of the world, to call his chosen to Paradise.

The *sacci* and the other embroideries of Constantinople epitomize, paradoxically, both deep religious fervor and sumptuous materialism. But neither the faith nor the luxury of the Byzantine Empire rested on a stable base of power. War succeeded war, until in 1453 Constantinople fell into the hands of the Turks, and no longer could the once-glittering capital serve as a funnel pouring Oriental ideas into Europe.

By then Europeans themselves had already begun to embroider real works of art, in which they portrayed their kings and saints, commemorated battles and miracles, and recorded their history. The most famous example is the Bayeux Tapestry *(right)*. (It is, in fact, not a tapestry at all—that is, not a woven wall hanging or floor covering into which designs are worked on the loom—but rather embroidery on linen.)

The work has hardly faded after nine centuries, probably because the worsted threads were dyed in the fleece, before they were spun. The whole masterpiece is only 20 inches high, but it extends more than 230 feet in length. This long band tells the story of the 11th Century Norman invasion, the Battle of Hastings and the conquest of England in a flow of dramatic pictures, complete with running captions in medieval Latin that serve to identify the characters and to describe the action.

The great episodes of William of Normandy's conquest are all there, but human details are also carefully recorded. For example, on the Norman beach, before William's marines wade out to their waiting transport ships, they pull off their stockings—a realistic touch preserved in the embroidery. Amid the fighting and carnage after William's invaders land in England, one soldier apparently taken for dead and stripped of his valuable armor is still alive—and at pains to cover his nakedness. All this sweep of action and intimacy of detail, a panorama with a cast of 626 men, women and children, 762 animals, with 41 ships and boats, is executed in basic stem stitch and filling stitches.

Continental and English embroidery not only depicted and recorded battles, it played a role in them. Fighting men distinguished friend from foe by the embroidered insignia on the cloth jackets worn over suits of armor or chain mail. The oldest surviving example is the overjacket of Edward the Black Prince (1330-1376), which is preserved at Canterbury Cathedral.

Just as distinguishing insignia were embroidered on fighting men's garments, it became the practice to repeat them on the trappings of soldiers' horses. And there is also evidence that the same crests and devices may have been emblazoned on the sails of medieval fleets. The insignia that were embroidered for historic warriors, mounted or seagoing, retain more peaceful significance even to the present day as family coats of arms.

Matching the distinction of the embroidery worn by men of war was that worn by priests celebrating the Mass. Embroidery was used to decorate Europe's abbeys and priories, for vestments and for altar trappings. Indeed the Bayeux Tapestry itself, although depicting secular conflict, was embroidered to adorn a Norman cathedral. In commissioning rich embroideries, the Roman Church was emulating the Byzantine. Though Western vestments seldom attained the splendor of ones imported from Constantinople, ecclesiastical patronage did advance the craft of embroidery in the West. Clerical embroidery is still the labor of some convents in Europe and America.

Historically, with the rise of the middle class and the leveling influence of democracy, embroidery moved from the throne room and abbey into the parlor and bedroom. There was an inevitable coarsening of theme and tone. But although much embroidery today is banal, or merely pretty, the tradition of embroidery with serious themes does persist. It is preserved not by the great institutions like Church and nobility, but by individuals expressing personal creativity (as, for example, in the dove of peace sometimes seen embroidered on students' jeans in the turbulent years of the 1960s).

There is a continuing interest in the copying of the old masterpiece embroideries.

Inscribed with Latin captions, the Bayeux Tapestry details high points of the Norman Conquest of England in 1066 in one of the most famous examples of crewel embroidery ever made. The segment above reads: "Here are the horses leaving the ships—and here the soldiers." The entire work was executed with only two types of stitches: an outline stitch for fine work, such as faces, and a filler stitch, which was employed to add texture.

Some of them are now reproduced stitch-by-stitch, exactly as they were originally made, but modern variations are increasingly introduced. And, most promising for the future, there is now a lively experimentation with abstract and nonrepresentational art in embroidery—an effort to do in needlecraft what has been created in painting by 20th Century artists ranging from Pablo Picasso to Jackson Pollock.

# Homespun themes of American needlework

American embroidery has always been marked by the homespun look rather than by cultural or historical significance. From Colonial times onward, when women did embroidery they portrayed simple images from the countryside around them.

The designs at right, dating from the 18th and 19th Centuries, are typical. They were embroidered on bedspreads, wing chairs and carpets. But as much as they differed in tone and character from the great Oriental and European embroidery, they were still worked in variations of the virtually universal basic repertory of stitches. The lovebirds, for instance, are embroidered with filling and stem stitches long familiar in Europe.

sunburst

a buck and a fruit tree

lovebirds

a country couple

Simple everyday themes like those above characterized American embroidery in the 18th and 19th Centuries.

oment and
techniques
for hand
embroidery

Some embroidery is done freehand, as in regular sewing, but many stitches are best worked with the material stretched taut on a hoop. This frame, an 8-inch round double ring with a thumbscrew to tighten it, should be made of wood because it grips the material tightly.

When embroidery is worked on a hoop, the material should be adjusted so that the crosswise and lengthwise threads are at right angles (right). At the end of each day's work, remove the hoop to prevent it from marking the material.

Embroidery needles and threads must be chosen to relate properly to each other as well as to the material to be worked on. The needle must be slightly larger than the thread to permit the thread to go through the material without fraying. But if the needle is too large for the thread and the weave of the material, it could make unsightly holes as you embroider. A guide to a basic selection of threads, needles and materials and hints on how to use them are given on the following pages.

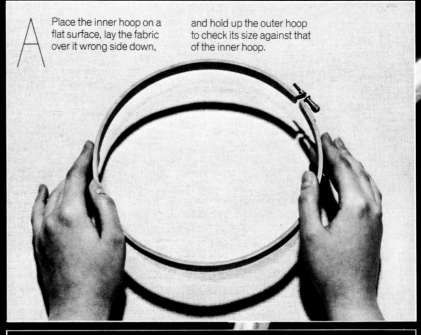

A Place the inner hoop on a flat surface, lay the fabric over it wrong side down, and hold up the outer hoop to check its size against that of the inner hoop.

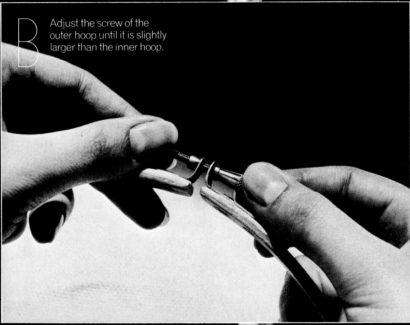

B Adjust the screw of the outer hoop until it is slightly larger than the inner hoop.

C Fit the outer hoop just over the edge of the inner hoop, making sure that it is even all around.

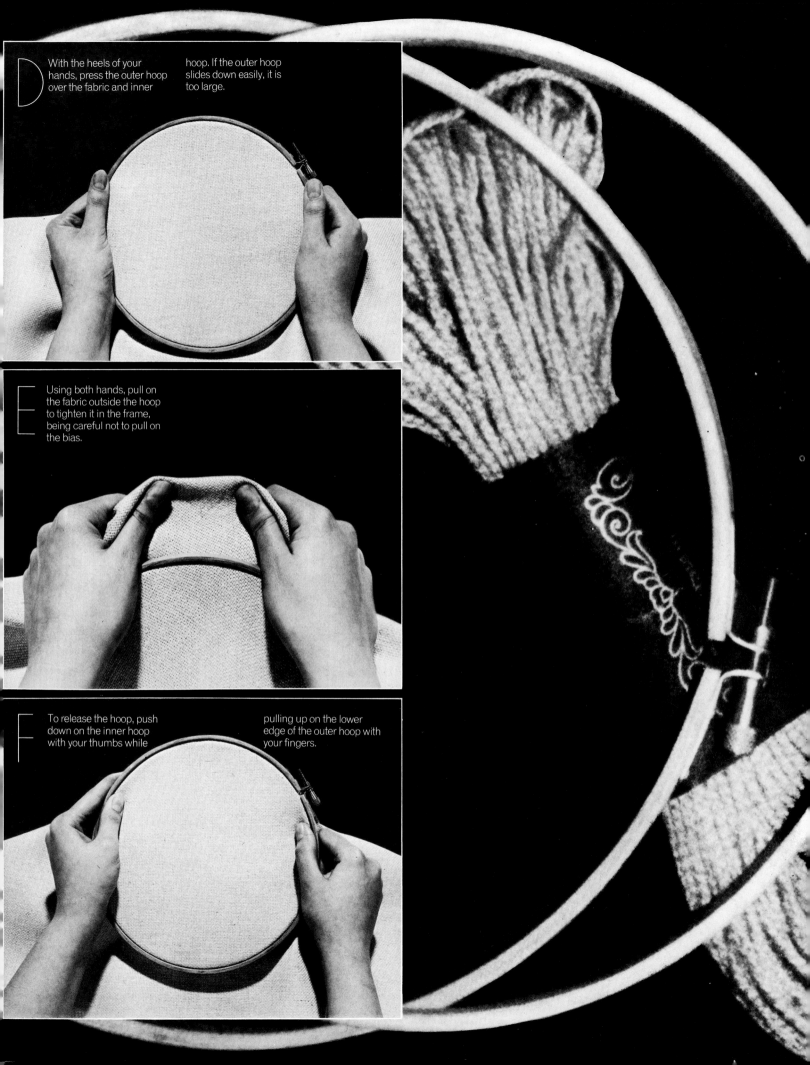

**D** With the heels of your hands, press the outer hoop over the fabric and inner hoop. If the outer hoop slides down easily, it is too large.

**E** Using both hands, pull on the fabric outside the hoop to tighten it in the frame, being careful not to pull on the bias.

**F** To release the hoop, push down on the inner hoop with your thumbs while pulling up on the lower edge of the outer hoop with your fingers.

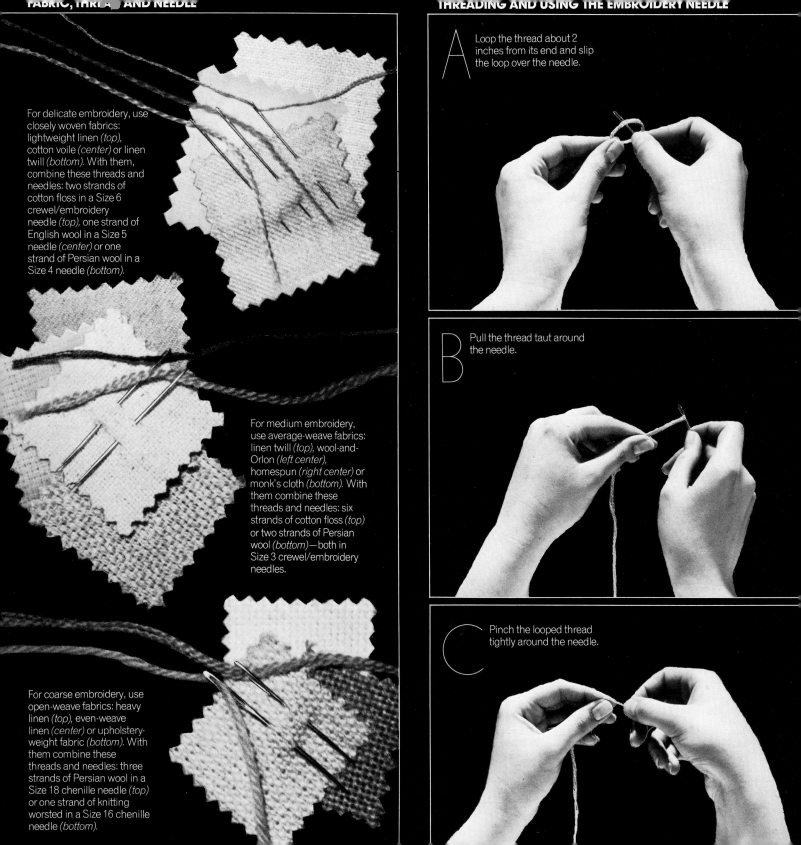

For delicate embroidery, use closely woven fabrics: lightweight linen *(top)*, cotton voile *(center)* or linen twill *(bottom)*. With them, combine these threads and needles: two strands of cotton floss in a Size 6 crewel/embroidery needle *(top)*, one strand of English wool in a Size 5 needle *(center)* or one strand of Persian wool in a Size 4 needle *(bottom)*.

For medium embroidery, use average-weave fabrics: linen twill *(top)*, wool-and-Orlon *(left center)*, homespun *(right center)* or monk's cloth *(bottom)*. With them combine these threads and needles: six strands of cotton floss *(top)* or two strands of Persian wool *(bottom)*—both in Size 3 crewel/embroidery needles.

For coarse embroidery, use open-weave fabrics: heavy linen *(top)*, even-weave linen *(center)* or upholstery-weight fabric *(bottom)*. With them combine these threads and needles: three strands of Persian wool in a Size 18 chenille needle *(top)* or one strand of knitting worsted in a Size 16 chenille needle *(bottom)*.

A Loop the thread about 2 inches from its end and slip the loop over the needle.

B Pull the thread taut around the needle.

C Pinch the looped thread tightly around the needle.

D Ease the needle out from the loop of thread.

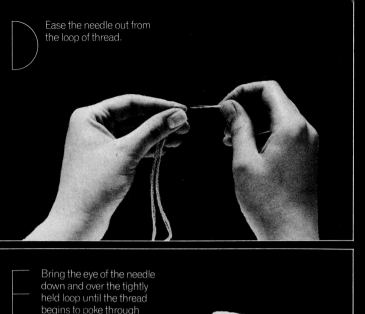

E Bring the eye of the needle down and over the tightly held loop until the thread begins to poke through the eye.

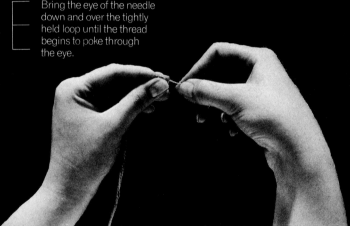

F Pull the loop of thread through the eye.

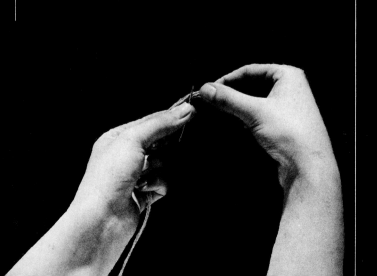

G Jab the needle straight up from the underside of the hoop.

H Pull it up through the fabric, then jab straight back down in whatever stitch you are using *(pages 162-163)*; use the bottom of the thimble to push the needle through.

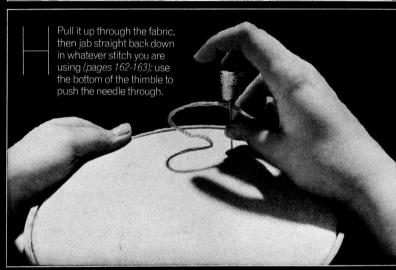

## RIPPING OUT

On the top of the hoop, slide one tip of a pointed scissors under the stitches to be removed; then snip them. Pull the threads out from the other side.

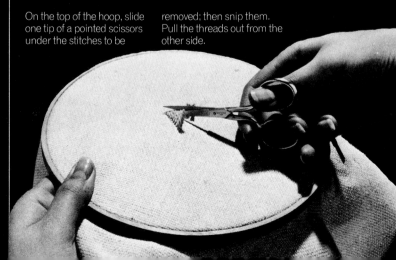

# A guide to the basic stitches

Even the most intricate embroidery designs can be created from a few basic types of stitches, all easily executed. Most stitches are best made with the material held securely in a standard 8-inch hoop, which prevents puckering or slipping. The hoop stitches, shown at right and opposite, are made with a stabbing motion: the needle darts vertically up and down through the taut material to produce precise patterns.

Some embroidery stitches require a hand motion more like that used in sewing: the needle must move almost horizontally, parallel to the material. These stitches, shown on pages 164-165, are done more easily and faster if the material is held loosely in the hand, not fixed in a hoop. While the tension on the material depends on the stitch, the tension on the stitch itself should always be uniform—neither so loose that the stitches are uneven nor so tight as to pucker the material.

**THE STRAIGHT STITCH:** For open or solid texture

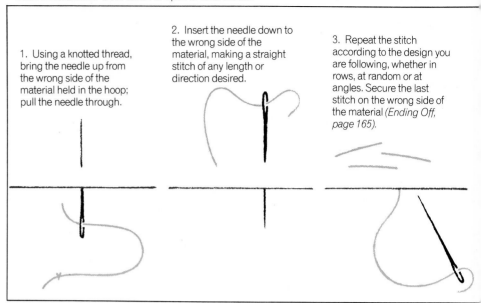

1. Using a knotted thread, bring the needle up from the wrong side of the material held in the hoop; pull the needle through.

2. Insert the needle down to the wrong side of the material, making a straight stitch of any length or direction desired.

3. Repeat the stitch according to the design you are following, whether in rows, at random or at angles. Secure the last stitch on the wrong side of the material (Ending Off, page 165).

**THE SATIN STITCH:** To fill small areas smoothly

1. Using a knotted thread, bring the needle up from the wrong side of the material held in the hoop and pull it through at a point on the left side of the design. This point should be 1/3 to 1/2 way up the design, depending on the angle desired.

2. Insert the needle down to the wrong side of the material at a point diagonally across the design, 1/3 to 1/2 way from the top, depending on the angle desired.

3. Bring the needle straight up from the wrong side of the material just above the hole made in Step 1, and insert it straight down just above the hole made in Step 2.

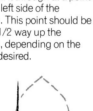

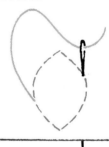

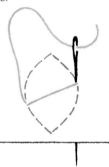

4. Continue to make long straight stitches diagonally across the design until the top half is filled. End at the tip by inserting the needle down to the wrong side of the material.

5. Bring the needle from the wrong side of the material just below the hole made in Step 1, and continue to make parallel diagonal stitches until the remaining area is filled. Secure the last stitch on the wrong side of the material (Ending Off, page 165).

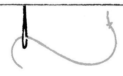

## THE FRENCH KNOT: To make flower centers or textural effects

1. Using a knotted thread, bring the needle up from the wrong side of the material held in the hoop; pull the needle through.

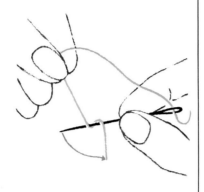

2. Put down the hoop and loop the thread once around the needle.

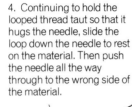

3. Holding the looped thread taut with one hand, push the needle tip into or just next to the hole from which it emerged in Step 1.

4. Continuing to hold the looped thread taut so that it hugs the needle, slide the loop down the needle to rest on the material. Then push the needle all the way through to the wrong side of the material.

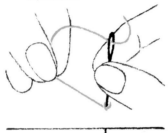

5. Bring the needle up from the wrong side of the material at a point that suits your design, and repeat Steps 2-4. Secure the last stitch on the wrong side of the material (*Ending Off, page 165*).

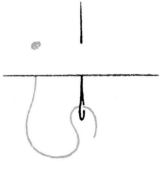

## THE SQUARED FILLING STITCH: For stylized petals or leaves

1. Using a knotted thread, bring the needle up from the wrong side of the material held in the hoop in the middle of one edge of the design; pull the needle through.

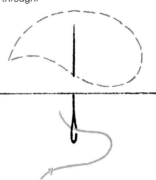

2. Insert the needle down to the wrong side of the material at a point directly across the design, as if for a straight stitch.

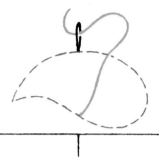

3. Bring the needle up from the wrong side of the material to the left of the hole made in Step 2. The distance separating the stitches is arbitrary, but should be consistent.

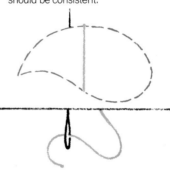

4. Continue to make parallel stitches, starting each on the same side of the design as the previous stitch ended. When the left-hand area is complete, bring the needle up to the right of the center stitch made in Steps 1 and 2, and complete the right-hand area.

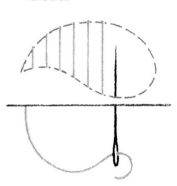

5. Bring the needle up from the wrong side of the material at the center of the far right end of the design, and insert the needle across the design to the far left end, making sure that the thread runs at a right angle to the stitches made in Steps 1-4. Complete the right-left stitches in the same fashion as the stitches in Steps 1-4.

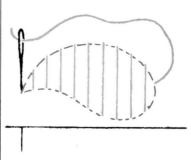

6. To lock the stitches at each crossing point, start in the upper right-hand corner. Bring the needle up near the point where the two stitches intersect. Insert the needle diagonally over the intersection to make a small diagonal locking stitch. Continue the locking stitches—working along one long right-left stitch at a time—until all intersections have been covered. Secure the last stitch on the wrong side of the material (*Ending Off, page 165*).

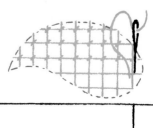

## THE STEM STITCH: For outlining and filling in designs

1. Using a knotted thread, bring the needle up from the wrong side of the material; pull it through.

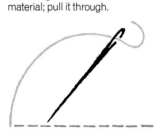

2. With your left thumb, hold the thread away from the needle. Point the needle to the left, but take a stitch to the right of the hole made in Step 1. The needle should emerge midway between the beginning of this stitch and the hole made in Step 1.

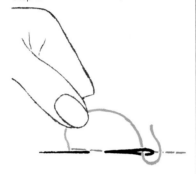

3. Pull the thread through taut, but not tight enough to pucker the material.

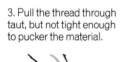
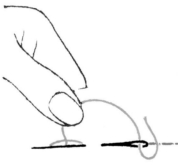

4. Take another stitch to the right the same size as that made in Step 2.

5. Continue making similar stitches along the design, and secure the last stitch on the wrong side of the fabric (Ending Off, opposite).

**IF YOU ARE LEFT-HANDED...**
Follow Steps 1-5, but point the needle to the right as below. Hold the thread away from the needle with your right thumb. Proceed from right to left.

## THE CROSS STITCH: For outlining and filling open areas

1. Using a knotted thread, bring the needle up from the wrong side of the material at the lower right corner of the design; pull it through.

2. Insert the needle down to the wrong side at a point diagonally across from and to the upper left of the hole made in Step 1. Bring the needle out as shown.

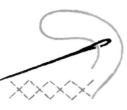

3. Continue to make stitches as described in Steps 1 and 2 to produce a diagonal pattern in a row.

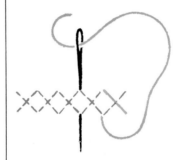

4. At the end of the row, reverse direction to go back over the row, inserting the needle through each previously made hole to form an X. Secure the last of these cross stitches on the wrong side of the material (Ending Off, opposite).

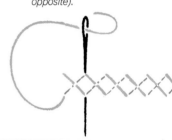

## THE CHAIN STITCH: To emphasize outlines and fill in broad areas

1. Using a knotted thread, bring the needle up from the wrong side of the material. Pull it through and loop the thread from the left to the right.

2. Hold the thread in a loop of the desired size with the thumb of your free hand, and insert the needle back in the hole from which it emerged in Step 1. Bring the needle out again directly below, keeping the loop under the needle point. Pull the needle through.

3. Again loop the thread from the left to the right and hold it down with your thumb. Insert the needle back in the hole from which it emerged in Step 2, and bring it out through the loop.

4. Complete the design. Anchor the last stitch by inserting the needle below its loop; secure on the wrong side of the material (Ending Off, opposite).

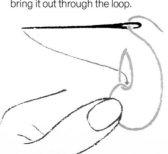

## THE LAZY DAISY STITCH: For outlining flower petals

1. Using a knotted thread, bring the needle up from the wrong side of the material at the pointed base of a petal. Pull the needle through and loop the thread from left to right.

2. Insert the needle back in the hole from which it emerged in Step 1 and bring it out again at the outermost curve of the petal, keeping the looped thread under the needle.

3. Pull the needle through, thus tightening the loop to the desired size and flattening it against the material.

4. Insert the needle below the loop to lock the loop in place, then bring the needle up again at the pointed base of the next petal to the left. Complete all of the petals. Secure the thread on the wrong side of the material *(Ending Off, lower right)*.

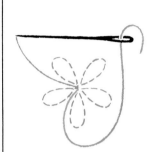

## THE FISHBONE STITCH: To fill in a leaf or petal

1. Using a knotted thread, bring the needle up from the wrong side of the material at the upper tip of the design; pull it through.

2. Insert the needle at a point about 1/4 of the way down the center of the design. Bring the needle up from the wrong side of the material at a point to the left and slightly below the hole made in Step. 1. Pull the thread taut, but do not pucker the material.

3. Loop the thread from left to right and insert the needle to the right of the stitch made in Step 1. Bring the needle out through the bottom hole of the center stitch as shown, keeping the looped thread under the needle.

## ENDING OFF

On the wrong side of the material, slide the needle underneath the nearest three or four consecutive stitches and pull it through. Snip off the excess thread.

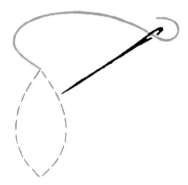

4. Pull the thread toward you and down, thus tightening the loop and flattening it against the material.

5. Insert the needle just below the loop, locking it in place, and bring the needle out to the left and slightly below the hole made in Step 2.

6. Complete the design by repeating Steps 2-5, finishing with a stitch that locks the base of the final loop. Secure the thread on the wrong side of the material *(Ending Off, at right)*.

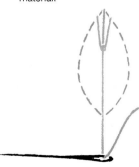

# Preparing the designs

Before you choose a design to embroider, consider the kind of project you want to do. If you are ambitious enough for a long, challenging task —perhaps hundreds of fine satin stitches—then choose a detailed, shaded design, such as a landscape from a photograph or painting. If, on the contrary, you want to dash off something informal in one day—in heavy thread on coarse fabric—then choose an open, simple design with strong lines, such as a sunflower, a fish or a cartoon character. Posters, fabrics, wallpaper and even children's coloring books are all good sources for such motifs.

It is easiest to embroider the same size as the original design. But you can enlarge or reduce the design by freehand drawing if first you break it into simple blocks with the grid system shown opposite.

To draw and transfer, clear off a hard, flat surface—say, the kitchen table. Get some dressmaker's carbon paper from your sewing supplies, plus these stationery items: drawing paper, a ruler, tracing paper, masking tape, a fine-point felt-tip pen and a pencil.

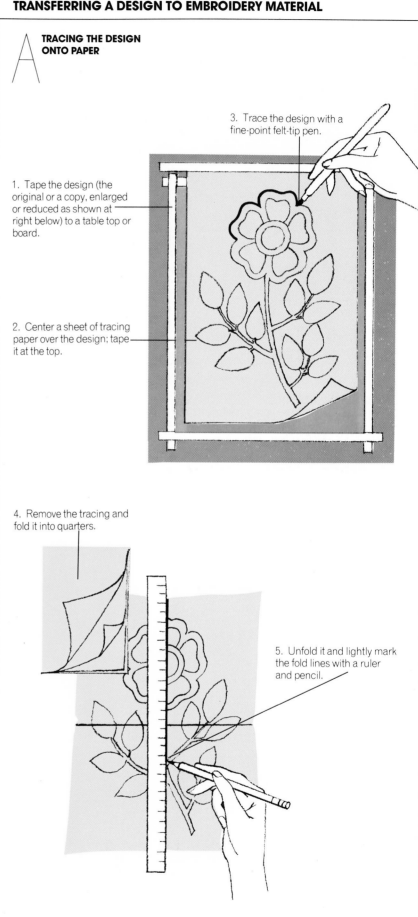

## A TRACING THE DESIGN ONTO PAPER

3. Trace the design with a fine-point felt-tip pen.

1. Tape the design (the original or a copy, enlarged or reduced as shown at right below) to a table top or board.

2. Center a sheet of tracing paper over the design; tape it at the top.

4. Remove the tracing and fold it into quarters.

5. Unfold it and lightly mark the fold lines with a ruler and pencil.

## B TRANSFERRING THE DESIGN TO FABRIC

6. Fold the embroidery fabric into quarters. Crease the fold lines with your fingers or an iron.

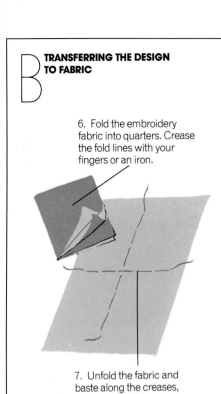

7. Unfold the fabric and baste along the creases, taking long stitches on the visible side for easily followed guide lines.

8. Tape the fabric, wrong side down, to the work surface.

10. Insert dressmaker's carbon paper, carbon side down, between the tracing and fabric. (If the carbon paper is smaller than the design, move it as you work.)

9. Lay the paper tracing over the fabric, aligning its fold lines with the basting on the fabric. Tape the tracing along the top. At the bottom corners, put tabs of tape that can easily be lifted as you work.

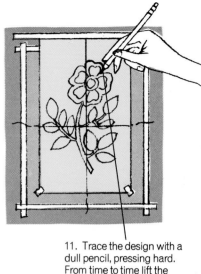

11. Trace the design with a dull pencil, pressing hard. From time to time lift the paper and check that the design is coming through distinctly on the fabric. Avoid smudging by working from top to bottom. Remove the fabric and baste around the edges to prevent fraying.

---

## ENLARGING OR REDUCING A DESIGN

### A PREPARING THE ORIGINAL

1. Trace the design onto a square piece of paper—it must be square to preserve proportions in rectangular designs—and fold the tracing, across its width, then across its length. Unfold and fold in quarters and eighths across its width and length to make a grid with eight squares on each side.

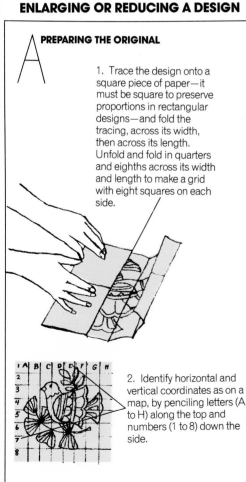

2. Identify horizontal and vertical coordinates as on a map, by penciling letters (A to H) along the top and numbers (1 to 8) down the side.

### B PREPARING DRAWING PAPER

3. Cut a sheet of drawing paper into a square approximating the size you want the embroidery to be.

4. Fold it just as you folded the original, and pencil in the same coordinates.

### C RENDERING THE ENLARGED OR REDUCED DESIGN

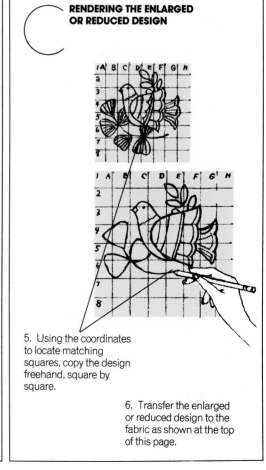

5. Using the coordinates to locate matching squares, copy the design freehand, square by square.

6. Transfer the enlarged or reduced design to the fabric as shown at the top of this page.

# Adaptable decoration for a border

The border pattern shown here, a repeated leaf, can be embroidered on almost anything from an eyeglass case to a vest *(opposite).* Different effects can be obtained by varying material, thread, stitches or even the number of petals sprouting from each stem. The delicate sample at right was made with a satin stitch and cotton floss on felt; the vest was rendered in wool on homespun, using a fishbone stitch and more abundant petals for a textured, rugged effect.

The secret of keeping the texture of this border raised is in proper pressing. After you take it off the hoop, press on the wrong side with a dry iron and a wet cloth over four layers of soft dry toweling.

## INSTRUCTIONS FOR THE LEAF DESIGN

To trace and enlarge the design, outlined on a grid above, follow the basic instructions on pages 166-167. If you are making the vest, first lay out your pattern pieces on the fabric so that the fabric extends at least 2 inches beyond the edges of the pattern pieces. This leaves enough fabric for a hoop to clasp. Transfer the design to the appropriate areas of the fabric and complete the embroidery before you cut out the individual pattern pieces.

For fabric, thread and needle suggestions, see page 160. The vest shown here is made of medium-weight homespun and embroidered with three strands of Persian wool in a Size 18 chenille needle.

All the embroidery stitches used here are demonstrated on pages 162-165. Embroider the outermost semicircle first, then the inner semicircles, all in satin stitches. Start each semicircle in the middle of its arc and work first to one side to complete a quarter-circle and then to the other side.

Next, make the stem in stem stitches. The leaves can be satin stitches or fishbone stitches.

After completing and pressing the embroidery, cut out the vest pieces and sew them according to pattern instructions.

# Flamboyant design for display

This design of a bloom on a radiating field is intended to show off the embroiderer's skill—it does not have to decorate a useful object but can stand on its own as an attractive display, framed like a painting or hung like a tapestry.

The underlying fabric will not be seen, but should be chosen with care—the coarser the fabric the bolder the finished design will be. The completed embroidery will show off to best advantage if it is at least 14 inches square. To hang the square, attach metal rings at the top and curtain weights at the bottom.

A hint for embroidering this or similar designs: do not jump from one area to another with the same color, extending the thread across the back of the work to each place where the color is used. Carrying the thread more than an inch will cause puckers. It is better to take the trouble to end off and begin anew.

## DIRECTIONS FOR THE SQUARE

To trace and enlarge the design outlined on a grid *(above),* follow the basic instructions on pages 166-167.

For a choice of fabric, thread and needles, see the chart on page 160. The square shown here varies from the chart's guidelines in order to achieve a particularly rough texture; it is made of medium-weight wool and Orlon and embroidered with three strands of Persian wool and a Size 18 chenille needle except for the pollen dots, which are done with six strands of Persian wool and a Size 16 chenille needle.

All the embroidery stitches used here are demonstrated on pages 162-165. Start by embroidering the background in satin stitches. Embroider the flower stem in two layers: stem stitches covered by slanting satin stitches. Embroider the leaf surfaces in satin stitches. Then add the outlines to indicate leaf sections with stem stitches. Embroider the surfaces of the flower petals in satin stitches. Then add fishbone stitches, spaced about 1/4 inch apart, to the foreground petals. Outline all petals with stem stitches. Cover the outline of the foreground petals with satin stitches.

Embroider the pollen with French knots, dotted at the center of the flower.

Press the finished work as described on page 168.

Granny squares were once the ingredients of an heirloom bedspread crocheted by somebody's real grandmother; a woman knitting long signaled the coming of a "blessed event" in Grade B movies. No more. Granny's square has been altered and haltered, pieced together into evening skirts and incorporated into bikinis. The women knitting on their way to work on the bus are not making boo-

# HIGH STYLE IN FISHERMEN'S KNOTS

ties; they are turning out boutique fashions. Just looking around you, you can see that both crafts have undergone revolutions.

Knitting began for strictly utilitarian purposes more than 2,000 years ago, probably in the Middle East. A pair of socks similar to the one overleaf was discovered in a Fourth Century B.C. Egyptian tomb.

Exactly how knitting reached Europe is unknown. Arab traders may have transported knitted pieces to Spain. However knitting was introduced, it soon flourished, particularly in British fishing villages.

That fisherfolk took to knitting is scarcely surprising. Knitting, basically, is knot making—pulling threads through loops—as in the making of a fisherman's net. And it produced garments well suited to the fisherman's life. Unrefined sheep's wool—wool from which water-resisting natural oils had not been removed—made warm sweaters adapted to a sea-swept homeland.

Among some fishing communities the practical craft of knitting gave rise to a true folk art. In the remote Aran Islands off Galway Bay, Ireland, for example, knitters did more than simply make weatherproof sweaters; taking their design inspirations from nature and legend, they created a repertoire of beautiful and intricate patterns that have been prized—and imitated—down to modern times. The Aran pattern names read like the titles of poems: Wheat Ear, Moss, Tree of Life, Scattered Oats, Bird Cage, Twisted Tree, Bridey's Braid. Patterns identified villages and families—and thus even drowned men washed ashore.

While the art of the humble sweater flourished among isolated fishermen, knitwear was serving the needs of the upper classes as well. Even Charles I of England found knitwear useful against the cold; en route to his execution on a January day, he called for a knitted shirt, lest he shiver and be thought afraid of the ax.

For generations, knitting remained the exclusive province of males. Women spun fibers into yarns; men knitted yarns into garments. But as time went on, increasing numbers of women learned the art. In the mid-18th Century, the division of labor between spinners and knitters broke down completely under the impact of a new technology—the hand-operated knitting machine. Men who had once knitted by hand now knitted on machines. Later, women were to tend power-driven knitting machines in infamous sweatshops, but in the interim they took up the hand knitting abandoned by men. Hand knitting remained for so many years in women's fingers that the craft took on exclusively feminine associations, some of them unflattering.

One woman who gave female knitters a bad name—at least in the eyes of the upper classes—was a fictional character: the ruthless Madame Defarge of *A Tale of Two Cities,* Charles Dickens' novel about the French Revolution. In the book, Madame Defarge knits incessantly as royal France hurtles toward revolution, and there is something almost sinister in the continuous click of her needles. Into the best and the worst of her knitwork she encodes the names of aristocrats who have been particularly harsh to peasants and commoners. When the king is overthrown and the guillotine is raised in the Place de la Révolution in Paris, the aristocrats neatly tallied in Mme. Defarge's knitting are brought to kneel beneath the blade.

The great social and political upheavals of the 18th Century had a more direct—and nonfictional—effect on the craft of knitting. Styles in dress changed drastically. Previously, commoners had been forbidden to wear such items of aristocratic apparel as buckled shoes, hose and knee breeches; conversely, no 18th Century aristocrat would have been seen in public in, say, long trousers. Now, clothing became more casual as members of the gentry, trying to dissociate themselves from opulence, began adopting clothes once worn only by the lower classes. This trend accelerated as the Industrial Revolution transformed the Western world in the 19th Century, and even such workingmen's clothing as the once-disdained sweater became modish.

Because of its resistance to dampness and cold, the fisherman's sweater had become the unofficial uniform of the European workingman. In the 1890s it was taken up by college students and athletes. Before long the sweater was stylish, for women as well as men. In the 1940s more than one Hollywood actress took the "sweater-girl" route to stardom, but it was not until after World War II that the humble sweater was transformed into a total wardrobe. Knitted long, it became a dress; longer, a coat; and even longer, an evening dress. In many cases, designers borrowed the intricate patterns of the fishermen of Aran, still knitting away in their remote islands as if encapsulated by time.

As the status of knitwear rose, more and more women found that the equipment needed for producing it was minimal and the techniques simple to learn *(pages 182-185)*. They took up the craft to make not only sweaters but ponchos, tank tops, caps, bags and bathing suits. Dresses began appearing that seemed to be simultaneously disappearing—knitwear made of little more than netting, its startlingly large interstices between knit and purl produced by fat needles some 3 inches in circumference.

If the oversized needles sometimes led to the ridiculous in knitting, larger hooks revolutionized crocheting. The cnange happened suddenly, during the 1950s. And crocheting, after centuries of being associated with lace doilies and antimacassars, acquired a new image.

The origins of crocheting are unknown, but it, unlike utilitarian knitting, evolved as a strictly ornamental art. For hundreds of years it was practiced mainly by European nuns, who made vestments and decorations for the Church. The patterns and stitches changed little over the centuries. Then, at the beginning of the 19th Century, a Frenchwoman, Mlle. Eleanore Riego de la Blanchardière, succeeded in using a crochet hook to imitate Venetian needlepoint lace, which was made by sewing a design onto a piece of paper. Mlle. Riego de la Blanchardière's patterns were seized upon by English ladies, including Queen Victoria herself. This development helped popularize crocheting—and oddly enough the growth of interest in crocheting, like that in knitting, owed something to the Irish.

In the 1840s Ireland was devastated by potato famine. As a charitable gesture, some English crochet fanciers offered to teach Mlle. Riego de la Blanchardière's patterns to Irishwomen in an effort to help the impoverished Irish earn money. The Irishwomen soon added new ideas of their own. Irish nuns in particular designed extraordinarily beautiful patterns that helped to establish delicate crocheting as a world-famous Irish specialty.

Even though the Irish work won renown, crocheting remained largely a pastime for genteel matrons. But after World War II, when someone discovered it was possible to crochet with heavier yarn and a larger hook, crocheting appealed to a much broader following. The heavier yarn and larger hook, used in conjunction with simple stitches *(pages 186-188)* made the work go much faster than it could with traditional equipment. Fashion designers became interested in crocheted hats and scarves, ponchos and small vests. Sales of crochet yarn and hooks increased so rapidly that in less than a decade crocheting began to rival knitting in popularity. Today little tops, dresses, even sweaters come tumbling off the crochet hook, and a few designers have turned dear old Granny's afghan squares into blazing works of art.

Although knitting and crocheting came out of opposite backgrounds, they now lend themselves to high fashion without reducing their usefulness, as demonstrated, for example, by the items on pages 192-195. Knitting and crocheting remain rooted in the lowly knot with which the men of Aran were so familiar, and many of the oldest techniques—such as the hand spinning and dyeing of yarns—enjoy new popularity among the most ardent practitioners of these ancient crafts.

  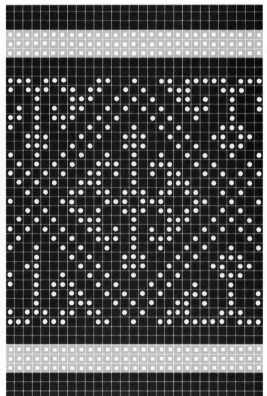

The sock above, dating from the 12th Century and ragged with age, suggests that knitting was not only a domestic art but an international trade. The sock was discovered in Egypt but is believed to have been imported from India. The evidence is in the pattern *(close-up, center, and diagram, right),* which resembles Indian designs. The heel was the last part of the sock knitted, so it could be replaced easily if it wore out.

# Elements of knitting and crocheting

Knitting and crocheting are techniques for creating fabric by knotting strands of yarn into loops. All knitting begins with a starter row of stitches *(page 182)* and is based on the knit stitch and the purl stitch. These can be "increased" or "decreased" to widen or narrow the fabric and "bound off" to prevent raveling. If stitches are "dropped" off a needle, they are "recovered." "Picked-up" stitches are used at an edge of the fabric to work in another direction.

Crocheting is based on a starter row of chain stitches, called a foundation chain *(page 186)*. On this foundation are built variations of the chain stitch, the single crochet stitch and double crochet stitch.

Before any stitches can be made, however, the size of the needle or crochet hook must be established; size is indicated by number or letter —higher ones for larger sizes of knitting needles and aluminum or plastic hooks, but, oddly, lower numbers for larger sizes of steel hooks. The size must suit the yarn weight *(charts, opposite)* as well as the number of stitches per inch called for in the pattern *(the "gauge," shown at right)*. Completed pieces must be fastened together. Three methods for joining knitwork and crochet work are shown on page 189, together with the final step of blocking the work to press it flat.

**A KNITTED SWATCH**

**A CROCHETED SWATCH**

## CHECKING THE GAUGE

All knit and crochet instructions are preceded by a stitch gauge, a specification of the number of stitches per inch (and often how many rows per inch) you must have if your project is to come out the proper size.

To check the gauge—to make sure your needle and yarn provide the desired number of stitches per inch—knit or crochet a sample swatch before beginning your project. It should measure at least 4 by 4 inches and be made with the yarn and hook or needles recommended in the pattern.

Remove the swatch from the hook or needles without binding off, lay it on a flat surface and count the stitches per inch, measuring with a ruler, not a tape measure. If the gauge calls for more stitches per inch, change to smaller needles or a smaller hook. If the pattern calls for fewer stitches per inch, use a larger hook or needle. This change of needle size will automatically adjust the row-per-inch guage.

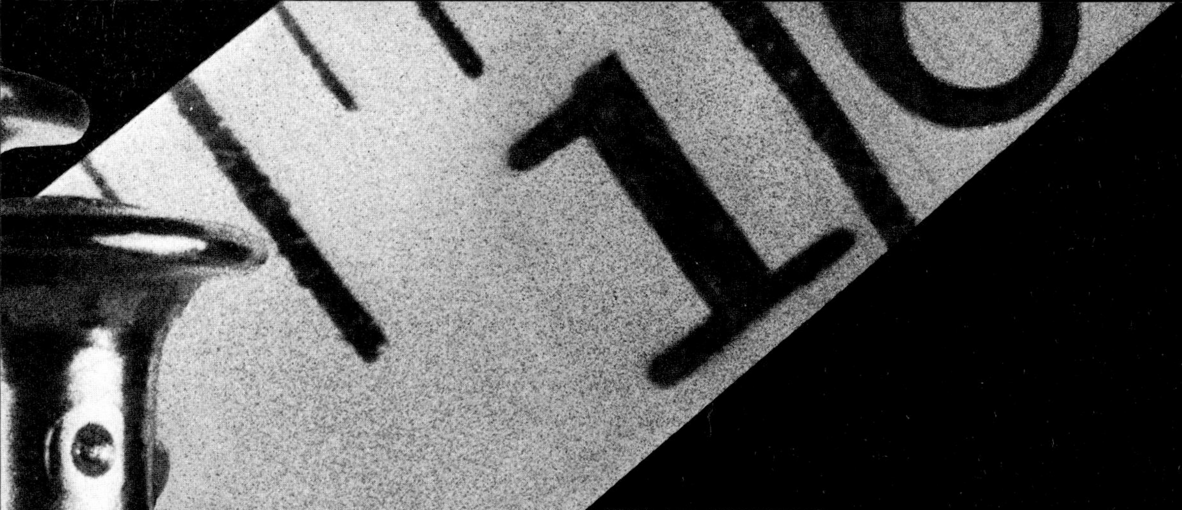

## MEASUREMENT CHARTS FOR KNITTED SWEATERS (For instructions on taking these measurements, see overleaf.)

**WOMEN**

| size | 10 | 12 | 14 | 16 | 18 |
|---|---|---|---|---|---|
| bust | 32" | 34" | 36" | 38" | 40" |
| waist | 24" | 25" | 26" | 28" | 30" |
| hip | 33" | 35" | 37" | 39" | 41" |
| shoulder | 4" | 4¼" | 4½" | 4¾" | 5" |
| shoulder back | 12¼" | 13" | 13¾" | 14½" | 15¼" |
| armhole depth | 7" | 7¼" | 7½" | 7¾" | 8" |
| waist to underarm | 7½" | 8" | 8" | 8½" | 8½" |
| underarm sleeve width | 11½" | 12" | 12½" | 13" | 13½" |
| underarm sleeve length | 17½" | 18" | 18" | 18½" | 18½" |

**MEN**

| size | sleeved | | | sleeveless | | |
|---|---|---|---|---|---|---|
| | small (36-38) | medium (40-42) | large (44-46) | small (36-38) | medium (40-42) | large (44-46) |
| chest | 37" | 41" | 45" | 37" | 41" | 45" |
| shoulder | 5" | 5½" | 6" | 4½" | 5" | 5½" |
| shoulder back | 16" | 17" | 18" | 15" | 16" | 17" |
| armhole depth | 8½" | 9" | 9½" | 9½" | 10" | 10½" |
| sweater length to underarm | 15" | 15½" | 15½" | 13" | 13½" | 13½" |
| sleeve width | 15" | 16" | 17" | | | |
| underarm sleeve length | 19" | 19¼" | 19½" | | | |

## RECOMMENDED COMBINATIONS OF KNITTING NEEDLES AND YARN

| needle size | 1 | 2 | 3 | 4 | 5 | 6 | 7 | 8 | 9 | 10 | 10½ | 11 | 13 | 14 |
|---|---|---|---|---|---|---|---|---|---|---|---|---|---|---|
| yarn | L | L | L M | M | M H | M H | H | H | H | H | H | H | H | H |

Key: L= lightweight 2-ply yarn; M= medium weight 3-ply yarn; H= heavy 4-ply yarn

## RECOMMENDED COMBINATIONS OF CROCHET HOOKS AND YARN

| hook size | ALUMINUM OR PLASTIC HOOKS | | | | | | | | | | STEEL HOOKS | | | | | | | | | | | | | | |
|---|---|---|---|---|---|---|---|---|---|---|---|---|---|---|---|---|---|---|---|---|---|---|---|---|---|
| | B | C | D | E | F | G | H | I | J | K | 14 | 13 | 12 | 11 | 10 | 9 | 8 | 7 | 6 | 5 | 4 | 3 | 2 | 1 | 0 | 00 |
| yarn | L | L | L M | M | M | M | M H | H | H | H | f | f | f | f | f | f | f | l | l | l | l | l | l | l | h L | h L |

Key: L= lightweight yarn; M= medium-weight yarn; H= heavyweight yarn; f= fine cotton thread; l= light cotton thread; h= heavy cotton thread

# MEASUREMENTS FOR MEN'S KNITWEAR

**1. CHEST:** Measure around the fullest part of the chest, holding the tape snugly against the body but not too tight.

**2. SHOULDER:** Measure from the base of the neck to the shoulder-bone point.

**3. SHOULDER BACK:** Measure each shoulder separately as directed in 2 above. Then measure across the back of the neck at the base from shoulder to shoulder. Total these three measurements for the shoulder back measurement.

**4. ARMHOLE DEPTH:** Measure straight up from just below the armpit to the shoulder-bone point.

**5. BOTTOM TO UNDERARM:** Measure straight up the side of the body from the desired length of the sweater—which is usually from 2 to 6 inches below the waist—to the armpit.

**6. SLEEVE WIDTH:** Measure around the fullest part of the upper arm, usually 1 to 3 inches below the armpit.

**7. UNDERARM SLEEVE LENGTH:** Holding the arm straight, measure up from the wristbone to the armpit.

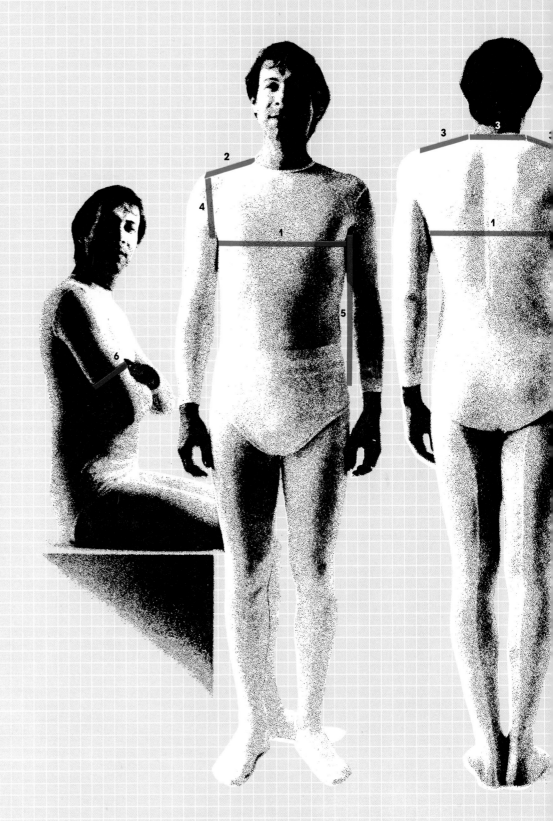

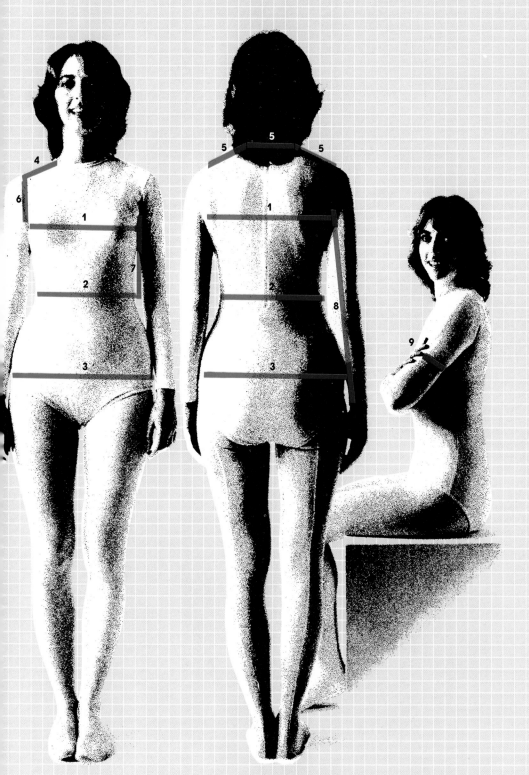

# MEASUREMENTS FOR WOMEN'S KNITWEAR

**1. BUST:** Measure around the fullest part of the bust, holding the tape snugly but not too tight.

**2. WAIST:** Measure around the narrowest part of the torso from back to front.

**3. HIP:** Measure from back to front around the fullest part of the hips, usually 7 to 9 inches down from the waistline.

**4. SHOULDER:** Measure from the base of the neck to the shoulder-bone point.

**5. SHOULDER BACK:** Measure each shoulder separately as in 4 above. Measure across the back of the neck at the base from shoulder to shoulder and total these three measurements.

**6. ARMHOLE DEPTH:** Measure up from just below the armpit to the shoulder-bone point.

**7. WAIST TO UNDERARM:** Measure up the side from the waistline to the armpit.

**8. UNDERARM SLEEVE LENGTH:** Holding the arm straight, measure up from the wristbone to the armpit for full length or start measuring from the desired length of the sleeve.

**9. UNDERARM SLEEVE WIDTH:** Measure around the fullest part of the upper arm usually 1 to 3 inches below the armpit.

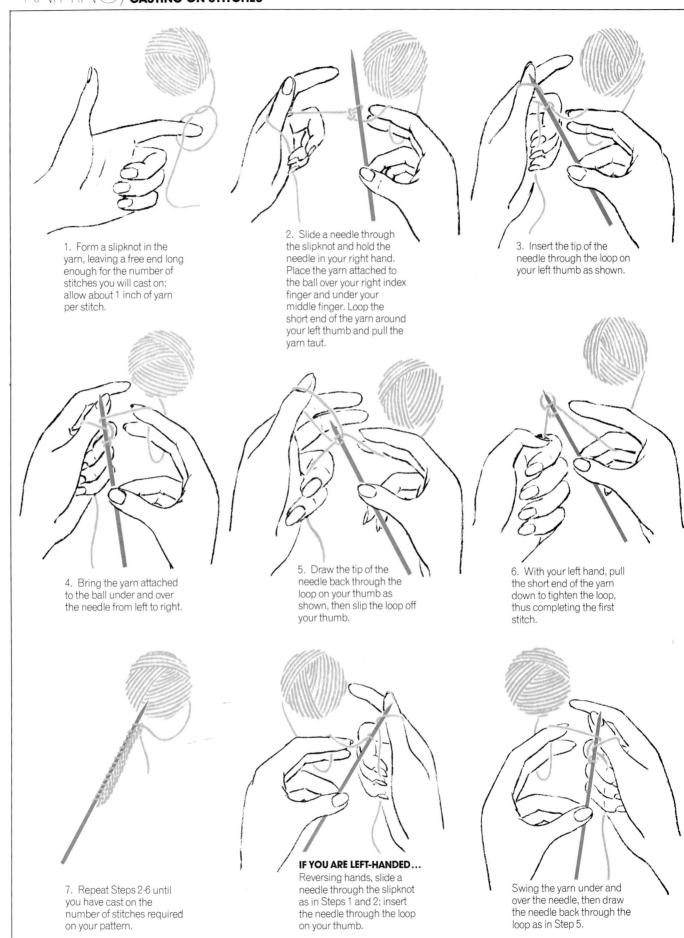

1. Form a slipknot in the yarn, leaving a free end long enough for the number of stitches you will cast on; allow about 1 inch of yarn per stitch.

2. Slide a needle through the slipknot and hold the needle in your right hand. Place the yarn attached to the ball over your right index finger and under your middle finger. Loop the short end of the yarn around your left thumb and pull the yarn taut.

3. Insert the tip of the needle through the loop on your left thumb as shown.

4. Bring the yarn attached to the ball under and over the needle from left to right.

5. Draw the tip of the needle back through the loop on your thumb as shown, then slip the loop off your thumb.

6. With your left hand, pull the short end of the yarn down to tighten the loop, thus completing the first stitch.

7. Repeat Steps 2-6 until you have cast on the number of stitches required on your pattern.

**IF YOU ARE LEFT-HANDED...**
Reversing hands, slide a needle through the slipknot as in Steps 1 and 2; insert the needle through the loop on your thumb.

Swing the yarn under and over the needle, then draw the needle back through the loop as in Step 5.

# THE KNIT STITCH

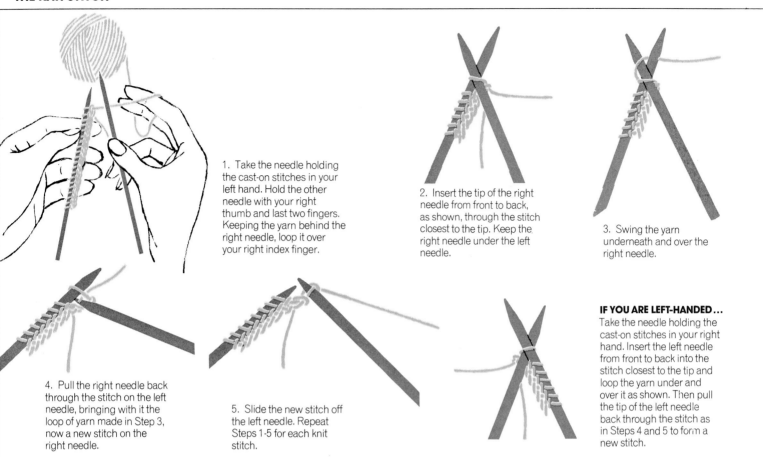

1. Take the needle holding the cast-on stitches in your left hand. Hold the other needle with your right thumb and last two fingers. Keeping the yarn behind the right needle, loop it over your right index finger.

2. Insert the tip of the right needle from front to back, as shown, through the stitch closest to the tip. Keep the right needle under the left needle.

3. Swing the yarn underneath and over the right needle.

4. Pull the right needle back through the stitch on the left needle, bringing with it the loop of yarn made in Step 3, now a new stitch on the right needle.

5. Slide the new stitch off the left needle. Repeat Steps 1-5 for each knit stitch.

**IF YOU ARE LEFT-HANDED...**
Take the needle holding the cast-on stitches in your right hand. Insert the left needle from front to back into the stitch closest to the tip and loop the yarn under and over it as shown. Then pull the tip of the left needle back through the stitch as in Steps 4 and 5 to form a new stitch.

# THE PURL STITCH

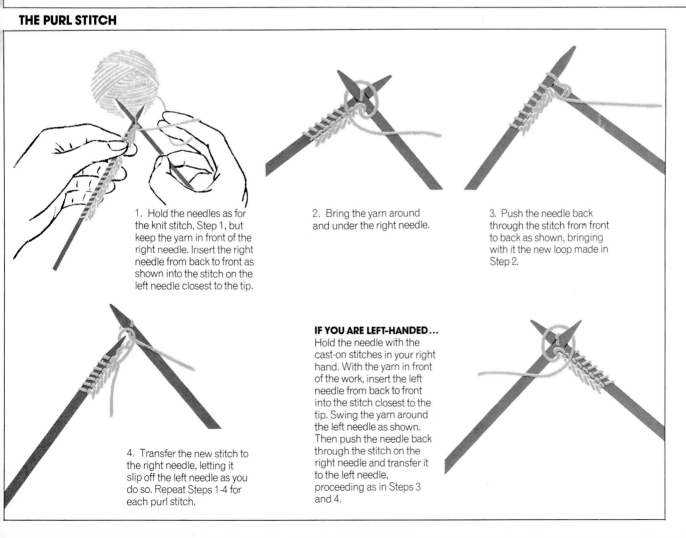

1. Hold the needles as for the knit stitch, Step 1, but keep the yarn in front of the right needle. Insert the right needle from back to front as shown into the stitch on the left needle closest to the tip.

2. Bring the yarn around and under the right needle.

3. Push the needle back through the stitch from front to back as shown, bringing with it the new loop made in Step 2.

4. Transfer the new stitch to the right needle, letting it slip off the left needle as you do so. Repeat Steps 1-4 for each purl stitch.

**IF YOU ARE LEFT-HANDED...**
Hold the needle with the cast-on stitches in your right hand. With the yarn in front of the work, insert the left needle from back to front into the stitch closest to the tip. Swing the yarn around the left needle as shown. Then push the needle back through the stitch on the right needle and transfer it to the left needle, proceeding as in Steps 3 and 4.

## INCREASING STITCHES ON A KNIT ROW

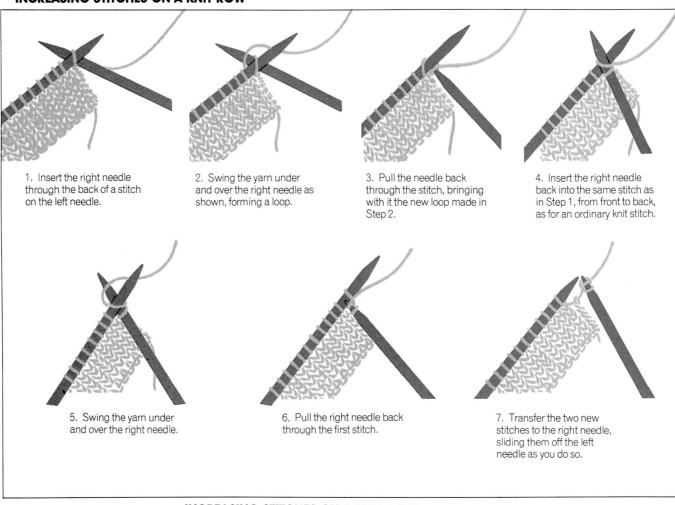

1. Insert the right needle through the back of a stitch on the left needle.

2. Swing the yarn under and over the right needle as shown, forming a loop.

3. Pull the needle back through the stitch, bringing with it the new loop made in Step 2.

4. Insert the right needle back into the same stitch as in Step 1, from front to back, as for an ordinary knit stitch.

5. Swing the yarn under and over the right needle.

6. Pull the right needle back through the first stitch.

7. Transfer the two new stitches to the right needle, sliding them off the left needle as you do so.

## INCREASING STITCHES ON A PURL ROW

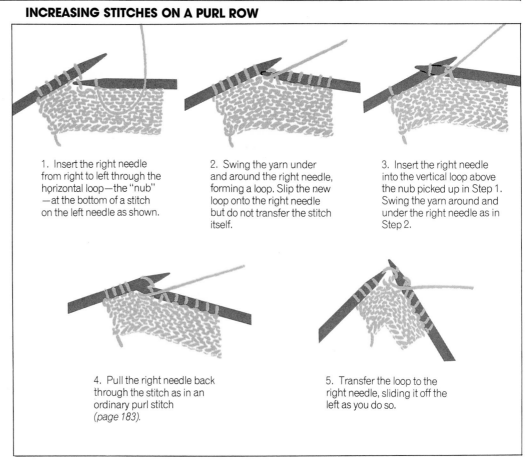

1. Insert the right needle from right to left through the horizontal loop—the "nub" —at the bottom of a stitch on the left needle as shown.

2. Swing the yarn under and around the right needle, forming a loop. Slip the new loop onto the right needle but do not transfer the stitch itself.

3. Insert the right needle into the vertical loop above the nub picked up in Step 1. Swing the yarn around and under the right needle as in Step 2.

4. Pull the right needle back through the stitch as in an ordinary purl stitch (page 183).

5. Transfer the loop to the right needle, sliding it off the left as you do so.

## DECREASING STITCHES

Insert the right needle into two stitches instead of one, either from front to back as for the knit stitch or from back to front as for the purl stitch *(page 183)*. Proceed as though you were knitting or purling one stitch at a time.

## BINDING OFF STITCHES

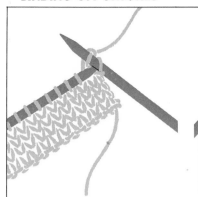

1. When the last row of your pattern is complete, start the next row by knitting two stitches. Then insert the tip of the left needle through the front of the second stitch from the tip of the right needle as shown.

2. With the left needle, lift this stitch over the other on the right needle, then drop it off the left needle. Knit another stitch and repeat the process. Continue until the required number of stitches are bound off.

3. Finish off by cutting the yarn from the ball, leaving a 2-inch end. Pull this end through the last stitch to secure it and weave it through two or three nearby stitches.

## RECOVERING A DROPPED STITCH

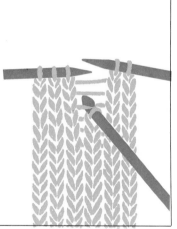

If a stitch slips off the needle and "runs," much as a stocking does, insert a crochet hook through the dropped loop. Then catch the loose cross thread with the tip of the hook and pull it through the dropped loop. Proceed up the "ladder" of cross threads until they are all pulled through the dropped loop. Place the last loop on the needle, making sure that the direction of the stitch conforms with the others on the needle.

## PICKING UP STITCHES AT AN EDGE

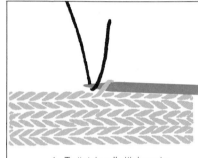

1. To "pick up" stitches at a neck or armhole to make a collar or sleeve, insert a needle from right to left into the first stitch to be picked up. Bring a new strand of yarn around the needle and draw it through the stitch.

2. Continue these operations along the row of stitches to be picked up, drawing the yarn through each stitch as you proceed.

## JOINING YARN

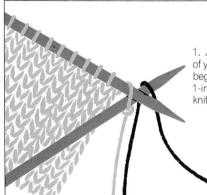

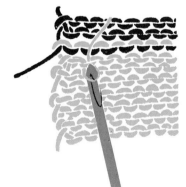

1. Join a new ball or color of yarn at the end or beginning of a row, leaving 1-inch-long ends. Continue knitting with the new yarn.

2. When you have knitted two or three rows, weave the loose ends of yarn through nearby stitches with the aid of a crochet hook.

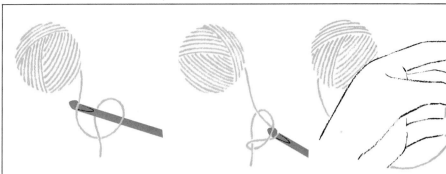

1. Form a loose slipknot in the yarn around the crochet hook, about 1 inch from the end of the yarn. Grasp the yarn attached to the ball with the tip of the crochet hook.

2. Pull the yarn through the slipknot with the tip of the crochet hook.

3. Hold the crochet hook in your right hand much like a pencil, and place the yarn from the ball around the left little finger, then up over the left index finger. Grasp the free end of the yarn between the thumb and middle finger of the left hand and pull it gently to secure the knot on the hook.

4. Swinging your left index finger to the right, bring the yarn from the back to the front of the hook and catch it under the tip of the hook.

5. Pull the tip of the hook through the loop on the hook, bringing the yarn with it to create one chain stitch in the foundation row.

6. Repeat Steps 4 and 5 for each chain stitch until you have chained the number of foundation stitches required for your pattern.

**IF YOU ARE LEFT-HANDED...**

Follow the directions in Steps 1-3, holding the crochet hook in your left hand and looping the yarn attached to the ball around the little finger and index finger of your right hand. Swing your right index finger to the left to place the yarn over the crochet hook as shown, then follow the directions in Steps 4-6.

## THE SINGLE CROCHET STITCH

1. To single crochet the first row of stitches after a foundation chain, first count back to the second chain stitch from the hook (arrow); do not count the loop on the hook itself. Insert the hook through this second chain stitch.

2. With two loops now on the crochet hook, bring the yarn over the hook from back to front, and catch it under the tip.

3. Draw the yarn caught under the tip through the loop closest to the tip, to form a new loop.

4. Bring the yarn over the hook again, as in Step 2. Draw the yarn through both loops on the crochet hook as shown, leaving only a single loop on the hook. Insert the hook into the top of the next chain stitch and repeat Steps 1-4 for each succeeding stitch across the row.

5. At the end of each row, chain one stitch (above). (If the first stitch of the next row is to be worked in a double crochet stitch as shown at right, chain two stitches.)

6. Turn the work to crochet back across the previous row. Insert the hook through both loops of the second stitch from the edge on this and all rows after the first.

7. Swing the yarn over the hook from back to front, catch it under the tip, and draw it through both loops of the stitch picked up in Step 6. Proceed as in Steps 4 and 5.

**IF YOU ARE LEFT-HANDED...**

Follow the instructions in Steps 1-7, holding the hook in your left hand and bringing the yarn around the hook as in the final picture of the chain stitch (above).

## THE DOUBLE CROCHET STITCH

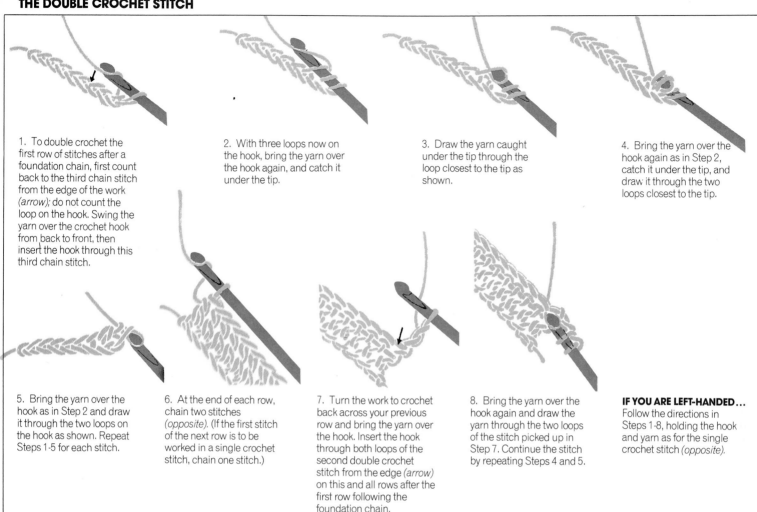

1. To double crochet the first row of stitches after a foundation chain, first count back to the third chain stitch from the edge of the work *(arrow);* do not count the loop on the hook. Swing the yarn over the crochet hook from back to front, then insert the hook through this third chain stitch.

2. With three loops now on the hook, bring the yarn over the hook again, and catch it under the tip.

3. Draw the yarn caught under the tip through the loop closest to the tip as shown.

4. Bring the yarn over the hook again as in Step 2, catch it under the tip, and draw it through the two loops closest to the tip.

5. Bring the yarn over the hook as in Step 2 and draw it through the two loops on the hook as shown. Repeat Steps 1-5 for each stitch.

6. At the end of each row, chain two stitches *(opposite).* (If the first stitch of the next row is to be worked in a single crochet stitch, chain one stitch.)

7. Turn the work to crochet back across your previous row and bring the yarn over the hook. Insert the hook through both loops of the second double crochet stitch from the edge *(arrow)* on this and all rows after the first row following the foundation chain.

8. Bring the yarn over the hook again and draw the yarn through the two loops of the stitch picked up in Step 7. Continue the stitch by repeating Steps 4 and 5.

**IF YOU ARE LEFT-HANDED...**
Follow the directions in Steps 1-8, holding the hook and yarn as for the single crochet stitch *(opposite).*

## INCREASING STITCHES

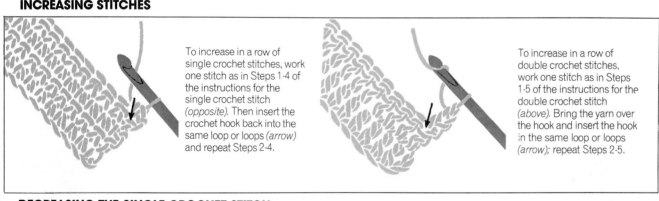

To increase in a row of single crochet stitches, work one stitch as in Steps 1-4 of the instructions for the single crochet stitch *(opposite).* Then insert the crochet hook back into the same loop or loops *(arrow)* and repeat Steps 2-4.

To increase in a row of double crochet stitches, work one stitch as in Steps 1-5 of the instructions for the double crochet stitch *(above).* Bring the yarn over the hook and insert the hook in the same loop or loops *(arrow);* repeat Steps 2-5.

## DECREASING THE SINGLE CROCHET STITCH

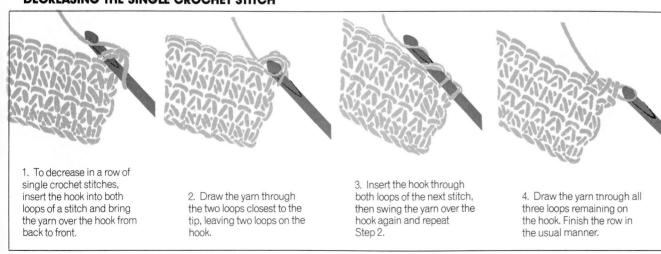

1. To decrease in a row of single crochet stitches, insert the hook into both loops of a stitch and bring the yarn over the hook from back to front.

2. Draw the yarn through the two loops closest to the tip, leaving two loops on the hook.

3. Insert the hook through both loops of the next stitch, then swing the yarn over the hook again and repeat Step 2.

4. Draw the yarn through all three loops remaining on the hook. Finish the row in the usual manner.

## DECREASING THE DOUBLE CROCHET STITCH

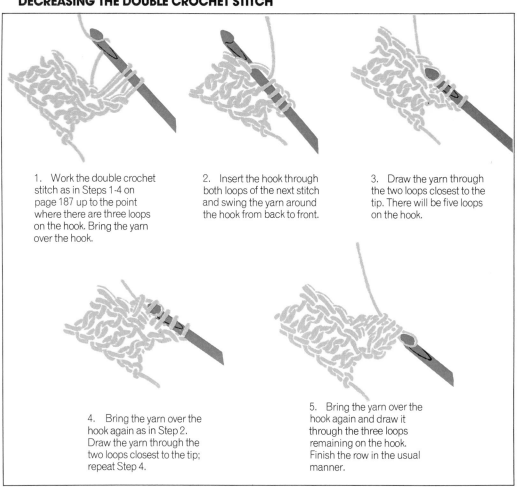

1. Work the double crochet stitch as in Steps 1-4 on page 187 up to the point where there are three loops on the hook. Bring the yarn over the hook.

2. Insert the hook through both loops of the next stitch and swing the yarn around the hook from back to front.

3. Draw the yarn through the two loops closest to the tip. There will be five loops on the hook.

4. Bring the yarn over the hook again as in Step 2. Draw the yarn through the two loops closest to the tip; repeat Step 4.

5. Bring the yarn over the hook again and draw it through the three loops remaining on the hook. Finish the row in the usual manner.

## FASTENING OFF

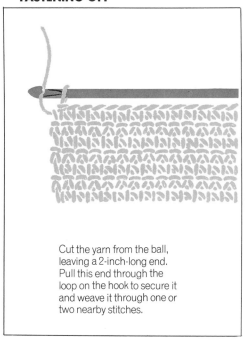

Cut the yarn from the ball, leaving a 2-inch-long end. Pull this end through the loop on the hook to secure it and weave it through one or two nearby stitches.

## JOINING YARN

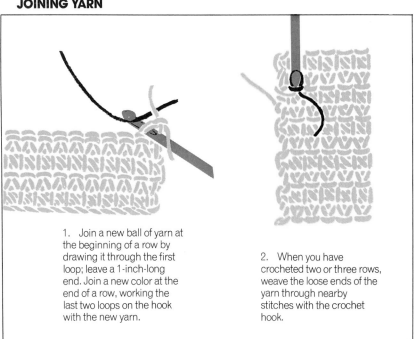

1. Join a new ball of yarn at the beginning of a row by drawing it through the first loop; leave a 1-inch-long end. Join a new color at the end of a row, working the last two loops on the hook with the new yarn.

2. When you have crocheted two or three rows, weave the loose ends of the yarn through nearby stitches with the crochet hook.

## JOINING KNITTED OR CROCHETED PIECES

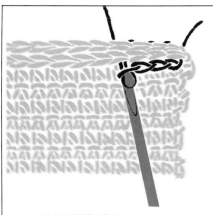

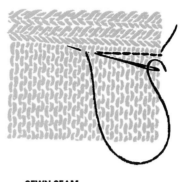

**CROCHETED SEAM**
With wrong sides facing out, hold the two edges of your work to be joined so that stitches and rows are aligned. Insert a crochet hook from front to back through the nearest whole stitch below both edges. Catch a fresh strand of yarn with the hook and draw it through both edges to form a loop on the hook. Insert the hook through the next pair of stitches, catch the yarn, and draw it through these stitches as well as through the loop on the hook. When the pieces are joined, weave loose ends into nearby stitches.

**WOVEN SEAM**
With the wrong sides of your work facing out, hold together the two edges of your work to be joined so that stitches and rows are aligned. Thread a blunt-edged tapestry needle with the same yarn used in your work, and insert it straight across both edges, through both loops of each edge —four loops in all. Turn the needle and repeat in succeeding loops to the left until the pieces are joined. Weave the loose ends into nearby stitches.

**SEWN SEAM**
With the wrong sides facing out, hold the two edges to be joined with stitches and rows aligned. Thread a blunt-edged tapestry needle with the yarn used in your work, and insert it through both pieces 1/4 inch down from the joined edges at one end. Leaving a 2-inch-long end of yarn, insert the needle from front to back 1/4 inch to the right (if you are right-handed) of the first stitch and bring it out from back to front 1/4 inch to the left of the first stitch. When the pieces are joined, weave the loose ends into nearby stitches.

## BLOCKING TO PRESS KNITTED OR CROCHETED PIECES FLAT

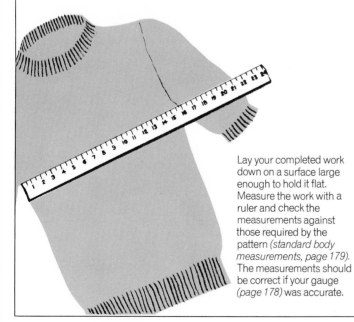

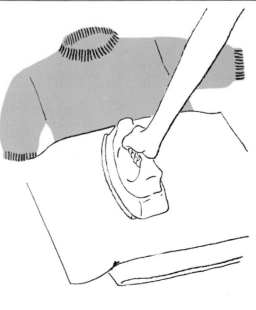

Lay your completed work down on a surface large enough to hold it flat. Measure the work with a ruler and check the measurements against those required by the pattern (standard body measurements, page 179). The measurements should be correct if your gauge (page 178) was accurate.

If the measurements are slightly off, you can press your work into the correct size by stretching or pushing it together a little as you lay it out here. Do not pin the work to your pressing surface; pins leave marks at the edges when you press. Cover the work with a damp cloth and press very lightly with a warm iron. Do not let the iron rest too long in one area or it will mat the finish and leave an impression.

# A wealth of patterns

Although it is entirely possible to knit or crochet a project using only one stitch pattern *(sweaters, pages 192-193, and afghan, pages 194-195)*, learning new combinations of stitches can add unexpected dimensions to the finished product. The variations can be slight, such as in the knitted seed pattern *(right)* or more complex, as in the ribbed crocheted pattern *(far right)*.

The samples at right have been made with knitting worsted yarn, using Size 8 knitting needles and a Size H aluminum crochet hook. By changing the size of the needles and the weight of the yarn, you can make even more variety in texture.

**KNITTED PATTERNS**

The Stockinette Pattern. Cast on the desired number of stitches. Row 1: Make a row of knit stitches. Row 2: Make a row of purl stitches. Alternate Rows 1 and 2 for the pattern.

The Seed Pattern. Cast on the desired number of stitches. Row 1: Alternately knit 1 stitch and purl 1 stitch across the row. Row 2: If the last stitch on Row 1 was a knit stitch, begin Row 2 with a knit stitch and alternate knit and purl stitches across the row. If the last stitch on Row 1 was a purl stitch, begin Row 2 with a purl stitch and alternate purl and knit stitches across the row. Repeat Row 2 for the pattern.

The Horizontal Stripe Pattern. Cast on the desired number of stitches. Row 1: Make a row of knit stitches. Rows 2 and 3: Make rows of purl stitches. Row 4: Make a row of knit stitches. Repeat Rows 1-4 for the pattern.

The Rib Variation Pattern. Cast on the desired number of stitches. Row 1: Alternately knit 1 stitch and purl 1 stitch across the row. Row 2: Make a row of knit stitches. Repeat Rows 1 and 2 for the pattern.

## CROCHETED PATTERNS

The Single Crochet Pattern. Make a foundation chain consisting of the desired number of stitches plus one. Row 1: Make a row of single crochet stitches. Chain 1 stitch and turn. Repeat Row 1 for the pattern.

The Textured Pattern. Make a foundation chain with an even number of stitches plus one. Row 1: Make a single crochet stitch, then a double crochet stitch, then another single crochet stitch. Alternate double and single crochet stitches across the row; end with a double crochet stitch. Chain 1 and turn. Row 2: Working through the front loops only of the stitches, alternate a single crochet stitch and a double crochet stitch across the row. Chain 1 and turn. Row 3: Working through both loops of the stitches in the usual way, alternate a single crochet stitch and a double crochet stitch across the row. Chain 1 and turn. Repeat Rows 2 and 3 for the pattern.

The Oxford Mix Pattern. Make a foundation chain with an odd number of stitches, plus one. Row 1: Single crochet across the row, chain 1 and turn. Row 2: Make a single crochet stitch, chain 1, skip a stitch; repeat this sequence across the row, ending with a single crochet. Chain 1, turn. Row 3: Single crochet across the row, going into each stitch and space below the chain of the previous row. Chain 1, turn. Repeat Rows 2 and 3 for the pattern.

The Ribbed Crochet Pattern. Make a foundation chain of any number of stitches, plus one. Row 1. Make a row of single crochet stitches. Chain 1 and turn. Row 2: Make another row of single crochet stitches, picking up the back loop only of each stitch on the preceding row. Chain 1 and turn. Repeat Row 2 for the pattern.

191

# Five timeless designs for sweaters

Each of the sweaters at left is worked in the same stockinette pattern *(page 190),* and is based on the same simple design. The shape in each case is a basic one, a loose-fitting body section. The variations that provide such different-looking fashions depend on the length of the sweater and the sleeve, the shape of the neckline, and the use of a single color or several in the pattern.

At far left is a short-sleeved slip-over, with a round crew neck and alternating stripes. The contemporary-looking sweater-dress beside it, bordered at the neck and armholes with the same vibrant contrasting color as the bottom of the skirt, is no more than an elongated tank-top. The round-neck long-sleeved sweater and its companion, the striped turtleneck, are masculine favorites that have in recent years been adopted by women as well. Last is a versatile V-neck slipover, appropriate in any color or combination of colors for men or women. Instructions for the sweaters are on pages 196-199.

# An afghan to crochet

The striking geometric design of the crocheted afghan shown below and its generous proportions (60 inches wide by 72 inches long) make it seem an ambitious project. But as can be seen in the close-up at right, it is based on classic lines and squares and requires just one type of stitch: the single crochet *(page 186)*. Each square is completed separately; the afghan is assembled when all the pieces are completed. Instructions are on page 199.

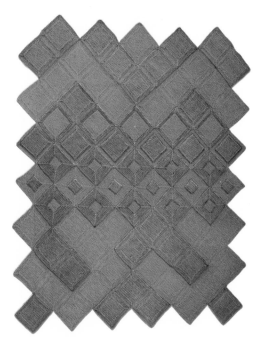

# Instructions for making sweaters and an afghan

The instructions for knitting or crocheting in this book describe each step fully in simple terms, but other books, magazines and patterns use a shorthand of standard abbreviations. Those translated here are the basic terms you will encounter in most other instructions for knitting or crocheting projects.

### KNITTING ABBREVIATIONS

**K**—knit      **REP**—repeat
**P**—purl      **PAT**—pattern
**ST**—stitch
*—starting point for a repeated sequence of steps: when instructions tell you to "rep from *," read back in the instructions to find the point (*) where you must begin to repeat.

### CROCHETING ABBREVIATIONS

**SC**—single crochet      **HDC**—half double crochet
**CH**—chain      **DC**—double crochet
**HK**—hook      **LP**—loop
**ST**—stitch      **SK**—skip
**REP**—repeat      **SP**—space
**PAT**—pattern
*—starting point for a repeated sequence of steps: when instructions tell you to "rep from*," read back in the instructions to find the point (*) where you must begin to repeat.

## KNITTING THE CLASSIC SWEATERS

Following are instructions for knitting the sweaters pictured on pages 192-193. All of the women's sweaters are in size 10; the changes in the number of stitches necessary for sizes 12, 14, 16 and 18 follow in parentheses in that order. The instructions for the man's slipover are for a small size (36-38); the changes necessary for medium (40-42) and large (44-46) sizes follow in parentheses in that order. All stitches used are demonstrated on pages 182-185 and the stockinette stitch pattern is detailed on page 190.

### THE SHORT-SLEEVED SLIPOVER

You will need 2 (2,2,3,3) four-ounce skeins of knitting worsted in color A (pink in the sweater on page 192) and 1 (2,2,2,3) four-ounce skeins of color B (gray in the sweater shown).

Use straight knitting needles in Sizes 7 and 9 and a tapestry needle for sewing seams.

Knit a sample swatch to check the gauge, which is 5 stitches per inch, 7 rows per inch.

**The back:** With the Size 7 needles and color A, cast on 80 (85,90,95,100) stitches. Knit 1 stitch, purl 1 stitch to make 1 inch of ribbing. Fasten off color A, attach color B and change to the Size 9 needles. Work the stockinette pattern for 4 rows in color B, then 4 rows in color A. Continue alternating colors until the piece measures 13 inches in all (or the length you want from the bottom edge to the underarm edge). End with a purl row.

**The armholes:** Bind off 5 (5,6,6,7) stitches at the beginning of each of the next 2 rows. Decrease 1 stitch at the beginning and end of every other row 4 (4,4,5,5) times. You should now have 62 (67,70,73,76) stitches on your needle. Continue the stockinette pattern until the back measures 7 (7 1/4, 7 1/2, 7 3/4, 8) inches above the start of the armhole.

**The shoulders:** Bind off 10 (11,12,12,13) stitches at the beginning of each of the next 2 rows and 10 (11,11,12,12) stitches at the beginning of each of the next 2 rows. Bind off loosely the remaining 22 (23,24,25,26) stitches for the back of the neck.

**The front:** Work as you did for the back until the piece measures 5 (5 1/4, 5 1/2, 5 3/4, 6) inches above the start of the armhole, ending with a purl row. Do not shape the shoulders at this stage.

**The neck:** Divide the front by knitting across 23 (25,26,27,28) stitches, joining a second ball of yarn, binding off the center 16 (17,18,19,20) stitches, then knitting across the remaining 23 (25,26,27,28) stitches. Work on both sides of the neck opening—across to the neck edge, picking up the second ball of yarn, ignoring the bound-off edge and work across the other side. Decrease 1 stitch at each neck edge every other row 3 times. Continue the stockinette pattern on the 20 (22,23,24,25) stitches on each side of the neck opening until the front measures the same as the back from the edge of the sweater to the shoulders. Shape the shoulders as you did on the back.

**The sleeves:** Continuing with the Size 7 needles and color A, cast on 54 (56,59,61,64) stitches. Knit 1, purl 1 to make 1 inch of ribbing. Attach color B, change to the Size 9 needles and work the stockinette pattern in alternating stripes as on the back and the front of the sweater for 1 inch. Increase 1 stitch at the beginning and end of the next row and repeat this increase after 1 inch: you will now have 58 (60,63,65,68) stitches. On these stitches continue the stockinette pattern until the piece measures 3 1/2 inches in all (or the desired length to the underarm edge). End with a purl row at the same point of the striped pattern that you reached when you began to shape the armhole—the stripes on the sleeve must match those on the sweater when they are joined.

**The sleeve cap:** Bind off 5 (5,6,6,7) stitches at the beginning of each of the next 2 rows, then decrease 1 stitch at the beginning and end of every other row for 4 (4 1/4, 4 1/2, 4 3/4, 5) inches. Bind off 2 stitches at the beginning of each of the next 6 rows. Bind off the remaining stitches.

**The finishing touches:** Using a tapestry needle and color A, sew the left shoulder seam. With Size 7 needles and color A, pick up and knit 70 (74,78,82,86) stitches around the neck. Knit 1 stitch, purl 1 stitch to make 2 inches of ribbing. Bind off loosely in the ribbing pattern. Sew the neckband opening and right shoulder seam. Sew the underarm and sleeve seams. Sew in the sleeves; block.

## THE STRIPED SHIFT

You will need 1 (2,2,2,3) four-ounce skeins of knitting worsted in color A (maroon in the shift on page 192), 1 (1,1,2,2) of color B (brown in the shift shown), 1 (1,1,1,2) of color C (orange in the shift shown) and 2 (2,3,3,4) of color D (pink in the shift shown).

Use straight knitting needles in Sizes 7 and 9 and a tapestry needle for sewing seams.

Knit a sample swatch to check the gauge, which is 5 stitches per inch, 7 rows per inch.

**The back:** With the Size 7 needles and color A, cast on 80 (85,90,95,100) stitches. Work evenly the stockinette pattern for 1 inch, then purl 1 row on the outside (the previously knitted side) of the work to make the hemline of the shift. Work 1 more row with Size 7 needles, then change to Size 9 needles and work evenly until the piece measures approximately 8 inches above the hemline; end with a purled row. Fasten off color A, attach color B and work with B for approximately 4 inches. Fasten off color B, attach color C and work with it for approximately 2 inches. Fasten off color C, attach color D and work with it until the piece measures 27 inches or the desired length from the hemline to the edge of the underarm.

**The armholes:** Bind off 8 (8,8,9,9) stitches at the beginning of each of the next 2 rows, then decrease 1 stitch at the beginning and end of every other row 6 (6,7,7,7) times. You now have 52 (57,60,63,68) stitches. Continue the stockinette pattern until the piece measures 3 inches above the start of the armhole edge.

**The neck:** Divide the back by knitting across 14 (15,16,17,18) stitches, joining a second ball of yarn, binding off the center 24 (27,28,29,32) stitches, then knitting across the remaining 14 (15,16,17,18) stitches. Work on both sides of the neck opening—across to the neck edge, picking up the second ball of yarn, ignoring the bound-off edge and work across the other side. Decrease 1 stitch at each neck edge every other row 7 times. Continue the stockinette pattern on 7 (8,9,10,11) stitches of each side of the neck opening until the piece measures 8 (8 1/4, 8 1/2, 8 3/4, 9) inches above the start of the armhole edge.

**The shoulders:** Bind off the 7 (8,9,10,11) stitches on each side of the neck.

**The front:** Work as you did for the back, checking to make sure the color bands align.

**The finishing touches:** Sew the left shoulder seam using color D and the tapestry needle. With Size 7 needles and color A, pick up and knit 178 (182,186,190,194) stitches around the neck. Knit 1, purl 1 to make a 3/4-inch ribbing, then bind off loosely in the ribbing pattern. Sew the neckband opening and right shoulder seam.

**The armhole band:** With Size 7 needles and color A, pick up and knit 116 (120,124,128,132) stitches around each armhole. Knit 1 and then purl 1 stitch to make a 3/4-inch ribbing, then bind off loosely in the ribbing pattern. Sew the side seams. Turn the hem under to the wrong side of the work and sew the hem into place with a catch stitch *(page 44);* block.

## THE CLASSIC MAN'S SLIPOVER

You will need 5 (6,7) four-ounce skeins of knitting worsted.

Use straight knitting needles in Sizes 7 and 9 and a tapestry needle for sewing seams.

Knit a sample swatch to check the gauge, which is 5 stitches per inch, 7 rows per inch.

**The back:** With the Size 7 needles, cast on 94 (104,114) stitches. Knit 1, purl 1 to make a 3-inch ribbing. Change to Size 9 needles and work the stockinette pattern until the piece measures 16 inches in all (or the length you want from the bottom edge to the underarm edge).

**The armholes:** Bind off 4 (5,6) stitches at the beginning of each of the next 2 rows, then decrease 1 stitch at the beginning and end of every other row 3 (4,5) times; you will now have 80 (86,92) stitches. Work evenly until the piece measures 8 1/2 (9, 9 1/2) inches above the start of the armhole shaping.

**The shoulders:** Bind off 13 (14,15) stitches at the beginning of each of the next 2 rows and 12 (14,16) stitches at the beginning of each of the next 2 rows. Bind off loosely the remaining 30 stitches for the back of the neck.

**The front:** Work as you did for the back until the piece measures 6 1/2 (7, 7 1/2) inches above the start of the armhole shaping.

**The neck:** Divide the front by knitting across 28 (31,34) stitches, joining a second ball of yarn, binding off the center 24 (24,24) stitches, then knitting across the remaining 28 (31,34) stitches. Work on both sides of the neck opening—across to the neck edge; picking up the second ball of yarn, ignoring the bound-off edge and work across the other side. Decrease 1 stitch at each neck edge every other row 3 times. Work evenly on the 25 (28,31) stitches of each side of the neck opening until the front measures the same as the back from the bottom edge to the shoulders. Shape the shoulders as you did on the back.

**The sleeves:** With Size 7 needles, cast on 42 (44,46) stitches. Knit 1, purl 1 to make a 2 1/2-inch ribbing. Change to Size 9 needles and work the stockinette pattern for 1 inch, then increase 1 stitch at the beginning and end of the next row and repeat this increase every 3/4 inch 16 (17,19) times more; you will now have 76 (80,86) stitches; work evenly until the sleeve measures 19 inches in all, or the desired length from the bottom edge of the sleeve to the edge of the underarm.

**The sleeve cap:** Bind off 4 (5,6) stitches at the beginning of each of the next 2 rows, then decrease 1 stitch at the beginning and end of every other row for 5 1/2 (6, 6 1/2) inches. Bind off 3 stitches at the beginning of each of the next 8 rows. Bind off the remaining stitches.

**The finishing touches:** Using the same yarn and a tapestry needle, sew the left shoulder seam. With Size 7 needles and with the outside of the work facing you, pick up and knit 92 (96,100) stitches around the neck. Knit 1, purl 1 to make a 1 1/2-inch ribbing, then bind off loosely in the ribbing pattern. Sew the neckband opening, the right shoulder seam, the underarm and sleeve seams. Sew in the sleeves; block.

## THE TURTLENECK SWEATER

You will need 3 (3,4,4,5) four-ounce skeins of knitting worsted in color A (brown in the picture on page 193) and 1 (1,1, 2,2) of color B (gray in the picture).

Use straight knitting needles, in Sizes 7 and 9, and a tapestry needle to sew seams.

Knit a sample swatch to check the gauge, which is 5 stitches per inch, 7 rows per inch.

**The back:** With Size 7 needles and color A, cast on 80 (85, 90,95,100) stitches. Knit 1, purl 1 to make a 2 1/2-inch ribbing. Change to Size 9 needles and work the stockinette pattern until the piece measures 11 (11, 11 1/2, 11 1/2, 12) inches in all, ending with a purl row. Fasten off color A, attach color B, and continue the stockinette pattern, alternating 2 rows of color B and 2 rows of color A until 11 contrasting color stripes have been completed. Fasten off color B and attach color A.

**The armholes:** Bind off 5 (5,6,6,7) stitches at the beginning of each of the next 2 rows, then decrease 1 stitch at the beginning and end of every other row 4 (4,4,5,5) times; you will now have 62 (67,70,73,76) stitches. Work evenly until the piece measures 7 (7 1/4, 7 1/2, 7 3/4, 8) inches above the start of the armhole shaping.

**The shoulders:** Bind off 10 (11,12,12,13) stitches at the beginning of each of the next 2 rows and 10 (11,11,12, 12) stitches at the beginning of each of the next 2 rows. Bind off the remaining 22 (23,24,25,26) stitches loosely for the back of the neck.

**The front:** Work as you did for the back until the front measures 5 (5 1/4, 5 1/2, 5 3/4, 6) inches above the start of the armhole edge.

**The neck:** Divide the front by knitting across 23 (25,26,27,28) stitches, joining a second ball of yarn, binding off the center 16 (17,18,19,20) stitches, then knitting across the remaining 23 (25,26,27,28) stitches. Work on both sides of the neck opening—across to the neck edge, picking up the second ball of yarn, ignoring the bound-off edge and work across the other side. Decrease 1 stitch at each neck edge every other row 3 times. Work evenly on the 20 (22, 23, 24, 25) stitches of each side of the neck opening until the piece measures the same as the back from the bottom edge to the shoulders. Shape the shoulders as you did on the back.

**The sleeves:** With Size 7 needles and color A, cast on 38 (40, 43,45,48) stitches. Knit 1, purl 1 to make a 2-inch ribbing. Change to Size 9 needles and the stockinette pattern. Increase 1 stitch at the beginning and end of the next row and repeat this increase every 1 1/2 inches 9 times more; you will now have 58 (60,63,65,68) stitches. When the piece measures 9 1/2 inches from the bottom edge, start a striped pattern as on the back and front of the sweater, al-ternating colors A and B until you have completed 11 contrasting color stripes.

**The sleeve cap:** Bind off 5 (5,6,6,7) stitches at the beginning of each of the next 2 rows. Then decrease 1 stitch at the beginning and end of every other row for 4 (4 1/4, 4 1/2, 4 3/4, 5) inches. Bind off 2 stitches at the beginning of each of the next 6 rows. Bind off the remaining stitches.

**The finishing touches:** Sew the left shoulder seam. With Size 7 needles and Color A, and with the outside of the work facing you, pick up and knit 70 (74,78,82,86) stitches around the neck. Knit 1, purl 1 to make a 6-inch ribbing, then bind off loosely in the ribbing pattern. Sew the neckband opening and right shoulder seam. Sew the underarm and sleeve seams. Sew in the sleeves; block.

## THE V-NECKED SLEEVELESS SLIPOVER

You will need 2 (2,2,3,3) four-ounce skeins of knitting worsted in color A (maroon in the picture on page 193) and 1 (1,1,1,2) two-ounce skein of color B (orange in the picture).

Use straight knitting needles in Sizes 7 and 9 and a tapestry needle for sewing seams.

Knit a sample swatch to check the gauge, which is 5 stitches per inch, 7 rows per inch.

**The back:** With Size 7 needles and color A, cast on 81 (85, 91,95,101) stitches. Knit 1, purl 1 to make a 2 1/2-inch ribbing. Attach color B, change to Size 9 needles and work the stockinette pattern for 2 rows. Fasten off color B and work evenly until the back measures 12 (12, 12 1/2, 13, 13) inches in all, ending with a purl row.

**The armholes:** Bind off 9 (10,10,10,10) stitches at the beginning of each of the next 2 rows, then decrease 1 stitch at the beginning and end of every other row 5 times; you will now have 53 (55,61,65,71) stitches. Work evenly until the piece measures 8 (8 1/4, 8 1/2, 8 3/4, 9) inches above the start of the armhole edge.

**The shoulders:** Bind off 8 (8,9,10,10) stitches at the beginning of each of the next 2 rows and 7 (8,9,9,10) stitches at the beginning of each of the next 2 rows. Bind off loosely the remaining 23 (23,25,27,31) stitches for the back of the neck.

**The front:** Work as you did for the back until the front measures the same as the back from the bottom edge to the armhole edge. Shape the armholes as on the back. When the shaping is completed and 53 (55,61,65,71) stitches remain, work 1 more row.

**The neck:** Divide the front by knitting across 26 (27,30,32,35) stitches, joining a second ball of yarn, binding off the single center stitch, then work across the remaining 26 (27,30,32,35) stitches. Work on both sides of the neck opening—across to the neck edge, picking up the second ball of yarn, ignoring the bound-off edge and work across the other side. Decrease 1 stitch at each neck edge every 6th row 2 (2,1,1,0) times, then every 4th row 9 (9,11,12,15) times. When 15 (16,18,19,20) stitches remain on each side, work evenly until the piece measures the same as the back from the beginning edge to the shoulder. Shape the shoulders as you did on the back.

Sew the left shoulder seam, using color A and a tapestry needle. With Size 9 needles and color B, pick up and knit 104 (108, 112,116,120) stitches around the neck. Place a marker before and after the bound-off center front stitch. Purl 1 row, then cut off color B, attach color A and transfer to Size 7 needles.

**The V-neck edge:** Row 1: Work in a knit 1, purl 1 ribbing pattern to within 2 stitches of the center marker. Then purl 2 together, knit 1, and purl 2 together. Continue in the ribbing pattern on the remaining stitches.

Row 2: Work in the ribbing pattern to within 2 stitches of the center marker. Then knit 2 together, purl 1, and knit 2 together. Continue in the ribbing pattern on the remaining stitches.

Repeat rows 1 and 2 twice more, then bind off loosely in the ribbing pattern. Sew the neckband opening and the right shoulder seam.

**The armhole bands:** With Size 9 needles and color B, pick up and knit 108 (112,116,120,124) stitches around each armhole. Purl 1 row, then fasten off color B, attach color A and transfer to Size 7 needles. Work in the knit 1, purl 1 ribbing pattern for 6 rows, then bind off loosely in the ribbing pattern. Sew the side seams; block.

## CROCHETING THE GEOMETRIC AFGHAN

The afghan pictured on page 194 is made up of 77 separately crocheted squares, assembled as shown on the numbered chart at right. Although they are made in 6 different patterns, all are based on the single crochet stitch (*page 186*). You will need 6 four-ounce skeins of knitting worsted for color A (blue in the picture) and 8 four-ounce skeins for color B (orange in the picture).

Use a Size K aluminum crochet hook. Crochet a sample swatch to check the gauge, which is 7 stitches equals 2 inches.

**Pattern 1** (make 22 squares): With color A, chain 17 stitches. Single crochet across the row of chain stitches, chain 1, turn. Continue to add rows of the same stitches—"work even on," in the jargon of many written instructions—until the piece measures 5 inches. Make 3 single crochet stitches in the last stitch of the last row, as though you are increasing. These extra stitches form the 1st corner of the square. Do not turn the work over at the end of this row, but continue working around the 4 sides of the square, making 3 single crochet stitches in each corner stitch in the same way. Be sure that you have the same number of stitches on each of the 2 sides as the number you have on the top and bottom of the square. Continuing in the same manner, work 3 more rows around the entire outer edge of the square.

Fasten off by cutting the yarn about 1 inch from the work, drawing the yarn through the last loop of the last stitch and pulling tight.

**Pattern 2** (make 28 squares): With color B, work in the same manner as Pattern 1.

**Pattern 3** (make 5 squares): With color B, work in the same manner as Pattern 1 up to the point where you have completed the 1st row of crocheting around the 4 sides of the square. Then fasten off color B, attach color A, and work 3

more rows of the single crochet stitch around the outer edge with color A. Fasten off.

**Pattern 4** (make 6 squares): Work in the same manner as Pattern 3, reversing the colors.

**Pattern 5** (make 10 squares): With color B, chain 9 stitches. Single crochet across the row of chain stitches, chain 1, turn. Single crochet for 7 more rows, then work 1 row of the single crochet stitch around the 4 sides of the square in the same manner as in Pattern 1. Fasten off color B, attach color A, and work around the square with color A for 7 rows, continuing to work 3 single crochet stitches in each corner stitch as you turn. Fasten off.

**Pattern 6** (make 6 squares): Work in the same manner as Pattern 5, reversing the colors.

When you have finished crocheting all the squares, arrange them according to the chart (*below*). Join the squares by sewing through the back loops of the final row of stitches on each, using a blunt-edged tapestry needle. Use a single strand of color A to sew color A squares together, and use color B where color B squares are being joined. Where different color edges are being joined, use either color.

When all the squares are joined, embroider a chain stitch (*page 164*) around the inner squares of Patterns 1, 2, 3 and 4—using color B yarn over color B, and color A yarn over color A. Embroider a chain stitch from each corner of the small inner squares to each corner of the outer squares. Trim the cut ends on the wrong side of the work; block.

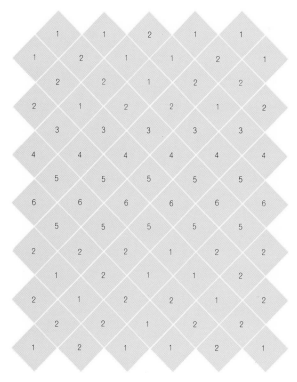

# GLOSSARY

**ADJUSTMENT LINE:** A double line printed on a pattern piece to indicate where it may be lengthened or shortened.

**ALL-PURPOSE FOOT:** See PRESSER FOOT.

**BAR TACK:** A hand-worked trim for reinforcing the ends of buttonholes and other openings.

**BASTE:** To stitch to hold fabric pieces together temporarily, or to indicate pattern markings on both sides of the fabric. Basting stitches can be made by hand or by machine, generally at six stitches per inch.

**BIAS:** A direction diagonal to the threads forming woven fabric—the warp and woof, or "grains." The true bias is at a 45° angle to the grains. Fabric is cut on a bias to make it drape in folds, as in a skirt, or to make it stretch slightly, as in a belt.

**BIAS TAPE:** A strip of cotton, cut diagonally to the fabric threads—on the bias—so that it will stretch to cover curved edges of a garment piece. It is available in 1/4-inch, 1/2-inch and 1-inch widths. The 1-inch width has edges folded 1/4 inch to the wrong side. It may be single fold, with edges that are folded to the wrong side and meet in the center, or double fold, with an additional fold just off center.

**BOBBIN:** The spool holding the lower of the two threads a sewing machine locks together in a stitch.

**CHALK MARKER:** A gauge used to set skirt lengths. It consists of an adjustable stand holding a rubber bulb that, when squeezed, emits a puff of chalk to mark a hemline.

**CLIP:** A short cut into the fabric outside a seam to help it lie flat around curves and corners.

**CLOSURE:** The area on which fasteners—such as buttons or zippers—are placed to open and close a garment; also, the fasteners themselves.

**CROCHETING:** The process of making fabric by using a hook to knot strands of yarn into a series of connected loops.

**CROSSWISE GRAIN:** See GRAIN.

**CUTTING LINE:** A long, unbroken line printed on a pattern, often accompanied by a drawing of scissors, that indicates where it must be cut.

**DART:** A stitched fabric fold, tapering to a point at one or both ends, that shapes fabric around curves.

**DRESSMAKER'S CARBON:** A marking paper, available in several colors and white, used with a tracing wheel to transfer construction lines from pattern to fabric.

**EASE:** The even distribution of fullness, without forming gathers or tucks, that enables one section of a garment to be smoothly joined to a slightly smaller section, as in the seam joining a sleeve to its armhole.

**EASE ALLOWANCE:** The extra material provided for in patterns to give room in a garment for comfort and ease of movement.

**EDGE STITCH:** Machine stitching on the visible side of the garment, close to the finished edges.

**EMBROIDERY:** The decoration of fabric with a needle and thread in a wide variety of stitches.

**FACING:** A piece of fabric, frequently the same as that used in the garment, that covers the raw fabric edge at openings such as necklines and armholes. It is sewn to the visible side of the opening, then turned to the inside so that the seam between it and the garment is enclosed.

**FASTENER:** Any device that opens and closes a garment—button, hook and eye, snap or zipper.

**FIBER:** Any wispy substance that can be twisted to make thread for sewing, crocheting or weaving, or a yarn for knitting.

**FLAT FELLED SEAM:** A double-stitched seam for tailored shirts and slacks in which the seam allowance of one piece forming the seam is trimmed and the seam allowance of the other piece is turned in and stitched on top of the first to give a finished effect on both sides of the garment.

**FOOT:** See PRESSER FOOT.

**GAUGE:** The number of stitches per inch in a piece of knitted or crocheted material.

**GRADING:** Trimming each seam allowance within a multilayer seam—the fabric, facing, interfacing, etc.—to a different width to reduce bulk and make the seam lie flat.

**GRAIN:** The direction of threads in woven fabrics. The warp—the threads running from one cut end of the material to the other—forms the lengthwise grain. The woof—the threads running across the lengthwise grain from one finished edge of the fabric to the other—forms the crosswise grain. Only if the two grains are at right angles to each other is the fabric aligned on the "true grain."

**GRAIN-LINE ARROW:** The double-ended arrow printed on a pattern piece indicating how the piece is to be aligned with the threads of the fabric, its grains. The line between the arrow heads must be placed parallel to either the lengthwise or crosswise grain, as specified on the piece.

**GUIDE SHEET:** Instructions included with a pattern to provide specific directions for using the pattern pieces to make the garment.

**HAM:** A ham-shaped cushion used for pressing shaped areas and curves.

**HOOP:** A two-part circular frame for embroidery, one part fitting snugly over the other to hold a section of fabric taut. Hoops are available in wood, metal or plastic, and in a variety of sizes.

**INTERFACING:** A special fabric sewn between two layers of garment fabric to stiffen, strengthen and support parts of the garment. It is usually used around necklines, in collars, cuffs, pockets or waistbands.

**INTERLINING:** A special fabric, sewn and shaped exactly like the garment and lining to add warmth.

**KNITTING:** The process of making fabric by using two or more pointed needles to knot strands of yarn into a series of connected loops.

**LAP:** To extend one piece of fabric over another, as at the connection of the ends of a belt.

**LENGTHWISE GRAIN:** See GRAIN.

**LINING:** A fabric, usually lightweight, constructed in the shape of a garment to cover the inside of part or all of the garment. It can also stiffen and strengthen the garment.

**MACHINE BASTE:** To insert temporary stitching for marking or preliminary seaming, working by machine rather than by hand. For basting, the machine is set at six stitches per inch.

**MERCERIZING:** A chemical treatment for cotton fabric and thread to add strength and luster, and make the material more receptive to dye.

**NAP:** The short fibers on the surface of the fabric that have been drawn out and brushed in one direction, such as on velvet or corduroy.

**NATURAL FIBERS:** The fibers of animal, vegetable and mineral substances; the most common are cotton, from the cotton plant; linen, from the flax plant; silk, from the cocoon of the silkworm; and wool, from the fleece of sheep or lamb.

**NEEDLEWORK:** A comprehensive term including all work done with a needle and thread, including embroidery, knitting, crocheting and sewing.

**NOTCH:** A V- or diamond-shaped marking made on the edge of a garment piece as an alignment guide. It is meant to be matched with a similar notch or group of notches on another piece when the two pieces are joined.

**NOTIONS:** Supplies used in sewing—needles, thread, pins, buttons, zippers, etc.

**OVERLAP:** The part of the garment that extends over another part, as at the opening of a blouse, jacket or waistband.

**PATTERN LAYOUT AND CUTTING GUIDE:** The instructions and diagrams showing how to place the pattern pieces on the fabric for cutting.

**PILE:** A surface of upright yarns found on fabrics such as corduroy, velvet and terry cloth. The pile tends to lie in a preferred direction, so that the fabric's orientation affects its appearance. To determine the direction of the pile, brush the fabric with your fingers; if the surface looks and feels smooth, you are brushing with the pile.

**PINKING:** A serrated edge at a seam, produced by special "pinking" shears to prevent woven fabrics from raveling.

**PLACEMENT LINE:** A line printed on a pattern to indicate where buttonholes, pockets, trimming and pleats are to be placed.

**PLACKET:** A garment opening with an overlapping edge covered by a visible strip of fabric running the length of the opening. It is used with openings that are equipped with fasteners.

**PLEATS:** Folds of fabric used to control fullness.

**PRE-SHRINK:** A chemical treatment that prevents fabric in the garment from shrinking when it is washed or dry-cleaned. If fabric is not labeled "pre-shrunk," it should be washed, if it is washable, or pre-shrunk by a dry cleaner.

**PRESSER FOOT:** The part of a sewing machine that holds fabric steady at the point it is being advanced and the needle is stitching it. The "all-purpose," or general-purpose, foot has two prongs, or "toes," of equal length, and is used for most stitching. The "straight-stitch" foot has one long and one short toe, and can be used for straight stitching and stitching over fabrics of varying thicknesses. The "zipper" foot has only one toe and is used to stitch zippers and cording.

**REINFORCE:** To strengthen an area that will be subjected to strain, such as the bottom of a pocket, with a small patch of fabric or extra stitches.

**RIBBING:** In knitting, an alternately raised-and-lowered effect created by a combination of knit and purl stitches across a single row.

**SEAM:** The joint between two or more pieces of fabric, or the line of stitching that makes a fold in a single piece of fabric, such as a dart.

**SEAM ALLOWANCE:** The extra fabric—usually 5/8 inch—that extends outside the seam line.

**SEAM BINDING:** Ribbon, 1/2 inch or 1 inch wide, of rayon, silk or nylon, that is sewn over fabric edg-

es to cover them, concealing their raw appearance and preventing raveling. Seam binding is also available cut diagonally to the fabric threads —on the bias—to sew over curved edges. See also BIAS TAPE.

**SEAM FINISH:** The treatment of raw seam edges to prevent fraying and raveling.

**SEAM LINE,** also called stitching line: The long broken line printed on a pattern to indicate where a seam must be stitched; it is usually 5/8 of an inch inside the cutting line.

**SELVAGE:** The finished edges on woven fabric.

**SHANK:** The link between the button and the fabric to which it is sewn. The shank can be made with thread or it can be part of the button, but it must be long enough to allow for the thickness of the overlapping fabric.

**SKEIN:** A length of yarn or thread coiled and packaged for knitting or crocheting. Usually the skein is wound into a ball before use.

**SLASH:** A long, straight cut to make a garment opening or to open a fold of fabric so that it will lie flat, reducing bulkiness.

**SLEEVE BOARD:** Two small ironing boards of different widths, connected at one end, for pressing garment areas (such as sleeves) that will not fit over a regular ironing board.

**SLIDE FASTENER:** See ZIPPER.

**STAY STITCH:** A line of machine stitches sewn at 12 stitches per inch on the seam line of a garment piece before the seam is stitched. Stay stitching is used as a reinforcement to prevent curved edges from stretching, and as a guide for folding an edge accurately.

**STITCHING LINE:** See SEAM LINE.

**STRAIGHT-STITCH FOOT:** See PRESSER FOOT.

**SYNTHETIC FIBERS:** Man-made fibers produced by forming filaments from chemical solutions, such as rayon, nylon and Dacron.

**TAKE-UP LEVER:** The lever on the sewing machine that raises and lowers the presser foot.

**TENSION:** The degree of tightness of the two threads forming machine stitches. Unless tension is properly adjusted in each, the threads will not lock evenly together in the stitch.

**THREAD:** Twisted strands of yarn used for sewing.

**THROAT PLATE:** A flat metal piece with a hole through which the needle passes as it stitches. A general-purpose throat plate has a wide hole to

accommodate sideways motion of the needle; many machines also have a second throat plate with a small hole, to prevent soft fabrics and knits from being pulled down into the machine and puckering during stitching. Throat plates have guide lines on the left and right sides to help you sew a straight seam.

**TOPSTITCH:** A line of machine stitching on the visible side of the garment parallel to a seam.

**TRACING WHEEL:** A small wheel attached to a handle, used in conjunction with dressmaker's carbon to transfer markings from pattern pieces to fabric. Tracing wheels with serrated edges are used for most fabrics, but plain edges are preferred for knits to avoid snagging the material.

**TRIM:** To cut away excess fabric in the seam allowance after the seam has been stitched. Also, a strip of fabric—such as braid or ribbon—used to decorate a garment.

**UNDERLAP:** A part of a garment that extends under another part, as at the connection at the ends of a belt.

**WARP:** The threads that run parallel to the finished edges of a woven fabric, from one cut end to the other, forming the lengthwise grain.

**WITH NAP:** A cutting direction on patterns to indicate how the pattern is to be aligned with fabrics that, because of their surface, napped weave or printed design, change in appearance with the direction in which they are set. When such fabrics are used, all pattern pieces must be laid and cut out in one direction—with the nap.

**WOOF,** sometimes called weft, filler: The threads that run from one finished edge of a woven fabric to the other, forming the crosswise grain.

**YARN:** A continuous strand of textile fibers, spun from short fibers or long filaments, and used in knitting and crocheting, in weaving fabric and in the manufacture of thread.

**ZIGZAG STITCH:** A serrated line of machine stitching used as decoration or to prevent raveling of raw edges, particularly on knits.

**ZIPPER,** sometimes called slide fastener: A mechanical fastener consisting of two tapes holding parallel lines of teeth or coils that can be interlocked by a sliding bracket, or slider. The zipper generally has a top stop, a small metal bracket or bit of stitching at the top to prevent the slider from running off the tapes; a guide line, a raised line woven into the tapes to show where they are to be stitched to the garment; and a bottom stop, a bracket at the bottom against which the slider rests when the zipper is open.

**ZIPPER FOOT:** See PRESSER FOOT.

CREDITS

*Sources for the illustrations in this book are shown below. Credits from left to right are separated by semicolons, from top to bottom by dashes.*

Cover—Fabric design by Abraham Silks Company, Zurich, Switzerland. 6,7—Ryszard Horowitz. 11—The National Museum, Denmark. 14,15 —Ryszard Horowitz. 16,17—Ryszard Horowitz. Skirts designed by Maxime de la Falaise for Blousecraft. 18,19—Ryszard Horowitz. Dresses and man's shirt designed by Maxime de la Falaise for Blousecraft. 20,21—Ryszard Horowitz. 22,23 —Tom Jackson. 27—Robert Colton, courtesy Smithsonian Institution. 28,29—Ken Kay. 30 —Ken Kay, except bottom left David L. Harrison. 31—Ken Kay, except bottom left David L. Harrison. 32,33—Ken Kay. 35—Collections of Greenfield Village and the Henry Ford Museum. 36,37 —Ken Kay. 39—The Colonial Williamsburg Collection. 40,41—Ken Kay. 42 through 45—Drawings by John Sagan. 46,47—Tom Jackson, tracing lines by John Sagan. 51—Paulus Leeser courtesy The Brooklyn Museum; right overlay by John Sagan. 52,53—Robert Colton, courtesy Museum of the City of New York. 54,55—Al Freni, courtesy Museum of the City of New York. 56 —Tasso Vendikos. 57—Drawings by Walter Johnson. 58 through 61—Tasso Vendikos. 62 through 67—Drawings by John Sagan. 69 —Courtesy The Oriental Institute, University of Chicago. 70 through 73—Tom Jackson. 74,75 —Drawings by Raymond Skibinski. 78,79—Ken Kay. 80 through 83—Drawings by Raymond Skibinski. 84,85—Ryszard Horowitz. 89—Smithsonian Institution. 90—Culver Pictures. 91—Wide World Photos; Studio Maywald, courtesy Christian Dior; H. Conant for LIFE; *Women's Wear Daily.* 90,91—Background photograph by Tasso Vendikos. 92—Tasso Vendikos. 93 through 99 —Drawings by Raymond Skibinski. 100—Ken Kay. 101 through 103—Drawings by John Sagan. 104—Tom Jackson. 105—Drawings by Thea Kliros. 106—Tom Jackson. 107—Drawings by John Sagan. 108—Tom Jackson. 109 through 115 —Drawings by Thea Kliros. 116—Tom Jackson. 117—Drawings by John Sagan. 118—Tom Jackson. 119 through 125—Drawings by John Sagan. 126—Tom Jackson. 127 through 129—Drawings by M. S. Jones. 130—Ken Kay. 131 through 133 —Drawings by M. S. Jones. 134—Drawings by M. S. Jones, except bottom right by Sanae Colton. 135—Drawings by Sanae Colton. 136—Tom Jackson. 137 through 139—Drawings by John Sagan. 140—Ken Kay. 141 through 146—Drawings by John Sagan. 146,147—Tom Jackson. 148,149—Tasso Vendikos; Drawings by John Sagan. 150,151—Tom Jackson. Embroidery by Erica Wilson. 155—Photo Giraudon, with special permission from the city of Bayeux. 158,159 —Ken Kay, background David L. Harrison. 160, 161—Ken Kay, except far left David L. Harrison. 162 through 165—Drawings by John Sagan. 166,167—Drawings by Raymond Skibinski. 168, 169—Tom Jackson. Embroidery by Erica Wilson. 170,171—Tom Jackson; Drawing by Carolyn Mazzello. Embroidery by Erica Wilson. 172,173 —Tasso Vendikos. Knitting and crochet by Del Pitt Feldman. 177—Enrico Ferorelli, courtesy Textile Museum of Washington, D.C.; far right drawings by John Sagan. 178,179—David L. Harrison; background Ken Kay. 180,181—Tasso Vendikos. 182 through 189—Drawings by John Sagan. 190,191—Tasso Vendikos. Knitting by Annette Feldman. 192,193—Tasso Vendikos. Knitting by Annette Feldman. 194,195—Tasso Vendikos. Crochet by Annette Feldman. 199—Drawing by Walter Johnson.

# ACKNOWLEDGMENTS

For their help in the preparation of this book the editors would like to thank the following: *in Colonial Williamsburg:* Sandra Shaffer, Assistant Curator; Jean Sheldon, Slide and Print Librarian; *in Dearborn, Mich.:* Carleton L. Safford, Curator of Textiles, Greenfield Village and Henry Ford Museum; *in New York:* Abraham Silks Company; Alamac/West Point Pepperell; Rose Ambersino; Ameritex/Cohn Hall Marx; Anglo Fabrics; Susan Bates; A. W. Bedell; Bloomsburg Fabrics; Boussac of France; Butterick Archives; Louise Cheney, Technical Research Division, Simplicity Pattern Company; Jeffrey Childs, Assistant Curator of Decorative Arts, Museum of the City of New York; Ann Coleman, Curator of Costumes, Brooklyn Museum; Dan River, Inc.; Ernst Eineger; Erlanger Blumgart Co.; Del Pitt Feldman; Fischer and Gentile Fabrics; Forte Fabrics; Friedes Associates; Greenwood Mills; Jax Manhattan, Inc.; Tracy Kendall; Kenneth Jay Lane, Inc.; Lady Continental Shoes; Lesur Inc.; Liberty Fabrics; McCall's Pattern Company; Jean Mailey, Associate Curator of Textiles, Metropolitan Museum of Art; Marvella Inc.; Mayar Silk Co.; Alice Maynard; Meyer Woolens; Violet Mock; Moygashel/Hamilton Adams Imports; John Noble, Director, Museum of the City of New York; Onondaga Silk Co.; Poli Fabrics; Robert Riley, Curator of Costumes, Fashion Institute of Technology; The Robeth Co.; Jane Schenck, Butterick Fashion Marketing Company; The Singer Company; R. S. Smith, Librarian, Fashion Institute of Technology; Spring Mills, Skinner Fabrics; Stern Merritt Co.; J. P. Stevens; Gordon Stone, Librarian, Costume Institute, Metropolitan Museum of Art; Pat Sukhaprayura; Texfi Industries; Veneziano Boutique; White Rose Fabrics; *in Washington:* Grace Cooper, Curator, The Smithsonian Institution; Louise W. Mackie, Associate Curator of Middle Eastern Textiles, The Textile Museum of Washington, D.C.; Rodris Roth, Curator, The Smithsonian Institution.

✗   Printed in U.S.A.